"Information through Innovation"

MS-DOS® AND PC-DOS™

A HANDBOOK OF ESSENTIALS

Second Edition

KENNETH S. CLOSE
President, Personal
Computer Instruction

bf
boyd & fraser publishing company

Publisher: Thomas Walker

Acquisitions Editor: James H. Edwards

Production Editor: Barbara Worth

Marketing Manager: Christopher Will

Composition: Custom Editorial Productions, Inc.

Cover Design: Lina Haddad

Cover Photography: © The Image Bank, Stanislaw Fernandes

A division of South-Western Publishing Company
Boston, MA 02116

Manufactured in the United States of America

Library of Congress Cataloging-in-Publication Data

Close, Kenneth S.
MS-DOS and PC-DOS : a handbook of essentials / Kenneth S. Close.—
2nd ed.
p. cm.
Includes index.
ISBN 0-87835-788-2 (pbk.)
1. Operating systems (Computers) 2. MS DOS (Computer file) 3. PC
-DOS (Computer file) I. Title.
QA76.76.063C56 1992
005.4′46—dc20 91-34386
CIP

1 2 3 4 5 6 MT 6 5 4 3 2 1

Contents

PREFACE

INTRODUCTION

Since the first edition of this book appeared, the use of the personal computer has continued to expand. The personal computer has become more complex internally, while manufacturers have tried to make it easier to use. The disk operating system, called DOS, makes the computer easy to use. It has been revised five times, and each revision has brought more capability and features.

Computer classes continue to emphasize application programs. While some emphasis is placed on learning the operating system, most students continue to learn DOS by trial and error on their own.

This revision maintains the three original goals of the book. The first goal is to introduce students to the disk operating systems used on IBM and IBM-compatible computers. The second goal is to provide hands-on practice with basic, intermediate, and advanced features of DOS. The third goal is to teach students to use personal computers more effectively. In addition, the book meets these goals by covering the latest versions of the updated disk operating system.

This book's target audience has not changed. It is written for several groups of users. The book provides an introduction to DOS for beginning computer users. It helps experienced users achieve maximum effectiveness. This text will improve users' understanding of and insight into DOS, which will improve their results. The book's structure moves from the simple to the advanced. Appendices provide introductory and reference material. The text provides valuable, relevant information to both experienced and inexperienced computer users.

FEATURES

This book presents DOS essentials in an easy-to-understand format. It is a learning guide rather than a technical reference manual. It provides a working understanding of how to use DOS to maximum advantage. The book offers three levels of learning; it begins with fundamentals and proceeds through intermediate topics to advanced features.

Throughout the book, hands-on exercises provide practice on the reading. The exercises cover the common operations, tasks, and problems that the DOS user will encounter. Completing the exercises will give the student practice with DOS operations.

The chapters provide increasingly advanced subjects. Students can find an appropriate entry point depending on their beginning level of skill. In addition, appendices are provided. These appendices contain information on

DOS commands, DOS editing keys, the EDLIN line editor, and other essential data. Information for beginning computer users has been expanded. The text now includes additional information on keyboarding. The fundamentals appendix has been slightly expanded to again help those who have had little exposure to computers.

This book is organized into three parts with two chapters in each part. Fundamentals are developed in Part 1, *Beginning DOS*. Students will learn about the basic DOS commands and how to enter and use them. Becoming familiar with DOS versions and performing basic file and disk operations are covered in Part 1. Part 2, *Intermediate DOS*, provides a more in-depth look at directories and subdirectories. It offers a chapter about hard disks and their use. Part 3, *Advanced DOS*, teaches students to create and use batch files. Part 3 also discusses other advanced DOS features that can improve effectiveness, and it provides information on common DOS problems. The book illustrates some of the common problems that users have and provides solutions to these problems.

DOS is now available in Version 5, but users probably use versions as early as Version 3.1. There may even be some earlier versions in use. This book tries to point out differences where these may be significant. However, not every feature of each version may be covered. The actual results you achieve or see on your screen may differ slightly from that shown in the text.

LEARNING AIDS IN THE TEXT

Each chapter has key features to enhance learning. Each chapter begins with learning objectives. These learning objectives describe what the student will be able to do after completing the chapter. A list of key terms is provided after the learning objectives. These terms will be defined and discussed in the chapter. A chapter overview follows the list of terms. This overview discusses the coming topics and their relationship to the chapter's objectives.

The chapter content follows a logical, progressive pattern. Students will learn about DOS commands and operations in the order they typically need to know them. The material builds upon previous material; a topic will not be introduced without the necessary prerequisites. Therefore, skipping material may cause difficulty later.

Each chapter contains examples to illustrate the concepts. These most often show students what should appear on the computer screen as they work with the disk operating system. Most chapter examples can be easily duplicated. Hands-on exercises are placed in each chapter. These reinforce learning and enable students to remember and understand DOS operations.

The chapters end with a summary and a series of exercises. The summary covers the key points developed in the chapter. It provides a concise review of the essential points. The exercises reinforce learning and have been expanded and enhanced in this revision. The questions and activities in the exercises demonstrate the understanding and competence that students achieve. An appendix offers possible answers to the exercises.

MESSAGE TO THE STUDENT

Using the computer effectively requires an understanding of how DOS works. This book will help you understand DOS and thus improve your computer effectiveness. If you are a new computer user, you should start at the beginning of this book. If you are a more experienced user, refer to the table of contents for your appropriate entry point. Then, work through the chapters and complete the hands-on exercises and the end-of-chapter exercises.

Do not be daunted by the complexity of computers or the many DOS commands. As you learn additional DOS features, share your learning with other users. Learning as much as possible about DOS will enable you to achieve better results with your computer. After you have achieved the goals of this book, you will be able to use your computer time much more efficiently.

ABOUT THE AUTHOR

Kenneth S. Close is an author of computer texts, including *INTEGRATED SOFTWARE: Principles and Applications Using Lotus® 1-2-3®*, edition 2, and *Electronic Spreadsheet Applications in Practice*, both published by South-Western Publishing Co. He has taught computer classes and seminars and has written articles for computer magazines. He is president of a computer consulting business. He has been a manager in a Fortune 100 consumer goods corporation, where he used personal computers to solve business and technical problems.

ACKNOWLEDGMENTS

The author would like to thank the following people for taking time to review and offer improvement suggestions for this revision. This type of support is invaluable in achieving high levels of effectiveness in textbooks.

JoAnne Autry
Collin County Community College

Karen L. Duda
Youngstown State University

Hussein Hoelscher
Professional Business School

LaVonne Huter
Southeast Missouri State University

Dennis J. Irwin
Illinois Central College

Roy Parkins
Portland Community College

Virginia Phillips
Youngstown State University

Carolyn M. Rainey
Southeast Missouri State University

REQUIREMENTS FOR USING THIS BOOK

This book discusses the disk operating system used on the IBM and IBM-compatible computers. PC-DOS™ is used on many of the IBM personal computers.[1] MS-DOS®, from Microsoft® Corporation, is available for many IBM-compatible computers.[2] Compatibles operate almost identically to an IBM computer. Except for a few, which have their own operating system, all of these compatibles use MS-DOS.

To complete all of the hands-on exercises in this book, you will need a computer and a copy of PC-DOS Version 3.1 or higher or MS-DOS Version 3.2. The version number refers to the level of features that are included. The digit 3 indicates the third major revision. The decimal digit refers to the different, smaller revisions.

Most of the illustrations in this book were produced using PC-DOS Version 3.1. Some have been produced with Versions 4 and 5. While Versions 4 and 5 are explained at places in the text, there are no hands-on exercises that depend on having these versions. In some cases, steps are explained if you are using one of these newer versions. You can work many of the examples with DOS versions earlier than 3.1. These earlier DOS versions do not contain all of the necessary programs to complete all of the exercises. When you work the examples and exercises, you will probably encounter differences between what is described and what you experience. Some of your screen displays may vary slightly from those shown in this book. Some DOS versions also use slightly different prompt messages. You should refer to the literature that accompanies the computer that you are using.

In addition, you will need several blank floppy disks, even if you will be using a hard disk. You should have at least four blank disks. These can be either 5¼″ or 3½″ depending on the drives available in your computer. Either high or regular density disks are acceptable. Finally, you will need to know how to use a basic word processor or a line editing program such as EDLIN or the new Edit command in Version 5. Appendix C provides the fundamentals of the EDLIN program.

[1]PC-DOS, Personal Computer XT, and IBM Personal System/2 are trademarks of International Business Machines Corporation. IBM, IBM PC, Personal Computer AT, and AT are registered trademarks of International Business Machines Corporation. Any reference to PC-DOS, IBM, IBM PC, Personal Computer AT, AT, Personal Computer XT, or IBM Personal System/2 refers to this footnote.

[2]MS-DOS and Microsoft are registered trademarks of Microsoft Corporation. Any reference to MS-DOS or Microsoft refers to this footnote.

Part 1

Beginning DOS

OVERVIEW OF PART 1

Beginning DOS introduces you to the operating system. You will benefit most if you are a beginning computer user. Part 1 consists of two chapters, which contain essential information about the basic DOS commands. Chapter 1 introduces the DATE, TIME, and DIR (directory) commands, and explains DOS commands in general. Chapter 2 introduces DOS topics such as the different DOS versions, disk basics, files, and subdirectories. Chapter 2 also illustrates the most commonly used DOS commands. It concludes with an explanation about application programs and how to set them up for your computer.

Chapter 1

Getting Started

◆ Objectives

After completing this chapter, you should be able to:

1. Understand and enter DOS commands.
2. Understand file names and know how to list them.
3. Display or print a directory of files.
4. Use the DATE, TIME, and DIR commands.

◆ Terms

operating system
hardware
software
user interface
command driven system
application programs
system prompt
command line
current (or logged) drive
booting the computer
internal command
external command
parameter
switch
delimiter
editing keys
text file
ASCII file
command file
program file
file name
root name
extension
directory
disk label
wild-card characters

◆ Overview

Chapter 1 gets you started using DOS. It introduces computer systems and the operating system. You will learn how DOS fills the role as a user interface. You will encounter the DATE and TIME commands immediately after you turn on the computer. This chapter tells you what to do and why you do it. You will learn about the DIR (directory) command and other DOS commands. Chapter 1 also discusses the proper use of file names. As you learn more about the directory command, you will learn how to control the screen display.

INTRODUCTION TO COMPUTER OPERATING SYSTEMS

Computers make it easy to accomplish many information-related tasks. Personal computers give the student or businessperson a tremendous amount of computing power. The computer's operating system makes it easy to harness this power.

The **operating system** is simply a computer program that manages the computer system. It allows you to run different applications and save your work for later use. It also allows you to print your results on a printer. The operating system manages the details of making all of the parts work together.

A computer and its parts must be directed to perform every step. The operating system manages these details for you. For example, DOS will interpret the keys you press and print the appropriate characters on the screen. DOS will perform file operations such as finding files on your disk, reading the data from the files, and later saving the data in the computer's memory back onto the disk. If you have a printer attached to your computer, DOS will control both the computer and the printer so that the characters in the computer are properly printed. The disk operating system allows every part of the computer hardware package to be controlled with relatively simple commands.

Typical Hardware and Software Systems

A computer system includes at least the computer, a keyboard, and a monitor. Many systems also include a printer and a **modem**, which is a device for connecting the computer to the telephone line. Some systems may also include a **mouse**, which is a device that makes it easier to point to data on the screen. Portable computers called "laptops" have built-in disk drives and screens, and they will run on battery power. These system units are called **hardware**. Today's computer systems have more hardware than ever before. While allowing work to be more easily accomplished, these devices add some complexity to the system. Manufacturers attempt to make their systems as easy to use as possible.

Hardware components must work together in order for anything useful to happen. In addition, each system should be as flexible as possible in order to satisfy multiple needs. The software determines how this hardware performs. **Software** refers to the programs that guide the computer and direct it to follow your instructions.

At one moment, you may use your computer as a word processor and develop letters or reports. Later, you may use a database program to look up the names and addresses of the members of your favorite club. Still later, you can use a spreadsheet to develop a club budget. These programs help you accomplish useful work. While you are using software and concentrating on the problem you wish to solve, the operating system is coordinating all the parts of the computer.

The User Interface

The operating system is the **user interface** between you and the computer hardware and software. An effective operating system is designed to be easy to use and to allow you to concentrate on your work. Ideally, it should seem invisible and allow the computer to be a tool for accomplishing useful work. For example, your objective may be to apply for a bank loan. A computer can help you and should not require special attention.

In creating a bank loan application, you could use a spreadsheet, a word processor, and perhaps a graphing program. Your attention is not on the internal workings of the computer system, but rather on the end result.

To accomplish your required tasks quickly and easily, you must have an understandable, easy-to-use user interface. An effective user interface will require few steps, and these steps will be easy to accomplish.

Two styles of user interfaces are available. A **command-based interface** uses text-based commands to control what the computer does. A **graphical user interface** (GUI) presents commands in picture or menu form on the screen. Commands are issued by selecting the right pictures or making menu choices. A mouse is required in order to derive the maximum benefit from a GUI.

PC-DOS and MS-DOS were written for IBM and IBM-compatible computers. They are the user interface between the application programs you use and the computer. DOS started as only a **command driven system**. Now, DOS and other operating systems offer menus or pictures that show the available options.

For the last several years, DOS users have enjoyed the benefits of the GUI. Windows™ is a graphical operating system shell, which means that the original operating system is still at work in the background. Windows allows the user to issue commands by pointing with a mouse. Windows is not a new operating system, but it allows DOS to perform differently. DOS Version 4 introduced DOSSHELL, which is still another means of giving DOS a graphics-like look. DOS Version 5 has improved on Version 4. This new program is discussed later in this book.

Graphical user interfaces such as Windows and DOSSHELL are usually easier to learn to use than previous systems. They allow you to produce more work with less effort. Figure 1-1 shows how the operating system coordinates the operations of the display, disk drive, keyboard, printer, and memory.

Figure 1-1.
The operating system at work.

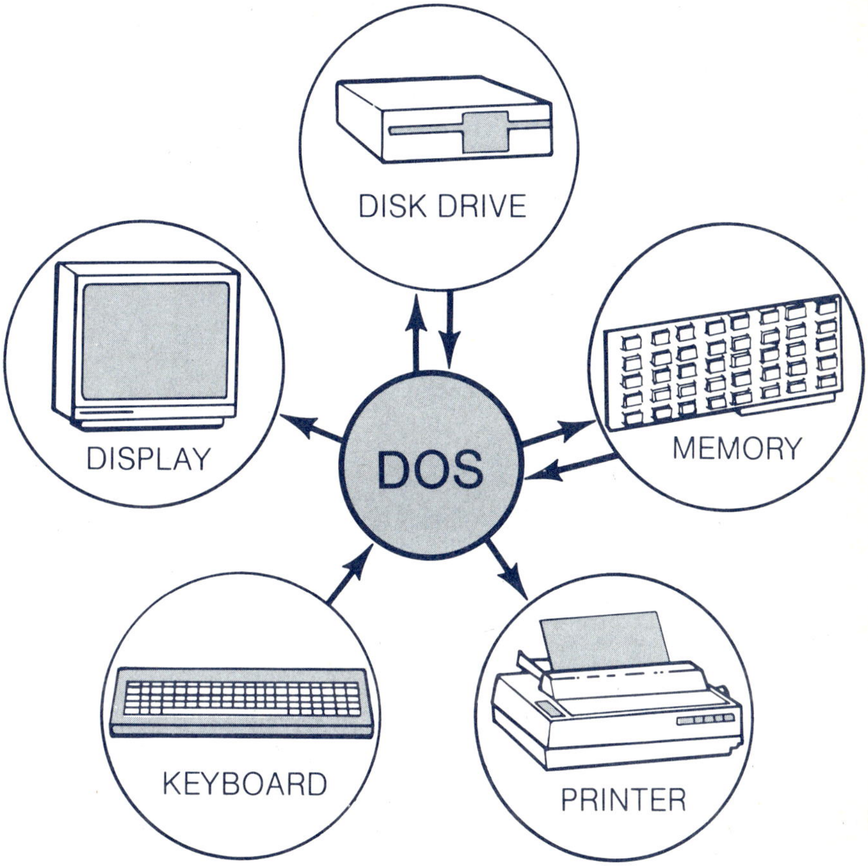

DOS—The Operating System

The disk operating system, called DOS, is itself a program. Programs, of which there are several types, are lists of computer instructions. **Application programs** direct a computer to perform functions such as word processing, spreadsheet use, or project planning. Machine language programs are very detailed lists of letter and number commands that accomplish tasks such as turning on a disk drive motor, moving paper in a printer, or changing the color of the display screen.

Operating system programs help application programs work with the machine language programs built into the computer. This allows application programs to work in a standard, uniform manner with the various parts of a computer system. Figure 1-2 shows how operating system programs

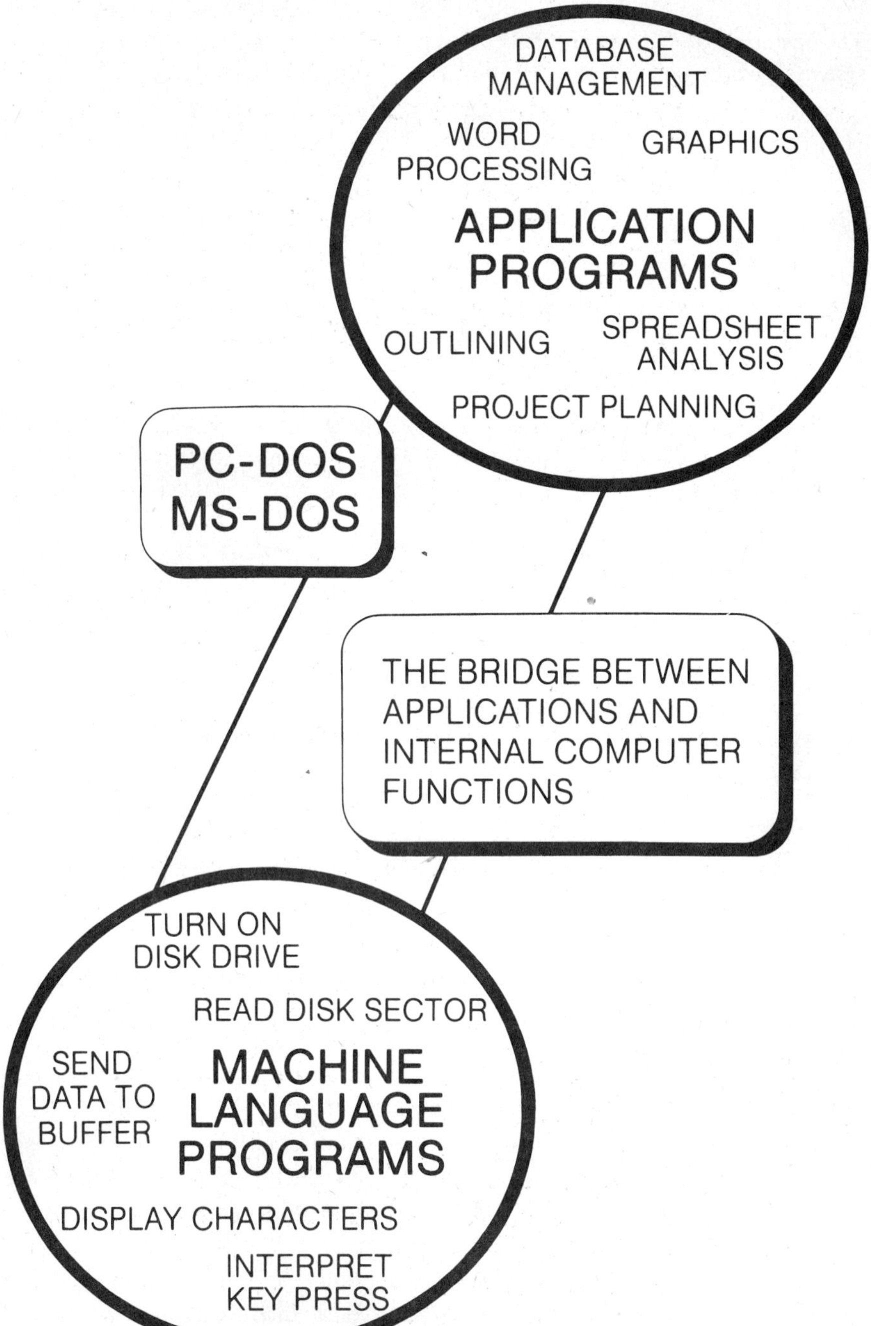

Figure 1-2. Operating system and other programs.

provide an interface or bridge between application programs and the computer's machine language programs.

DOS has operating rules that other programs must obey when they are run on the computer. The programmer must make sure that these rules are followed so that the computer system will perform the intended tasks.

In addition to providing operating rules for programs to follow, the operating system furnishes a number of housekeeping commands; these commands make it more convenient for the user to work with the system. They help accomplish repetitive tasks, such as copying files from one disk to another, changing the names of files, or preparing disks to receive data. Learning to use the disk operating system is like learning to use any other program. Specific commands produce specific results. Learning to use DOS involves knowing the results of all commands and using each command at the appropriate time. The first DOS commands you will encounter are probably the DATE and TIME commands.

DOS and Networks

Today's complex computer systems come in many varieties and configurations. One popular system configuration includes networks. Simply stated, a network is a system of personal computers, and sometimes larger computers, that are connected together. A network allows a group of people to use the same over-all computer system at the same time. A server is a central computer whose job is to manage all of the information on the network. User work stations allow individuals to connect to the server and to other parts of the network. These systems are often called Local Area Networks, or LANs.

MS-DOS and PC-DOS are available at the individual work stations to manage application programs. In a sense, each local work station behaves as if its computer were a stand-alone unit. It is beyond the scope of this text to explain the operation of networks or their operating systems. It will suffice to indicate that most networks can be configured so that individual users, at their own network work stations, can use MS-DOS and PC-DOS to perform useful tasks.

USING THE DATE AND TIME COMMANDS

When you first turn on an older-style computer, or one without a hard disk, the operating system asks you to enter the date and time. If you simply press the ENTER key, a meaningless date and time will be recorded. Newer (286- and 386-style) computers have built-in clocks that automatically read the date and time. On older computers, DOS will ask you to confirm the date and time, as measured by the built-in clock, or to enter a new date and time. The 286- and 386-style computers refer to the number of the computer chip that controls the computer.

If the disk with which you start the computer contains a special file called AUTOEXEC.BAT, the screen may not ask you for the date and time. As you will learn later in this book, the AUTOEXEC.BAT file can command the computer to perform different tasks when it starts. You will also create your own AUTOEXEC.BAT file. For now, you should ignore the AUTOEXEC.BAT file and its capabilities.

As you follow the examples in this chapter, use a DOS disk that does not contain an AUTOEXEC.BAT file. If you cannot find such a disk, refer to Appendix D or ask someone who is familiar with DOS to rename the AUTOEXEC.BAT file.

An Introduction to the Keyboard

If you are not familiar with a computer keyboard, the following will orient you and help get you started. You may also refer to Appendix D, which offers more computer hardware fundamentals, or to standard texts on keyboarding.

The keyboard of a computer is like that of a typewriter. Its purpose is to allow you to type letters, numerals, and punctuation marks, which the computer will recognize as commands. In addition, special keys that do not exist on a typewriter are included to help issue special commmands to the computer.

There are two styles of keyboards: regular and enhanced. A regular keyboard has fewer keys and ten function keys in two columns along the left side. An enhanced keyboard has more keys, including up to 12 function keys in a single row along the top of the keyboard. Figure 1-3 shows a typical computer keyboard.

When you strike a key, its character should appear on the screen. If it does not, you should seek expert advice. While the characters are on the screen, the computer cannot do anything with them. The ENTER key, when pressed, commands the computer to recognize the characters on the screen and to act on them.

Anything you type incorrectly must be corrected—using the BACKSPACE (←) key—before you press ENTER. Once you press ENTER, you cannot correct your entry. If your entry is incorrect, the computer will either carry out your command or issue an error message and give you another chance. See Appendix D for a complete list of keys and the functions they perform.

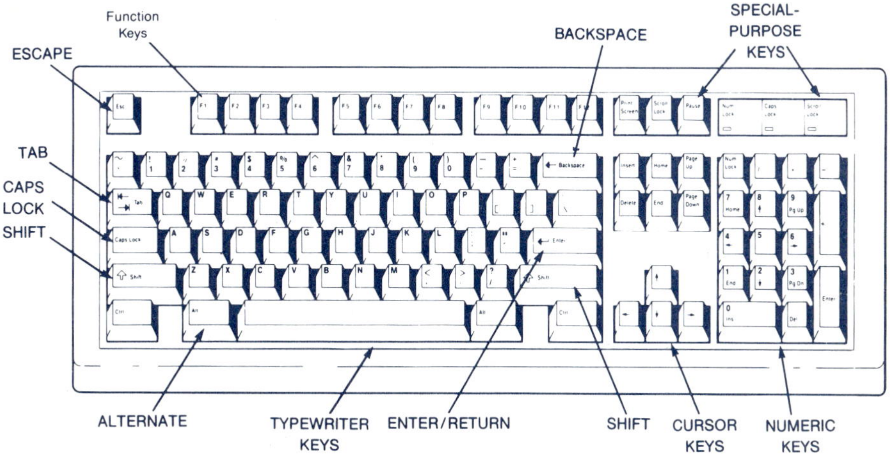

Figure 1-3. A computer keyboard.

Entering the Date and Time

Enter the date and time from the keyboard (do not bypass them). You must press ENTER (this key may be labeled with the word "Enter" or with a bent arrow) for DOS to run your command. This text often uses the term "key-enter" to mean keying text and pressing ENTER. After you have key-entered the current date, key-enter the time. For example, if the text asks you to key-enter 9:35, you should key 9:35 and press ENTER. Use hyphens or slashes for the date and colons for the time, as shown in the following display.

```
Current date is Sat 05-04-1991
Enter new date (mm-dd-yy):  5/9/91    ←Key-enter date.
Current time is 6:31:21.52p
Enter new time: 10:23    ←Key-enter time.
```

Once you have entered the date and time, the computer will save and continuously update them. The computer will maintain the correct time until you turn off the power. A calendar function also maintains the correct system date and time.

Changing the Date or Time

After you have started the computer and entered the date and time, you may discover that one or both of them are wrong. You can change them whenever you want using the DATE and TIME commands.

When you enter DATE, DOS will display the current date and give you the chance to change it. You may enter a new date or press ENTER to accept the date already in the system, as follows.

```
A:\>DATE   ←You key-enter this.
Current date is Sat 05-04-1991
Enter new date (mm-dd-yy):   ←The computer waits for you to key-
                              enter a new date or press ENTER to
                              accept the current date.
A:\>   ←The prompt returns and awaits your next command.
```

You can also change the time. The computer uses 24-hour time, so you must make your time entry in the following way. The time will range from 0:00 at midnight, to 12:00 at noon, to 23:59 at 11:59 P.M. Times from 0:00 to 12:00 indicate A.M. time. To calculate P.M. time, add 12 to the standard time notation. For example, 5:15 P.M. becomes 17:15 in 24-hour time. Time punctuation is more exacting than date punctuation. Hours, minutes, and seconds must be separated by colons, and a period must be used to separate seconds and hundredths of a second. However, it is rarely necessary to enter more than the hours and minutes. The following display shows how to change or maintain the time.

```
A:\>TIME
Current time is 6:48:52.85
Enter new time: 13:45   ←It is 1:45 P.M., so key-enter 13:45.

A:\>TIME
Current time is 13:45:15.24
Enter new time:   ←Press ENTER, because the time is correct.
```

Why Use the Date and Time?

DOS will automatically record the date and time when you save a disk file. The application programs that you use have commands that save the work you create using them. Saving a file records the results of your work on disk so that you may use the work at another time. You provide a file name (file names are explained later in this chapter), and the computer automatically attaches the date and time.

Date and time stamps on files become valuable when you have a large number of files. If you have files with similar names, the date and time stamps can help you find the file(s) you want. Some programs will arrange your files by date or time, listing the most recent file first.

In addition, many programs depend on having the current date and time, without which they cannot perform their functions. For example, programs that maintain calendars or budgets require the current date and time. With these programs, you must enter the correct date and time when you start, or have a computer equipped to provide them automatically.

Internal Clocks

Most computers have battery-powered **clock hardware** that automatically provides the correct date and time at start-up. These internal clocks are designed to tell DOS the correct time at start-up or whenever the TIME command is entered. Subsequently, the software clock in DOS maintains the time and date until the computer's power is turned off.

Older computers may use a short program to read the date and time from the battery-powered clock hardware. This data is automatically entered into the computer's software, as if it had been keyboard entered. Newer 286- and 386-style computers use an internal program for automatic reading of the battery-powered clock.

The System Prompt

After you have entered the date and time, DOS displays a copyright message and the system prompt. The **system prompt** consists of the characters A> below the copyright information. If you are using a hard disk system, the system prompt will be C> rather than A>.

The system prompt tells you several things. It lets you know that the computer is ready for input. If there is no prompt and no blinking cursor, the system is not ready for your input. Perhaps another operation is still underway, or the system is stuck because of a malfunction in the computer code (this is often referred to as the computer being "hung up" or "crashed").

The **blinking cursor** shows the location on the screen at which your input will appear, and it marks the beginning of the DOS command line. The DOS **command line** is where you enter commands to control the system. The system prompt also indicates the **current drive**. Your system can have several disk drives attached to it. In addition, electronic disk drives may be installed. The letter in the prompt shows you the current or "logged" drive unit.

DOS remembers the current drive and directs all operations there unless instructed to work with a different drive. Changing the current drive will change the letter displayed in the system prompt. If your computer has more than one disk drive, you can change the current drive. Simply enter a new drive letter and a colon. The system prompt will display the new letter. The number of drive letters that your computer system can handle depends on the configuration of your system. If you attempt to change to a drive that the computer system is not set to handle, you will receive an error message.

After you enter a DOS command, some computer activity should take place. If nothing happens, and you do not see the system prompt, the computer may be "hung-up" or "crashed." Causes and cures for a hung-up system will be described in a later chapter. For now, the following paragraphs will explain how to recover from a hung-up system.

Press ESC or CTRL-BREAK (hold down the CTRL and the BREAK or SCROLL LOCK keys together) and see if the system prompt returns. If it does not, try a "warm reboot." **Booting the computer** means to begin the start-up process. The first group of code that is loaded from the start-up disk contains instructions to load more code. This continues, and the computer "lifts itself by the bootstraps" to get going.

To perform a warm reboot, press CTRL-ALT-DEL. This means to press the CTRL, ALT, and DEL keys simultaneously. (These keys may be labeled slightly differently on the computer that you are using. For example, the DEL key may be labeled DELETE.) If the warm boot works, the screen will clear, and the regular start-up process will begin. Any data in memory will be lost, but there is no way to recover this data anyway if the system is "hung-up."

Finally, if nothing happens when you try a warm reboot, turn the power switch off, wait 30 seconds, and then turn it on again. This is called a "cold reboot" and solves all problems except those caused by a hardware malfunction in the unit. Remember that pressing CTRL-ALT-DEL from within an applications program will erase the program and all the work you have created using it. If an applications program "hangs" before you have saved your work, press ESC or BREAK to see if the program gets going again. If it does not, there is nothing else to try except a warm or cold reboot. To avoid losing work, save your work frequently as you progress, rather than just at the end of the session.

HANDS-ON EXERCISE

1. Place a DOS disk in drive A.
2. Start the computer with the DOS disk in drive A. (You may have to turn on the monitor.) After DOS is loaded into memory, the screen will display the prompt asking you to enter a new date. Do not press ENTER yet (if you do, the system date will remain as listed).

   NOTE: *The blinking underline is the cursor, and it indicates that the computer is ready to receive input.*
3. Key the current date. Use hyphens or slashes. If the computer cannot recognize the date, it will prompt you again. If you type the wrong key, press BACKSPACE to back up and erase the mistake, and then key the correct entry. After you press ENTER, the computer will prompt for the time.
4. Key-enter the time using a colon to separate minutes and seconds. To be consistent with the computer's 24-hour clock, enter all P.M. hours using digits from 13 to 24. For example, 3:25 P.M. would be entered as 15:25. After you press ENTER, the computer will display a copyright message followed by the current drive prompt.
5. The DOS command prompt A> is displayed on the last line if drive A is the current drive. If you started from the hard disk, C> will be displayed. DOS is now ready to receive your commands.

DOS COMMANDS

You already have some experience with the DOS commands. You have learned the DATE and TIME commands, which are used when the computer starts or when you need to change the system date or time. You will learn many additional DOS commands and how to use them.

Types of Commands

DOS commands are single words that are entered on the command line following the system prompt. DOS will recognize and respond to internal and external commands. An **internal command** is loaded when the computer starts, and it remains in memory with the rest of the DOS program. When you enter an internal command, it starts immediately. COPY, DATE, and TIME are internal commands.

The instructions for the **external command** reside on disk, not in the computer's memory. DISKCOPY, FORMAT, and CHKDSK are examples of external commands. You will learn these commands later. When the command is entered, the computer first loads the command's instructions from disk. Once these instructions are in memory, they are performed. When the external command's actions have been completed, its instructions are erased from memory. Figure 1-4 illustrates this difference between internal and external commands.

You can repeat some commands without re-entering the command word and wait for the instructions to be reloaded. You may enter a different command if you do not wish to repeat the command in memory. For example, DISKCOPY is an external DOS command that copies an entire disk onto a new one. After you have begun the command, you must insert your disks in the proper drives and proceed. Once the copy is complete, the program asks if you want to repeat the operation. You may copy additional disks or return to the system prompt. The following display illustrates the DISKCOPY command. When you key-enter this command, leave a space before A: and a space before B:.

```
A:\>DISKCOPY A: B:     ←Key-enter this command.

Insert SOURCE diskette in drive A:

Insert TARGET diskette in drive B:

Press any key to continue . . .
```

After the command has been completed (you will learn more about the DISKCOPY command later), the message shown below may be displayed. Some versions of DOS will display this prompt, whereas others will not. Selecting Y repeats the procedure, beginning with prompts to insert the source and target diskettes. Selecting N makes the system prompt reappear.

```
Copy another diskette (Y/N)?
```

A switch is turned on when it is included on the command line. Its action is determined by the letter following the slash. For example, /V is the "verify" switch for the COPY command, and /S tells DOS to transfer the system files (some of the DOS files) when it formats a disk. The following display illustrates the use of these two switches.

`A>COPY NEWFILE C: /V` ←*This is the command to copy NEWFILE on disk in drive A to drive C and verify that the copy has been made correctly. Without /V, the verification will not occur.*

`A>DIR B: /P` ←*This is the command to list the directory of the disk in drive B and pause after 23 file names have been displayed. Without /P, the pause will not occur, and the names at the top will scroll off the screen.*

The command name must be the first entry on the line. It may be entered in uppercase or lowercase letters. In this text, the command is shown in uppercase letters, but you may use lowercase or a combination of uppercase and lowercase letters. If no other parts of the command are to be used, press ENTER to initiate the command.

You can add the parts that you need. DOS will put an error message on the screen when it cannot understand your entry; it will usually tell you that you have entered an incorrect command or that the command cannot be completed as entered. If DOS indicates that it cannot find a file, you probably have mistyped the command or you do not have the proper disk in the disk drive.

If you are using DOS Version 5.0, add the /? switch to the command to see a description of the command. DOS will then display a brief description of the command along with some of its options.

Using DOS Commands

To use a DOS command, key it on the command line, add any parameters and switches, and press ENTER. If you make a mistake while keying the command, press the BACKSPACE key or the LEFT ARROW key to erase the characters already keyed. Once the mistake has been erased, finish keying the command.

The DOS **editing keys** make it easy to repeat or change previously entered commands. See Appendix B for a detailed explanation of these keys. DOS uses the FUNCTION keys as editing keys. On regular keyboards, the

FUNCTION keys are positioned in two columns along the left side of the keyboard. On enhanced keyboards, the FUNCTION keys are positioned in one row above the main keys.

FUNCTION key 3, F3, is the Copy-All editing key. The Copy-All key is useful if you must re-enter a command. Pressing F3, while the cursor is at the A prompt, will display the last DOS command, but will not enter it. You must press ENTER to begin the command. The following example shows how to repeat the COPY command using F3.

A:COPY OLDFILE B: ←*Copy OLDFILE in drive A onto the disk in drive B.*

1 File(s) copied. ←*Command has been completed.*

A:> ←*Now press F3 to repeat previous command.*

A:COPY OLDFILE B: ←*Press BACKSPACE twice, then key C:.*

A>COPY OLDFILE C: ←*The line will look like this. If you press ENTER, OLDFILE will be copied to drive C.*

DOS Version 5 provides DOSKEY, a program which lets you review your last 20 to 30 DOS commands. DOSKEY resides in memory and keeps track of each command you enter. Press the up or down arrow key to see each of these in turn, then use the left and right arrow keys to edit any part of the displayed command. INS and DEL and other keys may also be used to edit the command line. This feature is not available with any earlier version, although several commercial programs can do the same thing.

Canceling the Command

There are several ways to cancel a command. If you have typed the command but have not pressed ENTER, striking ESC, CTRL-C, or CTRL-BREAK will interrupt the command. ESC, alone, will terminate the command line. The other commands require you to press two keys simultaneously. CTRL-C means pressing CTRL and C at the same time. CTRL-BREAK means pressing CTRL and BREAK (BREAK may have Scroll Lock on the key face) simultaneously. The following example shows the result.

```
A>DISKCOPY ^C     ←Pressing CTRL-C terminates the command.

A>
```

FILES: FUNCTIONS AND NAMES

The subject of files is very important in computer use. DOS commands, such as MOVE, COPY, and TYPE, are often used to perform file operations. You will want to know where files are stored, how to make duplicates or backups, and how to find the file you need. All of this requires a knowledge of files, file functions, and file names.

File Functions

Files can be classified by the functions they perform. In the next chapter, you will learn about the technical differences among files. Here, you should pay attention to the functional differences among files—i.e., how they are used rather than how they are formed.

TEXT OR DATA FILES **Text files** contain data. They hold the results of work you or others produce. For example, you can use a word processing program to create the text for a newspaper article. When you finish the document and want to save it for future use, the word processing program will place the document into a file. Usually, this file is specific to the word processing program that created it. It will contain not only the words but also any formatting features you added to enhance the text, such as indentions, boldface terms, or underlined words. The word processor you use may also create an ASCII file. An **ASCII file** contains only letter and number characters; it does not contain any control or formatting codes. An ASCII file can be used by almost any program that works with plain text.

You cannot run a text file by entering its name on the DOS command line. Its name cannot be used as a command. You will use another program such as a word processing application program or a text editor to change or add to a text file.

You can, however, use DOS commands to perform operations on text files. As Figure 1-6 shows, DOS commands can copy, erase, or rename text files. Later, you will learn a command that will allow you to view a text file by printing it on the screen or on a printer.

Figure 1-6. Operations performed on a text file.

Programs	Perform Operations on Text Files
Applications such as word processors	Create Modify Add to
DOS commands	Copy Erase Rename Verify

DOS COMMAND FILES Unlike text files, DOS **command files** are run directly from the DOS command line. As mentioned previously, internal commands are DOS commands that are already built into the COMMAND.COM program. These commands are part of the instructions that are placed into the computer's memory when DOS is loaded. They are available instantly, and there is no delay in their execution. Typing the command and pressing ENTER bring immediate action.

External commands, in contrast, reside on disk and not in the computer's memory. When you enter an external DOS command, the system must find the command file, load it into memory, and run it. Only after these steps have been completed will there be any action.

After the external command has been executed, the instructions are erased from the computer's memory. DOS is then ready for a different command. As you will learn later, many external DOS commands allow you to repeat the command action before exiting. This saves time, because the file does not have to be loaded again.

PROGRAM FILES A **program file** contains a set of instructions that allows you to perform work with the computer. DOS external command files are simply program files that accomplish specific DOS operations. Both are executed by entering the file name on the command line.

Program files, sometimes called application programs, have COM or EXE as the last three letters in their file names. COM, EXE, and BAT files (which you will learn about later) are executable by DOS. Although command entry for any of these files is similar, the files themselves are very different. The results they produce are usually dissimilar.

You may see "overlay" files in your directory (OVL extension). These are portions of application programs that are so large that only parts of them are loaded into the computer at one time. Overlay files contain parts of the program, and the main section lays them into memory for when they are needed. You cannot run overlay files.

Word processing programs and spreadsheets are examples of application programs. They have been written to provide you with much capability and utility, but you must develop skill with each of them. DOS commands will allow you to perform most housekeeping functions on program files. For example, you may be able to copy program files. Some program files are copy-protected, however, and you cannot copy them. To run an application program, you do not need to know the programming language in which the program was written.

File Names

File names are an important part of the computer system. A computer manages information. This information, whether it is text, commands, or program instructions, is kept in a file. Files are manipulated by using file names. The computer hardware keeps track of the location of all information according to file names. File names are used to retrieve data and invoke commands.

THE FILE NAME The file name has two parts. The first part is the name itself, sometimes called the **root name**. The second part is the **extension** or suffix. Some file names do not contain extensions. When the full file name is needed (root name and extension), this will be stated. When this book shows the command syntax, sometimes the term "filename" (without a space) is used to mean the root name; this is used so that it will be clear that you should not key-enter a space.

The file name contains from one to eight characters. Only letters, numerals, and certain special characters are allowable file name characters. Characters that have special meanings in DOS commands are not allowable in file names. Examples of unacceptable characters would be the space, the colon, and the period. These characters will produce errors if they are used. Characters that are unacceptable vary slightly with the different versions of DOS, because the newer versions have additional commands and thus use additional characters.

THE EXTENSION The extension, also known as the suffix, contains from one to three characters, follows the file name, and is separated from it by a period. The same limitations that apply to file name characters apply to extension characters.

Two files can have the same root name, but DOS will treat them differently if their extensions are different. Many application programs do not require you to supply the extension when you create or save work. DOS command files and application files require you to enter only the root name. However, if you use a file name as a parameter in a DOS command, you must enter both parts of the name (if it has an extension). For example, if you want to copy a file to another location, you must enter the full file name. If the file name has an extension and you enter only the root name, DOS will display an error message stating that the file is not found. Figure 1-7 illustrates some of the features of file names.

Figure 1-7.
File names.

EXAMPLES OF ACCEPTABLE FILE NAMES

Without an extension

SALESRPT
1286LOSS
JAN_TURN

With an extension

MEMBERS.DAT
MARKT.LTR
SPEECH.TXT
PROPOSAL.DOC
MRK_PRO1.DOC
PRO1_RPL.DOC
DISK.COM
FILING.EXE
MENU.BAT

(DISK.COM, FILING.EXE, MENU.BAT ← *These are extensions used by files that DOS can run.*)

EXAMPLES OF UNACCEPTABLE FILE NAMES

Without an extension	*Unacceptable because*
SALESREPORT	More than 8 characters
1&2 CHAP	Contains space
With an extension	
DATES.1987	Has 4 characters in extension
MRKT PROPOSAL.DOC	Too long
1STRPT.D*C	Unacceptable character in the extension

THE DIRECTORY

To find data and instructions in computer memory or on disks, DOS maintains an up-to-date catalog of file names. DOS keeps the list of file names in a place called the **directory**. The directory contains a list of the files that are recorded or saved on the particular disk. Each floppy disk or hard disk has its own directory. The system will not work unless the disk contains a directory. DOS saves technical details about the location of each file on the disk in addition to other useful information.

The Directory (DIR) Command

The directory can be displayed on the screen or printed to give you a catalog of your files. The directory also shows the size of each file and the date and time each file was created. Finally, after all files in the directory have been listed, DOS will print the total number of files in the directory and the number of unused bytes remaining on the disk. The number of unused bytes remaining on the disk is known as "free space."

The directory (DIR) command is used to list the directory contents of a specified disk. In its simplest form, the DIR command is given by entering DIR on the DOS command line and pressing ENTER. The directory of the logged drive will be displayed. The display below shows the result of the DIR command and illustrates the different parts of a directory entry. Notice that the root name, the extension, the file size, and the date and time of creation are shown for each file. At the end of the directory is the number of files and the remaining free space on the disk.

```
A:\>DIR

 Volume in drive A is DF62
 Volume Serial Number is 1848-1DFB
 Directory of  A:\

ANSI     SYS     9105  10-14-88  12:00a
APPEND   EXE    11154  10-14-88  12:00a
ASSIGN   COM     5753  10-14-88  12:00a
ATTRIB   EXE    18263  10-14-88  12:00a
BACKUP   COM    36750  10-14-88  12:00a
 .
 .
 .
RESTORE  COM    36946  10-14-88  12:00a
SHARE    EXE    13424  10-14-88  12:00a
SORT     EXE     5882  10-14-88  12:00a
SUBST    EXE    18467  10-14-88  12:00a
```

```
SYS       COM     11456  10-14-88  12:00a
TREE      COM      6302  10-14-88  12:00a
XCOPY     EXE     17055  10-14-88  12:00a
GWBASIC   EXE     84544  02-01-88  12:00a
       42  File(s)     454656 bytes free

A:\>
```

The next chapter discusses disks in more depth. For now, you should know that a directory has room for a specific number of files. Most 5¼-inch floppy disks (using DOS Version 2.0 or higher) can hold 112 file names in the directory. A high-density disk can hold 244 directory entries. Attempts to save another file above this limit are met with a "directory full" error message. Chapter 3 discusses subdirectories and describes the way around this limitation.

The Directory Contents

The directory header displays two useful pieces of information. The first line shows the disk label. The **disk label** is a name that you can assign to the disk (also called a "volume"). The second line shows the full name of the directory that is being listed. The full name includes the name of any subdirectory. Recent versions of DOS also display the disk's unique serial number. The use of subdirectories will be explained in Chapter 3.

Following the directory header is the listing of all the files in the directory. All files will be listed, but only 23 files can be listed before the first file on the list disappears from the top of the screen. There are several commands that will give you time to read all of the file names, and these commands are explained later in this chapter.

After displaying the full file list, DOS displays the number of files in the directory, followed by the remaining free space on the disk. Because each floppy disk or fixed disk has a defined capacity, this free space number represents the difference between the number of bytes occupied by the files in the directory and the capacity of the disk.

Controlling Directory Output

DOS helps you work with your directories. "File management" is a term that refers to the organizing, listing, sorting, copying, and moving of files. In all of these operations, you must know the contents of the directories before and after the operation. The DIR command gives you the needed information. Displaying the directory contents either on the monitor or on paper is useful.

STOPPING THE SCREEN DISPLAY If there are more than 23 files in a directory, the first files listed will disappear from the top of the screen as more files are listed at the bottom. If you want to look at some of the first directory entries, you will have to stop the listing before they are lost from view. This can be done in two ways.

First, after key-entering DIR on the DOS command line, you can press either CTRL-NUM LOCK or CTRL-S to freeze the display. By pressing any other key, you can resume listing of the directory. You can press and re-press the letter S while continuously holding down the CTRL key to alternately start and stop the display. Pressing CTRL-NUM LOCK a second time will not resume the display; you must press another key.

Second, you can add one of two switches to the DIR command. The first switch, /P, causes the display to pause after 23 files. A message appears at the bottom of the screen requesting you to strike a key when you are ready for the listing to proceed. When you do this, up to 23 additional files will be displayed. The process continues until all files in the directory have been listed, or until you press CTRL-C to terminate the DIR command. The following display shows the use of the /P switch. Pressing any key will display the next 23 lines. Pressing a key a third time will complete the directory display for this disk.

```
A:\>DIR /P

 Volume in drive A is DF62                   }      { These lines will scroll
 Volume Serial Number is 1848-1DFB           }  ←   { off the top of the screen
 Directory of  A:\                           }      { before the display pauses.

ANSI     SYS      9105  10-14-88  12:00a
APPEND   EXE     11154  10-14-88  12:00a
ASSIGN   COM      5753  10-14-88  12:00a
ATTRIB   EXE     18263  10-14-88  12:00a
BACKUP   COM     36750  10-14-88  12:00a
CHKDSK   COM     17739  10-14-88  12:00a
COMP     COM      9459  10-14-88  12:00a
COUNTRY  SYS     12806  10-14-88  12:00a
```

```
DEBUG    COM     21574  10-14-88  12:00a
DISKCOMP COM      9857  10-14-88  12:00a
DISKCOPY COM     10396  10-14-88  12:00a
EDLIN    COM     14069  10-14-88  12:00a
EXE2BIN  EXE      7931  10-14-88  12:00a
FC       EXE     15807  10-14-88  12:00a
FIND     EXE      5941  10-14-88  12:00a
GRAFTABL COM     10239  10-14-88  12:00a
GRAPHICS COM     16693  10-14-88  12:00a
GRAPHICS PRO      9397  10-14-88  12:00a
JOIN     EXE     17813  10-14-88  12:00a
KEYB     COM     14727  10-14-88  12:00a
LABEL    COM      4458  10-14-88  12:00a
LINK     EXE     43988  10-14-88  12:00a
MEM      EXE     20005  10-14-88  12:00a
Strike a key when ready . . .
```

←The Pause switch causes this message to be displayed.

The second switch, /W, produces a wide display. File names are displayed in five columns across the screen. There is room, however, to display only the file name and the extension; the file size and creation date and time are not displayed. The /W switch allows more files to be viewed at one time on the screen. The following display shows the use of the DIR /W command.

```
A:\>DIR /W

 Volume in drive A is DF62
 Volume Serial Number is 1848-1DFB
 Directory of  A:\

DIAGS    COM   HIMEM    SYS   FASTOPEN EXE   FORMAT!  COM   COMMAND  COM
ANSI     SYS   APPEND   EXE   ASSIGN   COM   ATTRIB   EXE   BACKUP   COM
CHKDSK   COM   COMP     COM   COUNTRY  SYS   DEBUG    COM   DISKCOMP COM
DISKCOPY COM   EDLIN    COM   EXE2BIN  EXE   FC       EXE   FIND     EXE
GRAFTABL COM   GRAPHICS COM   GRAPHICS PRO   JOIN     EXE   KEYB     COM
LABEL    COM   LINK     EXE   MEM      EXE   MODE     COM   MORE     COM
```

```
NLSFUNC  EXE   PRINT    COM   RECOVER   COM   REPLACE  EXE   RESTORE  COM
SHARE    EXE   SORT     EXE   SUBST     EXE   SYS      COM   TREE     COM
XCOPY    EXE   GWBASIC  EXE
        42 File(s)   454656 bytes free

A:\>
```

PRINTING THE SCREEN Although it is essential to be able to display directory listings on the screen, you may also need a printed copy of the directory. Several commands allow you to print the directory listings.

Your first option is to use the printer control feature built into DOS. Pressing CTRL-P turns on the connection between the computer and your printer. Be sure that you have turned on the power to your printer and that the connection to the computer is properly installed.

Once you have turned on the printer connection, any characters displayed on the monitor will also be sent to the printer and will be printed. Therefore, one way to print a copy of a directory listing is to turn on the printer connection (CTRL-P) and then issue the DIR command. As the directory is displayed on the screen, it will also be printed.

After you have printed the directory listing, turn off the printer connection by pressing CTRL-P again. There will be no signal that the connection is on or off. A useful way of checking this is to press ENTER one time. If the printer advances the paper one line, then the connection is still on. This is illustrated below.

```
A>DIR   ←Press CTRL-P. Nothing will show on the screen.
A>   ←Press ENTER. The printer will advance one line.
A>DIR   ←Press ENTER and the directory listing will be printed.

 Volume in drive A has no label
 Directory of  A:\

APPEND   EXE    5825  03-17-87  12:00p
ASSIGN   COM    1561  03-17-87  12:00p
ATTRIB   EXE    9529  03-18-87  12:00p
```

```
BACKUP   COM    31913  03-17-87  12:00p
BASIC    COM     1063  03-17-87  12:00p
.
.
.
BASIC    PIF      369  03-17-87  12:00p
BASICA   PIF      369  03-17-87  12:00p
MORTGAGE BAS     6251  03-17-87  12:00p
      31 File(s)      55296 bytes free

A:\>
```
←*Press CTRL-P. Nothing will show on the screen, but the printer connection will be off.*

Another way to print the directory is to use the PRINT-SCREEN key. This key is labeled PrtSc on the IBM PC. Other computers may require that a special combination of keys be pressed in order to print the screen. Simultaneously pressing the SHIFT key and the PRINT-SCREEN key will print the entire contents of the screen. Therefore, to print a directory listing, you must first display the directory on the screen. Because the PRINT-SCREEN key prints only the display that is on the screen, the directory listing must fit entirely on the screen. Other lines of information on the screen besides the directory listing will also be printed.

If the directory listing is longer than 23 files and will not fit completely on the screen, press CTRL-PrtSc. This has the same effect as pressing CTRL-P and sends to the printer everything that goes to the monitor. Pressing CTRL-PrtSc a second time disconnects the printer.

Using Parameters and Wild-Card Characters

The DIR command by itself will display all the files in the requested directory. Because some directories contain many files, the DIR command alone is limited. For example, you may be looking for a certain file or for several similar files. These files can be scattered anywhere in the directory. If you use the DIR command, DOS will list all files rather than a select few. Wild cards and parameters are additional tools that can be used in conjunction with the DIR command to make file name selection and display more flexible.

PARAMETERS As with other DOS commands, you can add a parameter to the DIR command. For example, you can use the DIR command to check if a specific file is in the current directory. You do this by entering the DIR command followed by a space and then the file name on the same line. If the file is on the disk (or in the directory), using the DIR command with this parameter will display it. The following display shows how you can check if the BASIC file is on the disk. (Your version of BASIC may be named GWBASIC; if it is, you should key-enter GWBASIC instead of BASIC.)

```
A:\>DIR BASIC     ←Add BASIC as parameter to DIR command.

 Volume in drive A has no label
 Directory of  A:\

BASIC    COM     1063  03-17-87  12:00p  }
BASIC    PIF      369  03-17-87  12:00p  } ←Files listed
        2 File(s)      55296 bytes free  }

A:\>DIR BASCA     ←If you misspell the file name, an error message occurs.

 Volume in drive A has no label
 Directory of  A:\

File not found

A:\>
```

Another obvious method of using parameters is to list the directory of a disk in another disk drive. You do not have to change the logged drive in order to see the directory of a disk in another drive. This use of parameters is illustrated below.

```
A>DIR B    ←A is the logged drive, but this will display the directory
             of disk in drive B.
Volume in drive B has no label
Directory of  B:\

COMMAND  COM    23210   03-17-87  12:00p

         1 File(s)      300032 bytes free
```

WILD-CARD CHARACTERS This unusual term refers to special characters that can be used with the DIR command to make finding of files much easier. **Wild-card characters** are characters that may be substituted for one or more of the characters in the file name. Two wild-card characters are used: the question mark (?) and the asterisk (*).

The question mark (?) can be used to substitute for any character in the exact position where the question mark is placed. For example, DIR S?L? will list files such as SALE, SELL, SALT, and STLK. Placement of the question mark in the second and fourth positions tells DOS to list any file names having S in the first place, L in the third, and any characters in the second and fourth. Selected file names must have four characters. SELDOM, SOLITARY, and SWLM34 would not be listed.

The asterisk (*) can be used to substitute for any number of characters. DOS will accept any characters after and including the asterisk. For example, DIR PR* will list PROFITS, PROS, PRINCE, PR12__WIN, and PROTEST. The following displays show uses of wild cards.

```
A:\>DIR A*

 Volume in drive A has no label
 Directory of  A:\

APPEND   EXE     5825  03-17-87  12:00p
ASSIGN   COM     1561  03-17-87  12:00p
ATTRIB   EXE     9529  03-17-87  12:00p
        3 File(s)     55296 bytes free

A:\>
```

```
A:\>DIR *.EXE

 Volume in drive A has no label
 Directory of  A:\

APPEND   EXE     5825  03-17-87  12:00p
ATTRIB   EXE     9529  03-17-87  12:00p
FIND     EXE     6434  03-17-87  12:00p
```

```
JOIN     EXE      8969  03-17-87  12:00p
SHARE    EXE      8608  03-17-87  12:00p
SORT     EXE      1977  03-17-87  12:00p
SUBST    EXE      9909  03-17-87  12:00p
XCOPY    EXE     11247  03-17-87  12:00p
        8 File(s)      55296 bytes free

A:\>


A:\>DIR ?A*.*

 Volume in drive A has no label
 Directory of  A:\

BACKUP   COM     31913  03-17-87  12:00p
BASIC    COM      1063  03-17-87  12:00p
BASICA   COM     36403  03-17-87  12:00p
LABEL    COM      2377  03-17-87  12:00p
BASIC    PIF       369  03-17-87  12:00p
BASICA   PIF       369  03-17-87  12:00p
        6 File(s)      55296 bytes free

A:\>
```

Wild-card characters can be used with many DOS commands. Wild-card characters can be handy additions when you want to erase, copy, or verify groups of related files.

DOS Version 5 provides additional versatility in using the DIR command. Switches can be used to display files with specified attributes (files of one type). Also, directory entries can be sorted by name, date, extension, or size.

HANDS-ON EXERCISE

1. Place a DOS disk in drive A and turn on the computer if it is not already on.
2. Place a new disk in drive B. If you are using one of the early versions of MS-DOS, you may have to use a formatted disk for this exercise. If you use a formatted disk, use one containing data that you no longer want to keep. (If you have a single drive, place the original DOS disk in it.)

3. Key DISKCOPY A: B: and press ENTER. Be sure to place spaces before A: and before B:. A message will prompt you to insert the source diskette in drive A and the target diskette in drive B.

   NOTE: *If you have a single drive, key DISKCOPY or DISKCOPY A: A: and press ENTER. The messages for single drive systems will prompt you to swap the source and target disks. You will swap these several times before the operation is completed.*

4. Press any key to begin the copy process. If you are using a new disk, a message may appear telling you that DOS is formatting your disk.
5. Press N for no when the message appears asking if you want to copy another diskette.
6. Remove the DOS original from drive A, place it in its protective envelope, and store it in a safe place. Remove the copy from drive B, and place a label on it with a title such as "DOS Working Disk."
7. Insert your working copy of the DOS disk in drive A.
8. List the disk directory using DIR. Notice what happens to the directory header (the two lines above the first file name) and the first few file names.
9. List the directory again. Stop the display by pressing CTRL-S immediately after pressing ENTER. While holding down the CTRL key, press and re-press S to alternately start and stop the display.
10. List the directory again. Use the pause switch, /P. Key-enter DIR /P. Press any key to see the next file names.
11. List the directory again, this time using the wide switch, /W. Notice the differences between /P and /W.
12. Print a copy of the directory on your printer. (If you do not have a printer connected to your computer, either connect a printer or move to step 13.) Turn on the printer connection by pressing CTRL-P. Key DIR and press ENTER. Press CTRL-P after the directory has been printed to turn off the printer connection.
13. List all files in the directory that begin with F. Key-enter the following: DIR F*.
14. List all EXE files. These are files with EXE extensions. Key DIR *.EXE and press ENTER.
15. List all EXE files that begin with S. Key DIR S*.EXE and press ENTER.
16. List all files having OR in the second and third positions. Key DIR ?OR????? and press ENTER.
17. If you have DOS Version 5, list the directory sorted by size. Key-enter DIR /OS. Press CTRL-S to stop the display or key-enter DIR /OS /P.

Summary

1. The DATE and TIME commands are used to set or change the date and time that the system maintains.
2. The date and time are attached to a file name when a file is saved on a disk. This maintains a record of when the file was created or last updated.
3. DOS commands are entered on the command line. The DOS command line is located at the system prompt. The command is executed when you press ENTER.
4. A DOS command consists of the command name, parameters, and switches. Parameters follow the command and provide extra information that affects how the command operates. Switches turn extra features on or off.
5. DOS commands may be canceled with ESC, CTRL-C, or CTRL-BREAK.
6. Text files, command files, and application or program files are classifications of files according to function.
7. DOS commands may be either internal or external. Internal commands are loaded into memory with the rest of the DOS program. External commands reside on disk and must be loaded into memory from the disk.
8. In DOS Version 5, the /? switch can be used to display a description of the DOS command to which the switch is appended. DOSKEY is a Version 5 program which makes it easy to recall and edit commands.
9. File names consist of a root name, with no more than eight characters, and an extension, with no more than three characters. The root name and the extension are separated by a period.
10. The directory is the list of files on the disk. The DIR command will list the directory on either the screen or the printer.
11. DIR switches, /P and /W, control the directory's file display. The wild-card characters, the question mark and the asterisk, are inserted within a file name to help select particular files. DOS Version 5 allows you to sort file names using the /O switch.

Exercises

1. Assume that it is February 13, 1991. The computer system next to you has a February 12, 1991 system date. You wonder what the system date is on your computer. What command do you use to check your computer's system date? You find that the system date on your computer is also February 12, 1991. What do you key-enter to change the date?

2. In April, clocks are turned ahead by one hour for Daylight Savings. You turn on your computer at 8:30 A.M. on the Monday after the change. What commands would you use to change and then check the new time?

3. You have been creating data files from test experiments using your spreadsheet program. You enter data three times each day, five days a week, just after completing the experiments. Assuming that you create separate data files for each day, how can the date and time commands help you maintain consistency in your data file system?

4. Assume that you want to revise a letter file that you created several weeks ago. Before you start your word processor, you list the files in the directory. You discover three files: LETTER1.DOC, LETTER2.DOC, and LETTER1A.DOC. How would you decide which file is the most current?

5. You sit down at the system's work station to review a report file you created at least two weeks ago. The monitor is on and the system is ready to run. The system prompt is displayed as B>. You insert your data disk and key-enter DIR and get the following message.

```
B>DIR

 Volume in drive B has no label

Not ready reading drive B

Abort, Retry, Fail?
```

   Describe what has happened, why it happened, and what you will do to achieve your objective. What should you key-enter?

6. What is the difference between a parameter and a switch?

7. You mistype a DOS command but do not press ENTER. How do you correct your error?

8. You are looking at three files: SALES.DAT, SALES.BAT, and SALES.EXE. Which part of the file name is the same among these files? Which file probably contains the data that you want for budgeting, and why?

9. What command displays a disk directory? Assume that the directory contains 32 files. How do you view all files in the directory?

10. The data files from the experiments you have run are quite large, and there are dozens of them. To preserve the data in case a disk gets damaged, you begin to create duplicates

by copying files from the original disk. You want to get as many files on the backup copy as possible. How do you find the free space to tell if there will be room?

11. To guide your assistant in creating data files, you list a number of file names to go with the text reports that are being created. The small word processor requires the full file name. What are three legal DOS file names with extensions that can be used to keep test data, analysis data, and a summary report?

12. After following up, your assistant tells you that the word processing program has reported that an illegal file name prevented the file from being saved. What is wrong with the file names EXPERIMENT.DOC, TEST REPT.DAT, and CONCL%1.TEXT?

Use your working copy of the DOS master disk to answer the following questions.

13. Without displaying the entire directory, determine the number of bytes in each of the following files: ANSI.SYS, RECOVER.COM, MODE.COM, and VDISK.SYS.

14. Print the DOS master disk directory using the following methods.
    a. Wide display
    b. Complete listing
    c. Use the PRINT-SCREEN key to print the directory. If you do not have access to a printer, write the listing on a separate sheet of paper.

15. Using wild-card characters, determine how many files have only three characters in their names (do not include their extensions). Again, without manually counting, but using only wild-card characters, determine how many file names have exactly four, five, six, seven, and eight characters.

Chapter 2

Introduction to DOS

◆ Objectives

After completing this chapter, you should be able to:

1. Understand the differences among DOS versions.
2. Perform basic disk and file copying operations.
3. Use basic DOS commands such as FORMAT, LABEL, CHKDSK, DISK-COPY, COPY, TYPE, DEL (ERASE), and RENAME.

◆ Terms

hard disk	start-up disk	hierarchical tree
byte	hidden files	write-protect tab
high-capacity drive	system files	concatenation
format	disk label	printer driver file
track	executable files	
sector	subdirectory	

◆ Overview

In Chapter 1, you learned how to get started with DOS and how to use some basic DOS commands. In Chapter 2, you will learn some of the differences among DOS versions, and you will expand your knowledge of DOS. You will learn more about disks and how to prepare floppy disks for use. This chapter will introduce you to basic file and disk operations. You will also learn about commercial application programs and how they are installed for use.

DOS VERSIONS AND THEIR DIFFERENCES

The first edition of DOS for IBM computers was known as Version 1.0. It was introduced in 1981.

Major changes are usually announced with each new main version number. Each of these changes is generally accompanied by a major change in, or upgrading of, the system hardware. Lesser improvements rate changes in the decimal part of the version number. Sometimes, these lesser changes are repairs of bugs or mistakes.

Operating System Versions

The Microsoft Corporation introduced MS-DOS and sold rights to the operating system to IBM, which introduced PC-DOS. Essentially, MS-DOS and PC-DOS are identical, but they have a few differences in their commands, as explained below.

DOS 1.0 The first DOS version was introduced with the IBM personal computer in 1981. It handled single-sided disks. Version 1.1 offered greater speed in getting data to and from the disk. Version 1.1 also introduced double-sided disks, which held more data than single-sided disks.

DOS 2.0 The second major DOS revision occurred in 1983 when IBM introduced the Personal Computer XT, the personal computer with the hard disk. **Hard disks** contain platters that are sealed. Hard disks hold more data and operate faster than floppy disks. Version 2.0 also contained a series of commands that made it easier to manipulate files.

DOS 3.0 The next major change coincided with the introduction of the faster IBM Personal Computer AT. Version 3.0 had the capability of handling the new 1.2-megabyte (1.2M) floppy drive included with the AT. Version 3.1 added features permitting the use of networks. Version 3.2 introduced the capability of using the new 3½-inch drives, and Version 3.3 offered high-density 3½-inch disks.

DOS 4.0 Versions 4.0 and 4.01 provided greater disk capacities. Version 4.01 also introduced the new DOS Shell menu system as well as additional command improvements.

DOS 5.0 The latest DOS version is designed to use less memory, help manage the ever more complex computer systems, and be more convenient. Some fundamental commands for editing and recalling DOS commands have been added. The DOS Shell program has been improved.

MS-DOS AND PC-DOS DIFFERENCES PC-DOS is designed to work with IBM personal computers. MS-DOS is used with IBM-compatible computers. IBM-compatible computers are not made by IBM, but they work almost identically to IBM computers. Compatibility means that software that will run on IBM computers will also run on computers from other manufacturers.

MS-DOS and PC-DOS are identical in their detailed computer control commands. These are commands that programmers use. File management and disk management details are handled the same way in both operating systems. File names may differ between the two, and reserved characters may be slightly different. Differences appear at the user level in the commands that are used to carry out various operations.

The two DOS programs may differ in date and time commands and in time precision. Commands used to copy system files are also different. In general, however, the two operating system programs are quite similar. The majority of examples in this book use MS-DOS Version 4.01. Some examples are based on Version 3.3 or Version 5.0. Where significant, the differences between these versions will be explained.

It would be nearly impossible to mention all of the slight differences among the various versions of DOS. If you experience something different from what is described in this book, the difference may relate to DOS variations. The best approach is to read the documentation that accompanies the MS-DOS program. You may have to modify some of the exercises slightly. Some of the screen displays in this book may differ slightly from those on your screen. Also, in the later chapters, some of the programs are available only on the later DOS versions. In general, you will be able to work all of the examples using PC-DOS 3.3 and above or MS-DOS 3.3 and above. Examples using DOS 5.0 are called out and illustrate specific commands particular to 5.0.

Working with DOS Versions

It is important that you follow some guidelines when working with DOS. First, do not mix different versions. If you start up the computer with Version 2.0, you should not change to a disk containing Version 3.0. The COMMAND.COM file that controls most DOS operations will be different. DOS will let you know if you have the wrong DOS version. Each DOS version uses its own COMMAND.COM file. When you exit from an application program, DOS will discover that the COMMAND.COM file used to start the computer is not the same as the one on the disk. It will issue a message telling you to place the proper COMMAND.COM file in the disk drive.

DOS BASICS

A computer system helps you accomplish useful work. You can run an application program and save your work for later use. This is possible because of disks and the operating system's ability to manage and work with disks and disk files.

Basic operations with which you must be familiar include preparing and using disks. Files are the fundamental building blocks, and this section will increase your knowledge of files.

Disks

Work you do on the computer usually generates data. This data must be saved or recorded on a disk if you are to use it later. To use it, you retrieve it from the disk and load it back into the computer, where you may continue to work with it.

Disks are devices on which you can record the data produced by a computer. Three types of disks are used today: (1) the 5¼″ diskette, (2) the 3½″ diskette, and (3) the fixed, or hard, disk. The 5¼″ and 3½″ diskettes are both referred to as "floppy diskettes" or "floppy disks" even though the 3½″ disk is not flexible like the 5¼″ disk.

THE 5¼″ DISKETTE The 5¼″ diskettes (also called "floppy disks") are portable, inexpensive, and reliable. There are several types of floppy disks. In the early days of personal computers, single-sided disks were used. A single-sided disk allowed data to be recorded on only one side. Today's IBM and IBM-compatible computers are able to record on both sides of a floppy disk. DOS Version 1.1 provided the capability to use both sides of the disk.

Floppy disks are characterized by their capacity, or the amount of electronic data they can hold. Computer data, as mentioned above, consists of millions of electronic signals called **bytes**. A byte can represent a single character, although it also represents other types of computer signals. A thousand bytes is represented as 1K or 1 kilobyte. A million bytes is referred to as 1M or 1 megabyte.

Standard-capacity disks using DOS 2.0 or higher can hold approximately 360K. The **high-capacity drive** records both sides of the disk using a special recording device that places the signals closer together than they were on the older drives. In addition, special DOS 3.0 instructions are needed as well as disks made of the appropriate material. A high-capacity 5¼″ floppy disk will hold 1.2M of data, which is more than three times the capacity of a regular 5¼″ disk. Most personal computers today are equipped with high-density 5¼″ drives.

THE 3½″ DISKETTE Smaller disk drives are found on the growing number of portable, laptop computers.The 3½″ diskette was introduced for these smaller disk drives. Even though it is smaller, the 3½″ diskette allows more data storage than the 5¼″ diskette. The capacity of a regular 3½″ diskette is approximately 720K. The high-density 3½″ version can hold 1.44M, or about 20% more than a high-density 5¼″ diskette.

A 3½″ diskette is not flexible like a 5¼″ floppy diskette. The case, besides being smaller, is rigid and totally covered. A sliding door on the diskette opens when the diskette is inserted in the disk drive, thus exposing the disk surface to the recording head.

The 3½″ diskette is growing in popularity. First, it provides more storage than the larger diskettes. Second, it is more rugged and cannot be as easily damaged. Finally, it is more compact, which makes it easier to transport. It is compatible with IBM Personal System/2 computers and with laptop portable computers.

HARD DISKS The name "hard disk" derives from the hard, rigid platters on which the bytes from the computer's memory are recorded. Several rigid platters working together give the hard disk its high capacity. A hard disk is also called a "fixed disk." Whereas a high-capacity floppy diskette holds 1.2M bytes, a hard disk will typically hold 20M, 60M, 100M, or more. A 60M hard disk holds approximately the same amount of data as 41 high-density 3½″ diskettes.

Prior to DOS Version 4, the operating system would not recognize hard disks containing more than 32M, even if there was room for more. This was caused by the ways DOS identified the location or address of data on the disk. Thus, hard disks bigger than this limit had to be formatted in 32M parts called "partitions." Version 4 changed the addressing scheme and permits single large partitions.

Besides holding much more data than a standard floppy disk, a hard disk operates much faster. It does so because it spins faster and the recording heads that record or pick up the data move into position much more rapidly.

Once you have given the computer the correct instructions, you may use either floppy disks or hard disks, or both, to record your work. DOS commands operate the same on both.

The remaining parts of this chapter will guide you in working with disks in general, whether they are diskettes or hard disks. Hard disk operation is not specifically covered until Chapter 4. Even if you are working on a computer with a hard disk, you still must know basic disk operations for diskettes. You should follow the material and perform the exercises as given. You should have several diskettes available so that you can follow all of the examples. Chapter 4 will provide complete coverage of hard disks.

Preparing Disks (FORMAT)

Blank disks from the factory require that a special pattern of magnetic signals be recorded on the disk before data can be saved. Placing this pattern on the disk creates the **format** of the disk. As shown in Figure 2-1, the disk is formatted into **tracks**. These tracks provide storage zones, called **sectors**, into which data can be recorded. Figure 2-1 shows how characters are recorded within the sectors.

WHAT THE COMMAND DOES When the FORMAT command is executed, the computer controls the disk drive and records the track and sector pattern on the disk. These tracks and sectors contain codes that allow the computer to find any specific location.

When this special pattern is recorded on the disk, any data previously recorded is lost. (Of course, a new disk has nothing on it, so the format pattern is the first thing recorded.) Thus, before formatting a used disk, make sure that it does not contain any important data.

USING THE FORMAT COMMAND To format a disk in drive A, place the DOS disk in drive A and, at the DOS prompt, key-enter the word FORMAT. Remove the DOS disk, replace it with the disk to be formatted, and press ENTER.

Newer DOS versions ask you for a volume name at the end of the formatting process. When complete, the format program will report the number of bytes available on the disk and will allow you to repeat the operation. Occasionally, areas on the disk contain imperfections and cannot be formatted. You may see these reported as bad sectors. The following display shows the message you may see when you begin to format a disk in drive A.

```
A>FORMAT     ←Key-enter this command.
Insert new diskette for drive A:  }
and press ENTER when ready        } ←Insert disk and press ENTER.
```

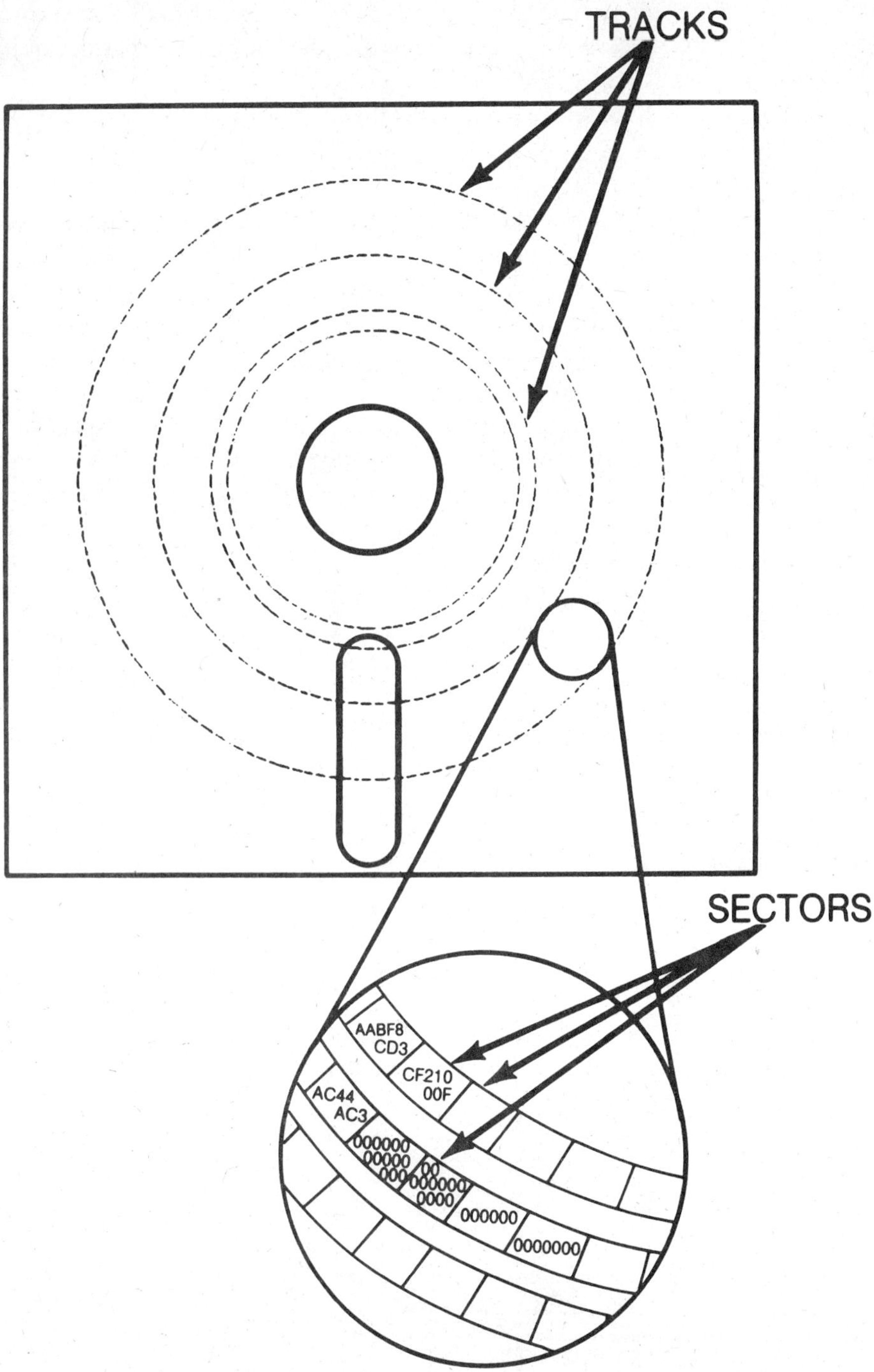

Figure 2-1.
Disk format and saved data.

USING PARAMETERS AND SWITCHES Following the FORMAT command, you can add parameters to control which disk drive will do the formatting. This allows you to load the FORMAT program from a DOS disk in drive A or drive C and format a disk in drive B.

Normally, the FORMAT command only records the pattern of tracks and sectors. This creates a data disk. If you include the switch /S with the FORMAT command, system files will be automatically transferred to the new disk. These files permit the computer to be started with this disk. In order to be transferred, these system files must be on a disk in one of the drives. Some versions of DOS require the system switch, /S, to be last on the command line, if more than one switch is used.

Some of the FORMAT switches allow you to customize the makeup of the disk sector and track capacity. These are advanced commands that apply only in special situations. You will not use these special switches while using this text.

Version 4 automatically pauses after formatting to allow you to enter a disk label, which is a disk's unique name. Version 4 will also create a unique serial number for your disk. Earlier DOS versions provided the /V switch to let you put a volume label on the disk during formatting. Still other switches let you format only one side of the disk (/1) and format a regular-capacity (360K) disk in a high-capacity disk drive (/4).

To format a 360K disk using a high-capacity disk drive, you must add the /4 switch following the command. If you do not, the FORMAT command senses the high-capacity drive and will automatically attempt to format a 1.2M disk. To create a 1.2M disk, you must use a special high-capacity diskette. These disks are made with a coating that has extra magnetic properties. These properties allow the extra sectors and tracks to be recorded within the same area as a regular disk. If you attempt to create a high-capacity disk from a standard diskette, it will be unreliable. The following display illustrates several ways of using switches with the FORMAT command.

`A>FORMAT B: /S` ←*Creates a start-up disk in drive B:*

`A>FORMAT B:` ←*Creates a data disk in drive B:*

`A>SYS B:` ←*Transfers the system files from the DOS disk in drive A to the disk in drive B. Then you must copy COMMAND.COM onto the disk in drive B:.*

TRANSFERRING THE SYSTEM (SYS OR /S) A **start-up disk** is one that will load DOS and start the computer when it is placed in drive A. It contains the DOS program in several special files. Two of these are **hidden files**, which cannot be displayed with the directory (DIR) command. When you start the computer with a data disk in one of the drives instead of a start-up disk, the computer will stop and ask you to replace the disk. Because a data disk does not contain the DOS files, it cannot start the computer.

There are two methods of creating a start-up disk. The first method uses the FORMAT command with the /S switch. This command works by first formatting the disk and then automatically copying the hidden **system files** onto it. The start-up files must be present on the original disk or be copied from the hard disk. The newly formatted disk contains the start-up files and is considered a start-up disk.

The second method of creating a start-up disk uses the SYS command to turn a data disk into a start-up disk. As long as no data occupies the specific disk locations where the start-up files will reside, the data disk can be converted. The COMMAND.COM file must also be copied onto the new disk if the SYS command is used. If a data disk does not have room, format a new disk with the system files and then transfer the data files to it. The following displays show how a data disk and a start-up disk are created.

```
C:\>FORMAT A:     ←Key-enter this command to create a data disk.
Insert new diskette for drive A:
and press ENTER when ready...

Format complete

Volume label (11 characters, ENTER for none)? FIRST DISK   ←DOS
                                                 4 automatically asks
                                                 for a disk label.

    1213952 bytes total disk space     ←Space on high-density
    1213952 bytes available on disk     5¼" diskette

        512 bytes in each allocation unit    ←Reported by DOS 4
       2371 allocation units available on disk

Volume Serial Number is 0B2B-0EEC   ←Automatically created

Format another (Y/N)?N
C:\>
```

```
C:\>FORMAT A: /S /V    ←Key-enter this command to create a start-up
                         disk.
Insert new diskette for drive A:
and press ENTER when ready. . .

Format complete
System transferred

Volume label (11 characters, ENTER for none)? FIRST DISK

   1213952 bytes total disk space
    108544 bytes used by system
   1105408 bytes available on disk    ←Additional space for start-up
                                        files

       512 bytes in each allocation unit
      2159 allocation units available on disk

Volume Serial Number is 144D-0EF1    ←Notice unique serial number.

Format another (Y/N)?N
C:\>
```

LABELING THE DISK DOS Version 2 introduced the **disk label**, an electronic name that can be written on a disk. The label is displayed during directory listings and while using the check disk (CHKDSK) command. A label is a convenience to help you manage your disks. It has no other purpose and is not used by any DOS commands. A disk label may be from one to 11 characters long. The label may use any letter or number character including the space, but it cannot include control characters or the escape character. The previous display illustrates the /V switch. The system switch, /S, is also used. (Different DOS versions will show slightly different messages and will also use different numbers of bytes for the system files.)

PC-DOS Version 3.0 and MS-DOS Version 3.1 introduced the LABEL command. Previously, you learned that FORMAT /V can install a disk label during the FORMAT process. With Version 3 and the new LABEL command, you may add or change the disk label without formatting the disk. Enter LABEL followed by the name you wish to use as the disk label, as follows.

```
A>LABEL B:DISK__NAME
```

LABEL is an external command and must be loaded from a disk, in this case, from drive A. If you enter an invalid name, an error message will appear telling you that the volume name contains illegal characters. The display below shows how you can check to see if the volume already has a label and change it if you desire. (Some DOS versions do not ask if you are sure that you wish to delete the current label.)

```
C:\>LABEL A:

Volume in drive A is FIRST DISK
Volume Serial Number is 144D-0EF1

Volume label (11 characters, ENTER for none)?   ←If you are not
                                                  satisfied with label, you can
                                                  change it here.

Delete current volume label (Y/N)?   ←You may see this if you press
                                      ENTER to previous question
                                      and the disk has a label. Press
                                      N to leave the current label.

C:\>
```

Checking Disks with CHKDSK

The line at the end of the directory listing tells you the remaining free space on the currently logged drive. The check disk command, CHKDSK, will provide additional information. It will show the number of bytes the current disk will hold, how the current space is allocated, and how much space is still free. In addition, it will report hidden files, bad sectors, and the amount of free memory left in your system. Hidden files are not displayed when the directory command is used.

In short, CHKDSK provides a convenient way to learn about the size and space availability of your system. This command can also adjust the way data is saved on your disk. This can help recover lost data in certain circumstances.

THE CHKDSK COMMAND Specify the disk drive, directory, or file you want to check, and CHKDSK goes to work. You may use two switches. The verbose switch, /V, tells the program to display more detailed results after checking the disk or files. The fix switch, /F, tells CHKDSK to rearrange or repair certain files if it finds that they have been disconnected from their main directory entry. CHKDSK will also determine how much space is lost by bad sectors on the disk. CHKDSK output is displayed below.

```
C:\>CHKDSK A:

Volume FIRST DISK   created 06-09-1991 7:42a
Volume Serial Number is 144D-0EF1

   1213952 bytes total disk space
     70656 bytes in 3 hidden files
     37888 bytes in 1 user files
   1105408 bytes available on disk

       512 bytes in each allocation unit
      2371 total allocation units on disk
      2159 available allocation units on disk

    655360 total bytes memory
    509520 bytes free

C:\>
```

USING CHKDSK The DOS CHKDSK command is an external command used to determine how many directories, subdirectories, and files the disk contains. It can determine and tell you how many hidden files your disk or directory contains. The CHKDSK command will report the memory status, including the amount of memory your computer contains as well as the amount of free memory left at the time you use the command.

The CHKDSK command can also make changes that will, in some cases, improve the speed of your disk drive. To understand how the CHKDSK command does this, visualize disk files stored in circular tracks which are broken into parts called sectors. Files are saved in "blocks" or pairs of sectors. A disk file is a series of sectors, each of which is filled with data until all of the work fits on the disk. The last sector may be only partially filled.

When DOS saves a file on a new disk, it records the data into each sector in a track. These sectors are called **contiguous** sectors, meaning that they are next to each other. The last sector of a file is the last sector in a line of contiguous sectors.

If you delete one or more files, the open and available sectors will be at various places on the disk. When the next file is recorded, it may be saved in noncontiguous sectors. The computer still knows the location of each sector, but it takes more movement of the reading head to read all the sectors.

The CHKDSK command can tell you how many noncontiguous sectors each file contains. It can determine if a file has "lost" sectors. Lost sectors can occur if each step in saving a file is not performed correctly. Finally, the CHKDSK command will try to fix the errors that produced the "lost" sectors. You can direct CHKDSK to look at entire disks or only at specified directories and subdirectories. It will list the number and total size of the files it finds, including hidden files. The following display shows a nearly full hard disk with many files, some of which have lost "chains." Note how much disk space can be recovered if this is adjusted.

```
C:>CHKDSK

Volume DOS400    created 12-22-1990 6:20p
Volume Serial Number is 156F-19DA
Errors found, F parameter not specified
Corrections will not be written to disk


   258 lost allocation units found in 11 chains.
Convert lost chains to files (Y/N)?N
    528384 bytes disk space would be freed

   31397888 bytes total disk space
      73728 bytes in 3 hidden files
     114688 bytes in 47 directories
   28833792 bytes in 1127 user files
    1847296 bytes available on disk

       2048 bytes in each allocation unit
      15331 total allocation units on disk
        902 available allocation units on disk

    655360 total bytes memory
    509520 bytes free

C:\>
```

HANDS-ON EXERCISE

1. Start the computer if it is not already on. Enter the date and time.
2. Insert your working copy of the DOS disk in drive A if you did not start the computer with this disk.
3. Key the FORMAT command as follows.

```
FORMAT A: /V /S      ←Key-enter this if your A drive is regular capacity.

FORMAT A: /V /4 /S   ←Key-enter this ONLY if your A drive is high-capacity.
```

4. Press ENTER to initiate the command. Insert a new disk in drive A when instructed to do so by the screen message. Press ENTER to begin formatting.

   WARNING: *If you leave the DOS disk in drive A and then press ENTER, you will format your DOS disk, thus erasing all files on the disk. Be certain you remove the DOS disk and insert a new disk before pressing ENTER.*
5. Enter the volume label FIRST DISK when prompted to do so by the screen message.
6. Respond with N for No when asked if you want to format another disk. By using the /S switch, you should have transferred the system files to your new disk. Confirm this by using the CHKDSK command, as shown in step 7.
7. Remove your newly formatted disk from drive A and replace it with the DOS disk. Then key-enter the following command.

```
A>CHKDSK B:    ←You must key-enter the parameter B: or the
                 CHKDSK command will immediately check the DOS
                 disk and will not give you a chance to insert
                 your new start-up disk.

                 (If you have two drives, insert the new disk
                 in drive B before pressing ENTER.)
```

If you have successfully transferred the system files, the CHKDSK command will indicate that the disk contains hidden files. If CHKDSK reports no hidden files, you may have forgotten to enter the /S switch on the command line along with the FORMAT command.

If you have forgotten this, use the following steps to transfer the system files.

a. Insert the DOS disk in drive A and your new disk in drive B.
b. Key-enter SYS B:. (Do not key the period.) (If your system has only one drive, insert your new disk in drive A when instructed to do so.)
c. The hidden system files will be recorded on your disk.
d. Copy COMMAND.COM from the DOS disk onto your new disk.

8. Test your start-up disk by inserting it in drive A and performing a warm boot. Press the CTRL, ALT, and DEL keys simultaneously, and the computer should restart from your new start-up disk.
9. You should make two more formatted system disks for backup copies and to use as you work through the examples and exercises in this book.

Files

The file is the single unit of instructions or characters that the computer uses for its work. A file has a beginning and an end and is known by its file name. It consists of either the special instructions written by programmers or the characters you create with programs such as word processors or spreadsheets.

SYSTEM FILES System files consist of hidden programs recorded in special disk locations. They are known as "hidden files" because you will not see their file names when you list the disk directory. They work with a visible file called COMMAND.COM, which controls the operation of DOS. COMMAND.COM is used before, during, and after any other program on the disk. The computer cannot work without COMMAND.COM being present on the disk.

EXECUTABLE FILES An **executable file** is a collection of instructions that is loaded into the computer and implemented. Running a program means instructing the computer to start the program. The program then operates either until you tell it to stop or until it comes to a built-in stopping point. To run a file, key the root name, which is the file name without the extension, and press ENTER. If you enter a root name that does not have an executable extension, DOS will tell you that the file is incorrect or missing.

Application programs, such as word processing, graphics, or database management programs, have COM or EXE extensions. The DOS external commands also have COM or EXE extensions. The only files that may be run have COM, EXE, or BAT extensions.

BATCH FILES Batch files, which have BAT extensions, contain a series of DOS instructions, listed one after the other. When you enter the batch file's root name, the list of DOS commands will be executed as if you had entered each one of them at the keyboard. Batch files provide a convenient way to execute a series of DOS commands over and over. Chapter 5 shows you how to write batch files for accomplishing useful tasks.

OTHER FILES You will encounter other file types when using your computer. Many of those you encounter will be programmed to work with COM or EXE files, such as the application programs that you will run. For example, text files created by a word processing program might have extensions such as DOC or TXT. Spreadsheet programs may use extensions such as WK1, SSP, or DAT. Graphics programs may create files ending with GRP, PIC, or DWG. If you name the extension for your file, you should use a descriptive extension to identify your file.

Today's commercial programs do so much and are so large that they normally will not fit in the computer's memory and still leave room for the work you create. Programmers have created overlay files to handle this. You may see an OVL file name extension. This refers to a part of the program code that is called into memory only when it is needed.

Directories and Subdirectories

You have learned how disks are formatted and how files are saved on the disk. You have learned the types of files and the rules for acceptable file names. Several examples have illustrated that the number of files on a hard disk can be large. You probably realize now that the number of diskettes can grow as more and more work is completed.

Directories and subdirectories help organize files. The file name is the link the computer makes with your work. The disk directory is the list the computer maintains of all files saved on the disk. Because the disk directory and its subdirectories are fundamental concepts in the way files are organized and manipulated, your mastery of this part of DOS is particularly important. The next chapter delves deeply into directories; the introduction presented here is intended to give you a basic understanding of how the many files you create can be managed.

The names, dates, and lengths of files are stored in the disk directory. Every disk has a directory; without it, the disk would not work in the computer. Each 5¼″ floppy diskette can hold a maximum of 112 file names in the directory. High-capacity disks can hold more file names. A one-file directory listing is illustrated below.

```
C:\>DIR A:

Volume in drive A is FIRST DISK
Volume Serial Number is 144D-0EF1
Directory of  A:\

COMMAND  COM    37557 12-19-88  12:00a
        1 File(s)   1105408 bytes free

C:\>
```

If the files are short, it is possible that they will fill up the directory before the disk itself is filled. To look through all of the file names, you may have to list many directory entries. Working with one long list of file names can become unmanageable. The hierarchical directory concept was created to solve this problem.

The directory is part of the disk format, and it is created when the disk is formatted. **Subdirectories** are similar to files; they contain directory information, including the file name, file size, date of creation or last update, and location codes. Subdirectories may contain as many files as the available disk space will allow.

The collection of directory and subdirectory entries is typically arranged in a particular order. This order is known as a **hierarchical tree**, and it provides a way to visualize the organization of many subdirectories as well as the files they contain. Trees and subdirectories will be explained in more depth in the next chapter.

BASIC OPERATIONS

This section presents five commonly used DOS commands. These commands are probably used most often in file management. It is very important for you to know how to use these commands. Although other commands that might have been included are not presented here, you will find most of the other popular and frequently used commands in other chapters of this book.

In the sections that follow, a similar format has been adopted to explain the commands in a uniform manner. First, the purpose of the command is explained. Then, an explanation of how the command is used, along with examples, is provided. Finally, other considerations are presented, such as difficulties to avoid and particular characteristics to keep in mind.

Copying Disks (DISKCOPY)

The DISKCOPY command is one of the most common DOS commands. It is used to make duplicates of disks. It becomes a key tool in keeping adequate backups of data or program disks.

PURPOSE DISKCOPY makes an exact duplicate of a disk, using one or two drives. It cannot be used with a hard disk or with copy-protected disks (commercial disks that are specially formatted to prevent duplication). It is most often used to make backup copies of data disks.

COMMAND USE This external DOS command uses parameters to specify the source and target disk drives. The source drive contains the disk to be copied. The target drive contains the disk that will receive the copy. The following two displays show the DISKCOPY commands for two-drive and one-drive systems. (The wording of the instructions may vary slightly depending on the version of DOS you are using.)

```
A>DISKCOPY A: B:        ←Common command form for two-drive system
                          when both drives are of the same type

Insert SOURCE diskette in drive A:

Insert TARGET diskette in drive B:

Press any key to continue . . .    ←Remove the DOS disk and insert
                                     the source and target disks.
Copying 80 tracks    ←May vary according to your computer and the
15 Sectors/Track, 2 Side(s)    types of drives you have. An exact
                               duplicate of the source is being made..

Copy another (Y/N)? N    ←Type N to stop or Y to copy another.
```

```
C:\>DISKCOPY A: A:


Insert SOURCE diskette in drive A:

Press any key to continue . . .

Copying 80 tracks
15 Sectors/Track,  2 Side(s)

Insert TARGET diskette in drive A:

Press any key to continue . . .

.
.   ←Swapping process continues until the entire source disk has been
     copied onto the target disk.
.

C:\>
```

If you are using DISKCOPY with a single drive, you will have to swap the target and source disks several times before the command is complete. The command first copies some of the source disk's information into memory. It then records it on the target disk. The amount of data that can be copied into memory at one time depends on the memory in your computer system. The less memory, the more times you will have to swap the disks. In a two-drive system, the two drives will come on and off as data is first loaded into memory and then copied; however, no swapping is required.

OTHER CONSIDERATIONS If you are using an early version of MS-DOS, you may have to format the disk prior to using the DISKCOPY command. If you are using PC-DOS, you may use a new disk as the target; it does not have to be formatted prior to using the DISKCOPY command. If the program does not find a format on the target disk, a message will appear on the screen telling you that the disk is also being formatted. The format of the source disk will be duplicated on the new diskette.

It is a safe practice to place a **write-protect tab** on the source disk before using the DISKCOPY command. This offers added protection against your data being damaged while the copying operation is in progress. Write-protecting of a 5¼″ diskette requires you to place an adhesive tab over the notch on the side of the diskette cover. When this notch is covered, the disk drive cannot record anything on the disk. Write-protecting of a 3½″ diskette involves covering the rectangular opening in the upper left-hand corner of the back of the disk. Expensive diskettes have a built-in piece of plastic which can be slid to the top of the slot. Cheaper diskettes require a piece of tape to be placed over the slot. Figure 2-2 illustrates write-protecting of two kinds of disks.

Figure 2-2. Write-protecting a diskette.

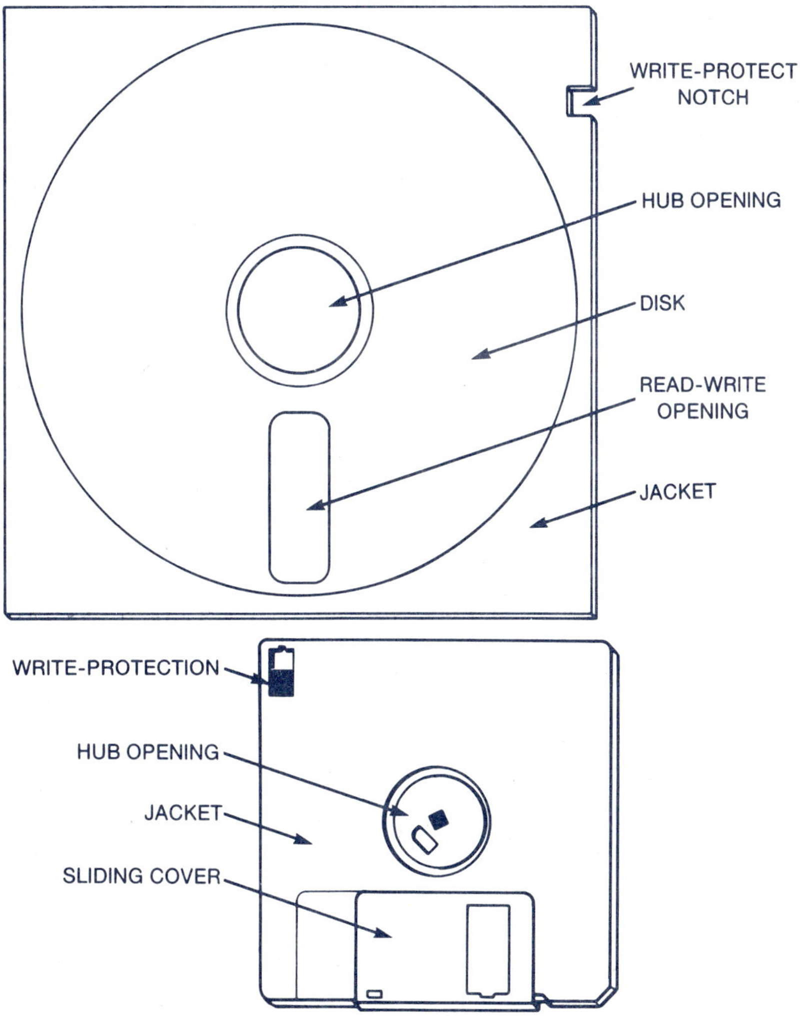

You will have to modify the way you use DISKCOPY if you have drives with different capacities. For example, you cannot copy a high-capacity disk onto a disk in a standard-capacity drive. You can, however, copy disks in the opposite direction; that is, you can copy one standard-capacity disk onto another in a high-capacity drive. The copy will be the same as the original.

If you attempt to use the DISKCOPY command with incompatible drives or disks, DOS will issue an error message. You then need to change the command or find a different system on which to complete the operation.

Copying Files (COPY)

Copy is an internal command used to create second copies of files or to move files from one place to another by first copying them and then deleting the originals. It may also be used to create new files or to add one file to the end of another.

PURPOSE The COPY command is used to create a duplicate of a file. The duplicate may appear on a different drive or device, such as a printer or screen. It may also appear on the same device if the file name is different from the original. The COPY command can also add one file onto the end of another in an operation called **concatenation**. A single file composed of the two files results.

COMMAND USE The COPY command is followed by the source file. If the source file is not in the current drive, the source file must be preceded by the drive designator. Wild-card characters may also be used. The target file and drive designator follow the source file. If no file name for the target is specified, the command will use the source file name. The following display shows some examples of the COPY command.

`A>COPY FIRST.DAT B:` `1 File(s) copied`	←*Copies file on drive A to drive B and gives copy the same name. Message shows 1 file copied.*
`A>COPY *.DAT B:` `8 Files(s) copied`	←*Copies all files on A with DAT extensions to drive B. All names are duplicated. Eight files had DAT extensions.*
`A>COPY MRKT.DAT B:MRKT.DOC` `1 File(s) copied`	←*The copy on B will have a new extension.*

The full file name must be specified for COPY to work. If you want to copy SALES.DAT from drive A to drive B, and you enter COPY A:SALES B:, DOS will indicate that it cannot find the file. To DOS, SALES is a different file from SALES.DAT.

You may specify any drive as the source and any drive as the destination. The source and/or destination drive may be the same or different from the current drive. DOS will not allow you to copy a file onto itself: i.e., you cannot copy the same file onto the original (target) drive without changing the file name. The following display shows more examples of the COPY command.

```
A>COPY C:MAIN.COM B:   ←This copies MAIN.COM from drive C to
                         drive B.
A>C:   ←This changes to drive C.

C>COPY B:MAIN.COM   ←This copies MAIN.COM on drive B (source) to
                     current drive C since there is no drive designator.

C>COPY B:MAIN.COM  MAIN2.COM   ←This copies file from drive B to drive
                                C and changes the file name.

C>COPY MAIN2.COM MAIN3.COM   ←This creates a third copy called
                              MAIN3.COM on drive C.
```

The COPY command can combine two or more files into one file. The command syntax would be as follows.

```
A> COPY FILE1.TXT+FILE2.TXT FILE3.TXT
```

FILE1.TXT and FILE2.TXT would be concatenated to form FILE3.TXT. The plus sign (+) between the file names tells DOS to combine these files. If you do not specify a destination file name, DOS will assign the first source file name as the new file name. You may also use wild-card characters when combining files. For example, you could concatenate FILE1.TXT, FILE2.TXT, and FILE3.TXT to form FILE4.TXT using the following command.

```
A> COPY FILE*.* FILE4.TXT
```

OTHER CONSIDERATIONS The COPY command will work with systems having only one drive. As you did with the DISKCOPY command, specify both an A drive and a B drive in the command, even though your system has only one drive. DOS will instruct you when to change the source and destination disks so that the copy is completed. This is shown as follows.

```
A>COPY BIGFILE.DAT B:    ←You can specify drive B as the target even
                           though you have a single drive.
```

If you have a high-capacity disk drive, you must be careful about which drive is used for the target diskette. If you have formatted a high-capacity diskette, the high-capacity drive must perform the copying. The regular-capacity drive will read the source disk. Therefore, to copy files from a standard-capacity diskette to a high-capacity one, place the source diskette in drive B and the target, high-capacity diskette in drive A. Drive A is almost always the high-capacity drive on AT computers.

Copies can be made from drives of different sizes as long as sufficient space exists on the target disk. The following display shows copying from a 5¼″ drive to a 3½″ drive and confirming the copy.

```
A:\>DIR    ←Drive A is 5¼″.

 Volume in drive A is FIRST DISK
 Volume Serial Number is 144D-0EF1
 Directory of  A:\

COMMAND  COM     37557 12-19-88  12:00a
TEST     TXT        25 06-15-91  10:54a
        2 File(s)   1104896 bytes free

A:\>COPY TEST.TXT B:    ←Drive B is 3½″.
        1 File(s) copied

A:\>DIR B:*.TXT    ←This shows that copying will work across different-
                     size drives.

 Volume in drive B is DF62__BU2
 Volume Serial Number is 0D37-1ECE
 Directory of  B:\

TEST     TXT            25 06-15-91  10:54a
        1 File(s)     641536 bytes free
```

To confirm that the file has been copied correctly, add the /V verify switch to the end of the command. DOS will compare the file copy with the original. If the copy is not the same, a message will appear. The command syntax is shown as follows.

```
A>COPY FILE1.EXE B: /V      ←/V tells DOS to verify that FILE1.EXE
                              is copied correctly.
   1 File(s) copied
```

If the file has been copied correctly, no error message appears. The command takes longer to complete because /V is on.

You must be careful when using the COPY command. First, the command will not warn you if a file with the same name as the original exists on the target diskette. For example, assume you have a file named WRITING.TXT on a backup diskette, but you have forgotten the name of this file. You create a new file called TEMP.TXT and decide to name its backup WRITING.TXT. After you execute the command to copy TEMP.TXT to B:WRITING.TXT, the contents of TEMP.TXT have replaced the original contents of WRITING.TXT. The file will still be called WRITING.TXT, but its contents will not be what you intended. Because DOS does not warn you when you are about to copy over a file with the same name, you must be sure you are entering the correct file names.

A second danger with the COPY command is reversing drive designators. You must remember that the first entry is the source and the second is the destination. For example, assume you keep backup copies of data files on a floppy diskette. These files have DAT extensions. At the end of a working session, you have created a number of new DAT files, which you save on your hard disk, drive C. You then want to make backup copies of these new data files and save them on the backup floppy in drive A.

Assume that when you copy the new files you reverse the drive designators. You key-enter COPY A:*.* C: instead of the correct entry COPY C:*.* A:. This mistake will copy all of the old files from drive A to drive C. The new work will be replaced by the old work and will be lost. There will be no way to recover the new work.

You can also copy keyboard entry directly into a disk file. This application of the COPY command is helpful if you want to create a batch file quickly without using a word processing program.

To copy from the console, the name for the keyboard, tell DOS to copy to a file from the console (CON). Key-enter the command COPY CON FILE NAME. (Do not key the period.) Instead of copying one file to another file, this command takes keyboard input and copies it to the specified file. The following illustration shows you how to do this.

```
A>COPY CON A:NOTE.TEXT    ← Key-enter this line.
-   ←The cursor waits for you to type.
This is the beginning of a note file on          ⎫   ⎧Key-enter each line.
quality performance in the assembly              ⎬←⎨(Press ENTER at the
operation. Special causes will be noted here.    ⎭   ⎩end of each line.)
^Z   ←After pressing ENTER after the last line, press F6.
      This produces a ^Z (Control-Z), the end-of-file
      marker. The file is copied to disk.

    1 File(s) copied

A>
```

Version 3.2 brought the new external command XCOPY to DOS users. XCOPY is an extended COPY command that makes file copying more flexible. For example, you can select more files to copy, such as those within a certain date range. You can select files across various subdirectories. The greater versatility of this command makes it an alternative to the DOS BACKUP command. It is also useful in maintaining up-to-date files when two or more computers are used.

XCOPY operates like COPY, but requires the use of more switches to invoke its additional features. The following command will copy all files in the MFG subdirectory that have been modified since the last copy operation was performed. In addition, XCOPY will wait for your approval before copying the file.

```
C>XCOPY C:\MFG\*.* B: /M /S /P    ←/M copies all modified files since
                                    last COPY operation. /S copies
                                    all files in designated directory
                                    and all its subdirectories. /P will
                                    pause until you approve copying
                                    of current displayed file.
```

Other XCOPY switches are explained in the command reference in Appendix A.

Displaying Files (TYPE)

The limits DOS places on file name length make it difficult to describe the file contents in the file name. You may wonder what is contained in a particular file, or you may want to find a file that contains specific information.

PURPOSE The TYPE command displays the contents of a file on the screen or printer. It is most often used to read the information in a data file or batch file. As mentioned earlier, batch files are special command files you create using DOS commands. You will learn about batch files in Chapter 5.

You can quickly review a letter or memo created with your word processor. Instead of entering the word processor program command, followed by the letter or memo file name, just use TYPE to display the file on the screen. You may see some funny characters along with the text you wrote. TYPE will display all characters in a file even if they are special computer commands inserted by the word processing program.

COMMAND USE Key TYPE on the command line followed by the file name you want to view. Press ENTER and the file will appear on the screen. If there are many lines, the text will scroll rapidly up and off the screen. You will not be able to read it quickly enough. Press CTRL-S to make the screen display pause. Press CTRL-S again to resume scrolling. The prompt will reappear when the entire file has been typed.

OTHER CONSIDERATIONS You can print the contents of a file by turning on the printer before completing the TYPE command. After keying TYPE and the file name, press CTRL-P. Then press ENTER. TYPE will begin listing the file on the screen and on the printer. After the entire file has been listed on paper, press CTRL-P again to turn off the printer.

If you list a program with the TYPE command instead of a text file, the screen will fill with many characters and symbols that make no sense. These characters represent the computer commands and special instructions that programs typically contain.

If you want to stop listing a file, press CTRL-C. This terminates the TYPE command and returns the prompt to the screen before you reach the end of the file.

Deleting Files (DEL/ERASE)

A necessary part of disk and file maintenance is removing old and unused files. You will also need to remove a new file if it contains bad data or has a file name you do not want to use (see the RENAME command next for another way to solve this particular need).

PURPOSE ERASE is used to remove a file name from the directory. This has the effect of removing the file from the disk. DEL is a shorter way to enter the ERASE command, and it does the same thing. DOS accepts either form of the command.

COMMAND USE Key-enter ERASE or DEL and the file name to be removed. Wild-card characters may be used in the file name specification, but this creates more risk. Once the file has been erased, there is nothing in DOS to allow you to bring it back. If you use a wild-card character in the file name specification and erase a file you really wanted to keep, with several exceptions described below, it will be lost. The following display illustrates the use of the DEL or ERASE command.

`A>DEL B:ADDRESS.DBF` ←*Pressing ENTER erases ADDRESS.DBF from the disk in drive B.*

`A>ERASE C:*.BAS /P` ←*This erases all files with a BAS extension on drive C. You will be asked to approve each deletion.*

`C>DEL *.*` ←*This erases every file on the hard disk. ISSUE THIS COMMAND WITH CAUTION!*

```
All files in directory will be deleted!
Are you sure (Y/N)?
```
←*DOS automatically supplies this warning. Key-enter Y to complete the command.*

OTHER CONSIDERATIONS Because ERASE is considered a dangerous command, exercise care when you use it. You can avoid erasing files you want to keep by first listing the file names with the DIR command. If you see a file name listed that you do not want to erase, do not use the ERASE command with that file name. In addition, Version 4 provides a new switch, /P, which requires approval before deleting the file or files designated in the command.

DOS versions prior to Version 5 do not provide any commands for recovering files that are erased. Utility programs do exist that permit you to recover the erased file. ERASE does not remove any part of the file from the disk. It marks the file name in the directory, and tells DOS that the space occupied by the deleted file is available to hold new data. As long as you do not record any other data on the disk after you mistakenly delete a file, you may be able to recover it using one of the file-recovery utilities.

DOS Version 5 provides UNDELETE, a command for recovering files that have been erased. This works with another command, MIRROR, which installs a memory-resident program to track all deletions as they are made. Use UNDELETE before saving any other files on disk. UNDELETE will in turn use the current list of deletions maintained by the MIRROR program. The display below shows the result of asking for a list of the undeleted programs maintained by MIRROR.

```
C:\DOS>UNDELETE /LIST

Directory: C:\DOS
File Specifications: *.*

   Deletion-tracking file contains   3 deleted files.
   Of those,     3 files have all clusters available,
                 0 files have some clusters available,
                 0 files have no clusters available.

   MS-DOS directory contains   3 deleted files.
   Of those,     3 files may be recovered.

Using the deletion-tracking file.

    TEST2    TXT   8  7-07-91   2:09p  ...A Deleted: 7-07-91   2:11p
    TEST1    TXT   8  7-07-91   2:06p  ...A Deleted: 7-07-91   2:10p
    TEST2    TXT   8  7-07-91   2:07p  ...A Deleted: 7-07-91   2:11p
```

Renaming Files (RENAME)

A common need is to rename an existing file. Although you could copy the file and give the copy the new name, this is time-consuming. Further, if you do not take the time to go back and delete the original file, you will have two copies of the same file with different names. This wastes valuable disk space and can ultimately slow DOS operation. A better approach is to rename the existing file.

PURPOSE The RENAME command lets you change file names in the directory. Doing this is useful when you change your mind, or when the contents of a file change so much that a different file name is better.

COMMAND USE RENAME or REN will be accepted by DOS. The command form is RENAME D:OLDFILE NEWFILE. The letter D designates the drive where the file to be renamed is located. The file name to be changed is entered next, followed by the new name. Extensions must be entered, and they may be changed. An example of the use of RENAME is shown in the following display.

```
A:\>DIR

 Volume in drive A is FIRST DISK
 Volume Serial Number is 144D-0EF1
 Directory of  A:\

COMMAND    COM    37557 12-19-88  12:00a
TEST       TXT       25 06-15-91  10:54a
         2 File(s)  1104896 bytes free

A:\>RENAME TEST.TXT EXPER.MNT    ←This changes the file name.

A:\>DIR TEST.TXT    ←The file will not be found because the name was
                     just changed.

 Volume in drive A is FIRST DISK
 Volume Serial Number is 144D-0EF1
 Directory of  A:\

File not found

A:\>
```

OTHER CONSIDERATIONS A drive designator should always be entered unless the file to be renamed is on the current drive. The new file name should never have a drive designator because the location of the file to be changed is entered with the old file name.

Wild-card characters may be used with RENAME. The command will change names according to the entry you make on the command line. However, if applying the wild-card character will result in a duplicate file name, DOS will display an error message and will end the command. If some files were not changed before the command stopped, you must re-enter the command, renaming from the point at which the message appeared.

HANDS-ON EXERCISE

1. Turn on the computer if it is not already on. Use your new start-up disk to do this.
2. Insert your start-up disk in drive B.
3. Insert the DOS disk in drive A. If you have only one drive, you will have to swap your disk and the DOS disk in and out of the drive. If you have a hard disk and one floppy drive, and all of the DOS disk files have been transferred to the hard disk, follow the instructions in step 6.
4. Copy the following files from the DOS disk to your start-up disk.

   NOTE: Some of these programs are not available on versions prior to PC-DOS 3.0 or MS-DOS 3.2, and some of the programs may have EXE extensions rather than COM extensions on your version of DOS. Also, your version of BASIC may be GWBASIC. Therefore, modify this exercise if necessary.

BASIC.COM	DISKCOMP.COM	FORMAT.COM	SORT.EXE
BASICA.COM	DISKCOPY.COM	LABEL.COM	TREE.COM
CHKDSK.COM	EDLIN.COM	MODE.COM	VDISK.SYS
COMP.COM	FIND.EXE	MORE.COM	

   For example, use the following commands to copy the first two files.

```
COPY A:BASIC.COM B:

COPY A:BASICA.COM B:
```

5. If you have a single floppy drive, insert the DOS disk in drive A and enter the same commands. You will then have to swap disks when prompted.
6. If you have all of the DOS files on the hard disk in drive C, insert your start-up disk in drive A and use the following commands to copy the first two files. Copy the other files listed in step 4.

```
COPY C:BASIC.COM A:

COPY C:BASICA.COM A:
```

If the DOS files are in a subdirectory called DOS, for example, you would enter the first command as follows: COPY C: \DOS \BASIC.COM A:. This way of entering the file name uses the file name's path name. It tells the computer how to find the subdirectory holding the file and then the file itself. You will learn how to use path names in the next chapter.

7. Place your start-up disk in drive A. Copy a text file from the keyboard. It will contain a brief summary of some of the DOS commands we have covered so far.
8. Key-enter the following command: COPY CON DOSINSTR.
9. Key-enter the following lines. (They must not exceed the width of the screen.)

```
DIR: Lists the directory

DISKCOPY: Duplicates an entire diskette

COPY: Creates a duplicate file

TYPE: Lists a file's contents on the screen

ERASE: Removes a file from the directory

RENAME: Changes a file's name
```

10. After entering the sixth line, press F6, followed by ENTER. The new file, DOSINSTR, is now on your start-up disk.
11. Confirm that the file has been created. Key-enter the following command: TYPE DOSINSTR. Your list of DOS instructions should appear on the screen.
12. Copy these DOS instructions and give the new file a different name. Key-enter the following command: COPY DOSINSTR DOSINST2. The copy will be on the same disk as the original.
13. Delete the original file. Key-enter the following command: ERASE DOSINSTR.
14. Rename the copy by key-entering: REN DOSINST2 DOS__SUMM.
15. Confirm that it is the same file by key-entering: TYPE DOS__SUMM.

APPLICATION PROGRAMS

An application program instructs the computer to perform certain work. Word processing is a typical application. This kind of program will let you type letters, edit reports, and generally use the computer for text management. When the computer is running a word processing application program, it cannot do a different task, such as spreadsheet calculations. Other typical application programs include spreadsheet, graphics, database management, and project management.

Several programs, called "multitasking," allow multiple tasks to be performed in the computer at the same time. The computer must have the proper hardware and sufficient memory, and the programs must be compatible with the multitasking environment. Then it is possible, for example, to begin a long calculation on a spreadsheet program and then switch to the word processing program to complete a letter.

Windows 3.0 is the latest graphical version of the program that permits multitasking. It works best if the hardware includes a 386 processor and at least 1M of memory. DesqView is a text-based windowing environment that allows the same thing. In fact, DesqView can run Windows 3.0 in one of its windows. In turn, Windows 3.0 can run DesqView in one of its windows. Setting up productive multiwindow situations can be challenging, and requires advanced knowledge of DOS, the windowing program, and the application programs involved.

Application programs help you accomplish work using the personal computer. We discussed earlier the benefits of using the computer to help manage information and solve problems. Because these programs run on the personal computer, they are under the general control of DOS, the computer's operating system.

This chapter has introduced some basic, commonly used DOS commands. These are the commands you will use repeatedly as you work with the personal computer. One of your most prevalent uses of the computer may be for application programs. The remainder of this chapter will tell you how to set up, in general terms, the application programs you will be using. If you are working with a system in which all or most of the application programs have already been installed or loaded, you may want to skip this part. You can refer back to it later if you have a specific need.

Setting Up Application Programs

When you first purchase commercial programs, they probably will not be in easily usable form. The programs themselves will perform, but you must adjust them to work with your system. Because computer equipment can be hooked together in so many different ways to form a system, vendors may sell their programs in "building block" form.

Building blocks are series of files that must be put together to match the system equipment you are using. You must put these blocks together so that you have a series of programs that will work in your system. Most manufacturers today include a setup or install program on the disks that you buy. These are special programs that you run once to set up or configure the software to match your hardware. Usually, you can modify your configuration after it has been installed.

Installing Programs

This section will describe briefly the typical approaches used to help you install an application program in your system. You will not have an opportunity to practice these steps until you have a new program to set up. Nevertheless, you will find this introduction useful because it raises your awareness of the start-up requirements. If you are working with a system with programs installed, attempt to talk with the person who did the actual installation.

If appropriate, you may want to use the install programs to modify one or more features. However, write down the original settings in case you need to reset the original configuration.

Most software vendors follow a similar approach. In following the program manual, you will be instructed to run the install program. This requires you to insert the proper disk in drive A and enter a command such as INSTALL or SETUP. Most install programs will instruct you on each step. The following are some typical questions you might be asked to answer while setting up an application program.

- Do you have a hard disk?
- Which drive will hold your data disks?
- Do you have a color monitor?
- Does your color monitor support enhanced graphics?
- Do you have a modem?
- If you have a modem, how is it hooked to your computer?
- Do you use an impact printer or plotter?
- Which printer or plotter do you use?
- How is your printer or plotter hooked to your computer?

Many of today's installation programs have the ability to analyze your entire system with no intervention from you. The program will then tell you what it has found and suggest that these features be included in the setup process. Most times, these self-analysis programs will understand your system better than you do. It is best to accept the suggested responses to the installation choices.

The most friendly and effective programs provide small paragraphs of information, give you several choices of action, require you to indicate and confirm your choice, and then ask you to indicate whether you are ready to continue. When the procedure has been completed, you are shown all of the choices you have made and are asked to confirm them again.

The install program then copies files from the disks you have purchased onto your working diskettes or your hard disk. Often, the install program will also "decompress" the files on the new disks; these files are compressed to save space on the disks sent to you. So 500K of compressed files can become 1600K or more on your hard disk. Many large programs will not work unless you have a hard drive to hold all of the files. The program literature will tell you ahead of time if this is the case.

Your responses to questions such as those listed above will determine which files are copied. Vendors supply many more files than you will need. For example, several different printer driver files may be supplied. A **printer driver file** is a program containing the special codes that control how your printer performs. You will need only the one that corresponds to your own printer. The install program copies the appropriate printer driver file onto your working disk.

This general procedure is repeated until all of the necessary files have been copied onto a working set of floppy disks or onto your hard disk. In most cases, the install program will even set up any required subdirectories and will copy the files at the correct locations.

Copy Protection

If you use a copy-protected program, it is illegal and unethical to attempt to make additional, unauthorized copies of the software. You are often entitled to have one backup copy to use if the original becomes damaged. Vendors often will supply backup copies of their program disks with the packages you purchase. Some vendors may require you to send a coupon to them before you receive a backup copy. Still, the trend today is the sale of commercial programs without copy protection. Instead of copy protection, the program requires that you enter your name and company, if you work for one, and then it permanently writes this information within the program. Usually, you cannot skip this step, nor can you change the information that is recorded. If you share copies of your program with others, which is illegal, the copies will carry your name on them.

If you do not have a hard disk, you will use the diskette supplied by the vendor. The diskette is already copy-protected. If you use a hard disk, the vendor will, in many cases, provide a way for the installation program to copy special files onto your hard disk. These special files allow you to use the program on the hard disk but prevent any unauthorized copying from the hard disk. Special menu selections may allow you to "uninstall" the special files so that you can move the program to another hard disk.

◆ Summary

1. Newer DOS versions include improved and additional commands as well as fixes for program bugs.
2. Computer data is recorded on either floppy disks or hard disks. Hard disks hold millions of characters or bytes, whereas 5¼″ floppy diskettes can hold about 360K, 3½″ diskettes approximately 720K, high-capacity 5¼″ diskettes approximately 1200K (1.2M), and high-capacity 3½″ diskettes about 1440K (1.44M).
3. The external FORMAT command records a pattern of tracks and sectors on a disk surface, erasing any data previously recorded. Extra care is required to avoid erasing important work.
4. A label is an electronic name given to any disk. DOS Version 2 allows you to label the disk only when it is formatted. Version 3 provides the LABEL command, which allows the label to be added or changed at any time.
5. CHKDSK will display the total size of all files on a disk, including any hidden files. In addition to showing the size of current memory, CHKDSK will repair files that may have been recorded improperly.
6. Files are units of program instructions or user-generated characters from an application program. System files are used by DOS to control the computer. The computer runs executable files to perform work, and the results are saved in data files.
7. A disk directory holds the file name, the time and date of creation, and the size of all files on the disk. Subdirectories are branches from the root directory and hold file groupings. The entire file directory system is known as a hierarchical tree structure.
8. Some fundamental DOS commands are:

   DISKCOPY, which creates a duplicate disk

   COPY, which duplicates or appends files from one location to another

   TYPE, which displays a file's contents on the screen or printer

   ERASE, which removes a file name from the disk directory

   RENAME, which lets you change a file name
9. Setup or install programs help you select the building block files to allow an application program to run on your system.

◆ Exercises

1. You type the command XCOPY /M /S, and receive the message "Unknown command." What might be the problem? How would the DOS version you are using affect this situation, and how would you determine what version of DOS you are using?

2. You learn that several subdirectories of document files contain over 6M of data. You have several blank 5¼″ and 3½″ diskettes on hand on which you could make backup copies. Some of the 5¼″ diskettes, and some of the 3½″ diskettes, are labeled "high-density." Assume that you have two of each type (eight in all). What is the total amount of disk capacity you have, and will the document files fit on these diskettes?

3. As you begin to copy the files mentioned in exercise 2, what command must you use to prepare the new disks to hold data? Someone tells you to be sure to use "/S" with this command. For the task you are doing, explain why this is bad advice.

4. After you are halfway through copying files from the hard disk, you learn that a start-up disk is needed. However, you have no more blank disks. What command would you use to turn a data disk into a start-up disk? Assume that you have formatted all of the disks but have not begun copying to all of them.

5. You are asked to put a label on each disk. All disks are formatted. You have made one into a start-up disk. What is the best way to label the disks? Name another method you could have used if you had been told earlier to name the disks.

6. Which command would you use to determine if any hidden files are on your disk? If this command tells you there are 25528 bytes in hidden files on your disk, what might you conclude about these files?

7. Returning to the situation introduced in exercise 2, you observe that the files to be copied are in the DOCS subdirectory, which in turn contains two subdirectories, THISYEAR and LASTYEAR. First, explain the difference between a directory and a subdirectory. Then explain why XCOPY could have been used to advantage to copy files from these subdirectories.

8. You have a 5¼″ high-density disk and must copy all of the files it contains onto both another high-density 5¼″ disk and a high-density 3½″ disk. Your computer has a high-density 5¼″ drive A and a high-density 3½″ drive B. Describe what commands you would use to satisfy this request and why you would use them.

9. What command should be used to copy SMALL.COM from a disk in drive A to a disk in drive B and verify that the copy is acceptable?

10. You display the directory and see the three files ADDR1.TXT, ADDR2.TXT, and ADDR3.TXT. You know that these files contain names and addresses but are not alphabetized, and you do not know where the address you are looking for is located. What DOS command could you use to display these files? Describe how you could ensure that you would have enough time to look for the address you want.

11. After copying three files (MON.DAT, TUE.DAT, and WED.DAT) onto floppy disks from a hard disk, you want to remove them. What command will accomplish this? How can you remove all three of these files with one command? What big danger exists with this approach?

12. What command would you use to change TAX88.WKS to TAX89.WK1? The file is on a disk in drive B. The current drive is drive A.

13. You are handed five installation disks for a new word processor and are asked to copy them to the hard drive. What is at least one thing that is wrong with these instructions?

Part 2

Intermediate DOS

OVERVIEW OF PART 2

Part 2 takes you further into DOS operations and provides skills that will improve your effectiveness with the computer. Directories help manage the many disk files that you will create. Chapter 3 will show you how to use directory and subdirectory commands to your advantage. These commands are especially important when you use a hard disk, because the number of files can become very large. Chapter 4 will show you how to manage your hard disk efficiently and will discuss the important tasks of file control and backup.

Chapter 3

Deeper into DOS

Objectives

After completing this chapter, you should be able to:

1. Use directories more effectively.
2. Use the PATH command.
3. Create, move among, and remove subdirectories using MKDIR, CHDIR, and RMDIR.

Terms

subject disk
root directory
subdirectory
disk capacity
multilevel subdirectory
network
current subdirectory
parent directory
path
path name
metastring command
subdirectory handling command

Overview

Directory trees provide a way to organize and efficiently use large numbers of computer files. Whether you use floppy disks or a hard disk, you should be able to understand and apply directories and subdirectories. This chapter introduces you to the benefits of good directory organization and shows you how to plan your directory system. It introduces you to the basic directory commands and provides you with practice in using these commands.

SYSTEM STRUCTURE

Choosing the organization and structure of your directory is an important decision. Having an effective directory system will increase your efficiency, whereas a poorly organized system will cause wasted time and confusion.

Good disk organization will help you in at least three ways. First, by avoiding frustrating searches through unneeded files, you will save time in finding the data you need. Second, you will conserve disk space. Instead of having obsolete files or current duplicates, you keep only the data you need. Finally, an organized file system makes it easy for others to use your files.

ORGANIZING YOUR COMPUTER FILES

Your file organization depends on your hardware and whether you will use floppy disks or a hard disk. If your system does not have a hard disk, floppy disk capacity will restrict the organization method you can use. Hard disks (or network storage) give you much more freedom in selecting an organization method.

Floppy Disk System

Added features have made applications programs larger, at least by the standards of several years ago. Printer support files, printer font files, and dictionary files quickly fill floppy disks and leave little space for data files. Therefore, systems without hard drives depend on having two floppy disk drives. The A drive contains the program disk with its program files. The B drive contains the data disk.

In a floppy disk system, it is common to keep separate data disks for each application program. For example, if you regularly use a word processor, a spreadsheet, and a graphics program, you will have separate data disks for each. Whenever you change the program disk, you will change the data disk.

Another technique is to place all data files about a single subject on a separate data disk. Each disk becomes a **subject disk**. You might have separate disks for finances, maintenance issues, school topics, and work subjects.

Hard Disk System

The hard disk has space for many programs and data files. The **root directory** or main directory of any disk is limited to a fixed number of files depending on the type of disk used. Therefore, it is essential to use **subdirectories** to maximize disk capacity. **Disk capacity** is the disk space available. The number of subdirectories and their files that a disk can hold is limited only by the amount of disk space available.

Subdirectories can function like floppy disks. A separate subdirectory can be designated to hold all of the program files for a particular application.

The organization of your data files will affect your efficiency. Most of your work will involve creating, changing, moving, and copying data files. These files must be properly arranged to achieve maximum effectiveness. There are two basic approaches to organizing data files. The first approach is to use a separate subdirectory for each subject or project. The second approach is to use a separate data subdirectory for each application program. With the first approach, you might store word processing, outline, calendar, and database files in the time management subdirectory. With the second approach, you would keep each of these files in the data subdirectory associated with each program. The file's title would be used to identify the time management files.

Multilevel subdirectories allow a combination of these two approaches. Each application program has its own subdirectory. Within the application subdirectory, a separate subdirectory is created for each general topic. Thus, your word processing subdirectory would have subdirectories for business letters, proposals, personal notes, and research reports. Figure 3-1 illustrates this approach.

Figure 3-1. Multilevel subdirectories.

Word Processing Subdirectory	Spreadsheet Subdirectory	Database Subdirectory
Business	*Personal*	*Personal*
STARTUP.DOC	HOMEBUD.WK1	PHONE.DBF
AGENCY1.DOC		DATES.DBF
Personal	*Account*	*Clients*
ENTERTAI.DOC	INVEN.WK1	CURRENT.DBF
ALUMNI.DOC	TRAVEL.WK1	INACTIVE.DBF
Proposal	*Productn*	*Sales*
SALES.DOC	PROWEEK1.WK1	NOREAST.DBF
		SOEAST.DBF

Networks

A network is a system in which computers are connected together with cables. There is a network operating system as well as an individual computer or work station operating system. A detailed explanation of networks is beyond the scope of this text. Nonetheless, you may be in a situation in which your computer is part of a network.

A network usually has a central computer, called a "server," which manages the actions of the network. Satellite computers are the work stations that can operate essentially like stand-alone units. The only differences are those related to the network operating system and its requirements. See the network administrator for training about the specifics of how your network works and how you start your computer.

For the purposes of the remainder of this text, it will be assumed that DOS is present on the work station and that the DOS commands perform as described. One difference that you may encounter involves the concept of the virtual disk. Your work station may have one or two floppy drives. It may not contain an actual physical hard drive. Yet, you can access drive C or D as a virtual disk. This means that you use the physical hard drive on the network server as if it were in your computer. Actually, you will use a subdirectory on the server, but you will think you are using the hard disk itself.

HANDS-ON EXERCISE

1. With pencil and paper, arrange the list of file names that follows step 2. Use all of the files listed, even if you are not personally familiar with all of the represented programs. Write down headings to represent subdirectories. Use only one level of headings. Place under these headings the programs that you believe belong there. Do not use any file name from the list below as a heading. Use a heading that is a legal file name. (It should have no more than eight characters, and it may have a three-character extension.)

2. Assume for now that you have an unlimited amount of disk space, which is similar to having a new, large-capacity hard disk. The following list shows the file names with an explanation of the contents of each file.

LOTUS.COM	(A spreadsheet program)
GRADES.WK1	(A spreadsheet data file)
123.EXE	(A spreadsheet program that works with LOTUS.COM)
LORDFLY.DOC	(A document file)
BIBLIO1.DBF	(A database data file)
BOOKRPT1.DOC	(A document file)
PERSBDG.WK1	(A spreadsheet data file)
GASMILES.WK1	(A spreadsheet data file)
EDITOR.EXE	(A word processing program)
FRIENDS.DBF	(A database data file)
POEMS-OL.DOC	(A document file)
POEM12.DOC	(A document file)
MOMDAD1.DOC	(A document file)
CHEMLAB1.WK1	(A spreadsheet data file)

DICTION1.OVL	(A word processing companion file)
DUNGEON.COM	(A game program)
DBASEIII.EXE	(A database program)
MELTPNTS.PIC	(A graphics file)
RESUME.DOC	(A document file)
GRAPH.COM	(A graphics program)
DBASEIII.OVL	(A database companion file)
ZAPIT.EXE	(A game program)
BOOKRPT2.DOC	(A document file)
CLUBMBRS.DBF	(A database data file)

3. Create a second list having more than one level of headings. It might look similar to the multilevels in Figure 3-1.
4. Create a third list, assuming that you will be using floppy disks. Disk space will be limited. Assume that each floppy disk can hold only one application program (including companion files) and no more than 15 data files.
5. Compare the advantages and disadvantages of each of the approaches you designed in your lists. How would you want to set up your own files?
6. If instructed to do so, prepare a final list of your own files. Arrange them in the manner in which you want to use them.

DIRECTORIES

The essential start-up files used to start the computer must be located in the root directory. The application files and data files can be located in subdirectories.

You should be able to move quickly and easily from program to program. This is especially important if you are using many different programs. In the next section, you will learn how to create a directory tree and use directories and subdirectories. If you are just setting up your files, you can organize your system according to this method. If you are already using a nonorganized hard disk or a floppy disk system, organizing your files in this manner may take some effort, but will save time later.

Subdirectory Characteristics

Subdirectories are similar to files, but look and act differently. Subdirectory names follow the same rules as file names. Most alphanumeric characters are allowed. The exact list of characters may vary with the computer used. Any character that has special meaning to DOS cannot be used in a subdirectory name. For example, characters such as the colon (:), the slash (/), and the asterisk (*) cannot be used. In addition, subdirectories may have extensions in their names. Figure 3-2 indicates some acceptable subdirectory names. Subdirectory names should not match regular DOS command names.

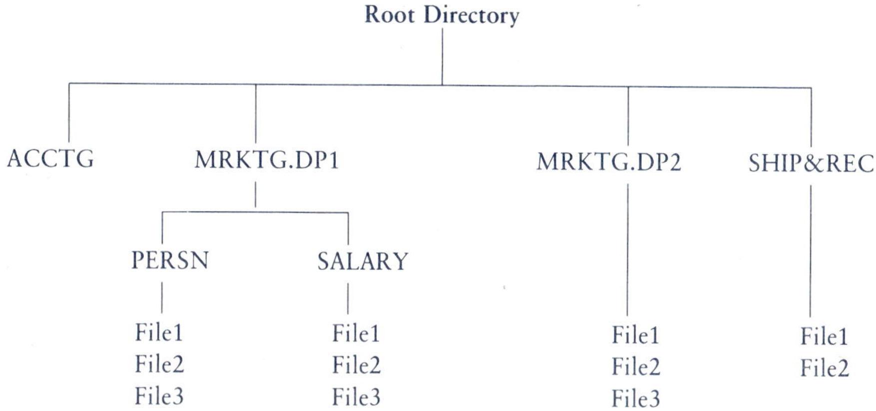

Figure 3-2. A typical subdirectory structure with typical subdirectory names.

Directory Listing

The DIR command lists the contents of a disk or the current directory. DIR, followed by the subdirectory name, will display the files in the named subdirectory. Additional subdirectories will be displayed at the same time as directory files. You will learn how to move from subdirectory to subdirectory later in this chapter.

The first line in a directory listing gives the name of the subdirectory specified in the DIR command. The following display shows examples of several directory listings. Additional information will appear on your screen display.

```
A>DIR

 Directory of A:\    ←This indicates the root directory.

(names of files in directory)
```

```
A>DIR \SALES     ←Lists the SALES subdirectory.

Volume in drive A is REGION1
Volume Serial Number is 15D5-34E2
Directory of A:\SALES     ←This indicates the SALES subdirectory.

.          <DIR>        12-10-90   8:10a  }  ← { Special lines in
..         <DIR>        01-13-91  12:10p  }    { subdirectory
(names of files in subdirectory)
```

The first two lines in the SALES subdirectory are the names of two directory entries created automatically by DOS. The period is an abbreviation for the current directory, and the double period is an abbreviation for the parent directory.

The **current** (or active) **subdirectory** is the one into which you are logged. Therefore, in a hierarchical directory tree, the current subdirectory is always within a directory known as its parent. The **parent directory** is one level immediately above the current subdirectory. The current subdirectory is the parent of the subdirectories it contains. The double period is a shorthand name for the parent directory. For example, CD .. moves from the current directory to its parent, and DIR .. displays the parent directory.

LOCATING FILES

You tell the computer the name of the file you need. DOS uses the file name to find the file. Because the file may be in a subdirectory, the path to the file and the path name are important concepts in locating and using files.

The Path to a File

When you think of a path, you probably visualize a trail in the woods. The concept of a path in your hierarchical tree is similar. A file's **path** is the route from the root directory, through any subdirectories, to the specific file you are seeking. A file's **path name** is the list of the subdirectory names from the root directory to the file.

To illustrate this important concept, refer to Figure 3-3. Notice that there are four files called File2. Without subdirectories, only one File2 could

Figure 3-3.
The path to a particular file.

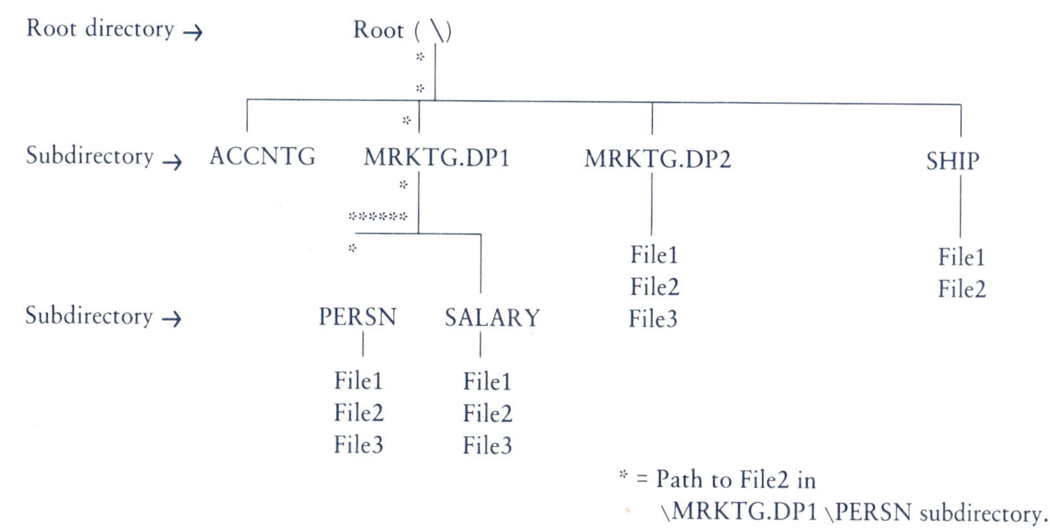

exist. However, each file is distinct, even with the same file name, because each resides in a separate subdirectory. Files having the same name cannot exist within the same subdirectory.

To describe the path to the second personnel file in the first marketing department, use the path name. The path name for this file is \MRKTG.DP1 \PERSN \File2. The subdirectory names, which are on the path to the file name, are separated by reverse slashes and are placed in front of the file name. Notice how this file is unique. It is different from \MRKTG.DP1 \SALARY \File2 and from \SHIP \File2 because the path names are different. Using path names in this manner allows the computer to find any file in any subdirectory at any level in the hierarchical tree.

To use the path name correctly, start with a reverse slash, followed by each subdirectory name along the path. The subdirectory names are separated by reverse slashes. The file name you want is entered last in the string of characters. No spaces are allowed anywhere in a path name.

The PROMPT Command

DOS will show you the current subdirectory. To make it display your location, issue the PROMPT command with two metastring commands. **Metastring commands** tell DOS to alter the display in specified ways.

The command used to show the current subdirectory location is PROMPT pg. The $p tells DOS to display the current path, and thus your location in the directory tree. The $g tells DOS to display a ">" sign after the path name and thus separate the path name from the next command that may be entered. The > is a matter of preference and could be some other character. To remove the path from the display, issue the command PROMPT without any parameters.

The Current Directory

You learned in Chapter 1 that DOS needs to know the current drive. Similarly, DOS needs to know the current directory. A directory or subdirectory will remain current until changed.

Any command you enter will use the current directory unless a different directory name precedes the command. DOS looks in the current directory for the file name you enter. If the file is there, DOS executes it. If it is not, DOS will indicate that the file does not exist.

To execute a file in a directory other than the current one, the path name, starting from the root directory, must be entered. The named file will be executed, but the current directory will not be changed. When you exit from the program, you will find that you are still in the directory that was current when you entered the execution command.

A problem can occur when you run a program in a directory other than the current directory. Many application programs use other programs or files in their operation. To do this, the main application program will issue its own command to run or load the needed file. Many applications operate as if any of the files they need are in the current directory. Therefore, if you start a program from another directory, that program will look for its companion programs, be unable to find them, and stop with an error. The best procedure is to make the directory containing the application you want to run the current directory. You will learn how to do this in the next section. In addition, the DOS PATH command gives you a way to instruct DOS to look in other directories if it does not find a file in the current directory.

The PATH Command

The PATH command allows any executable file to be found regardless of the current directory designation. DOS will search first in the current directory when it is directed to use a particular file. If the named file is not there, DOS tells you that it cannot find the file. To use the file, you will have to enter the file name along with the path name.

By entering the PATH command when you start the computer, you tell DOS to search every subdirectory named in the PATH command until it finds the named file. If the specified file name is not in any of these subdirectories, DOS will stop with a message informing you that it cannot find the file.

To illustrate this, assume that you are in the DOCMNT subdirectory. The OUTLINE.EXE program is in the PRGMS subdirectory. Both DOCMNT and PRGMS are first-level subdirectories, as shown in Figure 3-4. You have not used the PATH command. To run the outline program, enter \PRGMS \OUTLINE. If you enter just OUTLINE, DOS will tell you that it cannot find the file because it looks only in the DOCMNT subdirectory. If you key-enter the command PATH=C: \PRGMS; at the prompt, you will then be able to issue the command OUTLINE while in the DOCMNT subdirectory. When DOS cannot find the specified file in the current directory, it looks in all of the subdirectories specified in the PATH command.

Figure 3-4. PRGMS subdirectory with OUTLINE.EXE file.

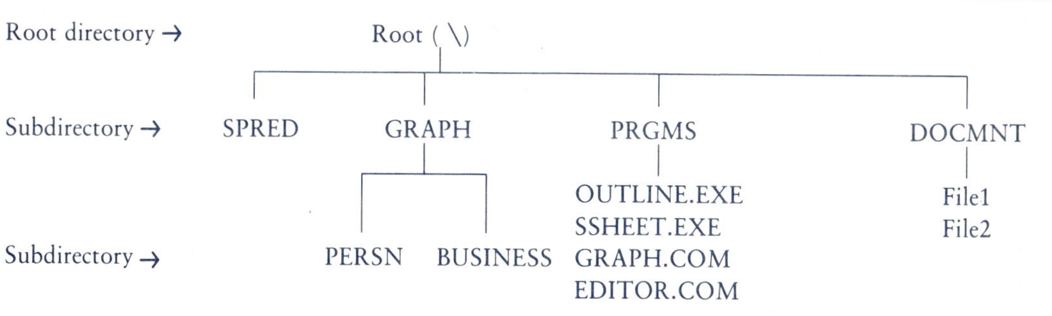

You must specify in the PATH command every subdirectory you want DOS to search, starting with the root directory. You have to do this only once, at the beginning of your work session, and it will stay in effect until changed or until the computer is turned off. Separate the subdirectory names with semicolons, and include the complete names of the paths you want DOS to search. If you specify only first-level subdirectories in the PATH command, DOS will not search the second level for your file.

Finally, the PATH command will work only when you specify an executable file—that is, any EXE, COM, or BAT file. Entering a data file from the DOS command line does not make sense and will be rejected by DOS.

The proper syntax is PATH= \subdirectory; \subdirectory;. (Do not use the period at the end, but do use the semicolons.) Start with C: \; to have DOS search the C drive root directory. The PATH command works only if it is entered from the DOS command line. If you are within an application program and want to store the data in a file in another subdirectory, you must use the commands provided in the program. If you just enter the name of the data file, it will be stored in the current subdirectory; the PATH command will have no effect.

The APPEND Command

The PATH command causes DOS to search directories for executable files, such as EXE, COM, or BAT files. However, DOS will not look for other types of files.

The APPEND command causes DOS to search for nonexecutable files in subdirectories other than the current directory. This is useful when you use an application with data files in different locations on the hard disk.

To search the PRGMS and DOCMNT subdirectories for data files, enter the following commands at the start of your work.

```
APPEND /E /X
```

←*This loads the command, directs the use of special DOS commands, and includes the disk drives in the environment.*

```
APPEND C: \PRGMS;C \DOCMNT
```

USING SUBDIRECTORIES

The number of subdirectories is limited only by disk space. A subdirectory can contain other subdirectories as well as any types of program or data files. Special DOS handling commands are used to create and manipulate subdirectories and aid you in working with your files. You will learn to use these **subdirectory handling commands** in the following discussion.

Subdirectory Handling Commands

Regular file commands will not work with subdirectories because of the special nature of subdirectory files. Three subdirectory commands allow you to create, move among, and delete subdirectory files.

MKDIR—MAKE DIRECTORY Using the MKDIR, or MD, command is the only way to create a subdirectory. DOS will set up the subdirectory file and its internal linkages to the hierarchical tree. It even creates the period and double period subdirectory names.

Creating a subdirectory is like listing the directory of a disk. The proper procedure is to enter MKDIR, or the abbreviation MD, followed by the name of the subdirectory you are creating. To create a subdirectory within a subdirectory, you must enter the path name after entering MD. The following example shows the commands needed to create a subdirectory called UTIL. The DIR command is used to show a partial directory before and after creating UTIL.

```
A:\>DIR

 Volume in drive A is FIRST DISK
 Volume Serial Number is 144D-0EF1
 Directory of  A:\

COMMAND  COM    37557  12-19-88  12:00a
EXPER    MNT       25  06-15-91  10:54a
        2 File(s)    1104896 bytes free

A:\>MD UTIL     ←Creates the UTIL subdirectory

A:\>DIR

 Volume in drive A is FIRST DISK
 Volume Serial Number is 144D-0EF1
 Directory of  A:\

COMMAND  COM     37557   12-19-88  12:00a
EXPER    MNT        25   06-15-91  10:54a
UTIL        <DIR>        06-29-91   5:52p
          3 File(s)   1104384 bytes free   ←Subdirectory treated
                                             as a file
```

Listing the contents of the new subdirectory will show that DOS has created two new subdirectories known as period (.) and double period (..): These may be used as abbreviations for the current directory and the parent directory, respectively. For example, assume that you have changed to the UTIL subdirectory created in the previous example. (The next section shows you how to change to another subdirectory.) The following example shows how to use the period and double period with the DIR command.

```
A:\UTIL>DIR    ←A:\UTIL>means that the PROMPT $p$g command
                has been used to display the current path.

 Volume in drive A is FIRST DISK
 Volume Serial Number is 144D-0EF1
 Directory of  A:\UTIL

.            <DIR>       06-29-91    5:52p
..           <DIR>       06-29-91    5:52p
        2 File(s)    1104384 bytes free

A:\UTIL>DIR ..    ←The double period refers to the parent directory.

 Volume in drive A is FIRST DISK
 Volume Serial Number is 144D-0EF1
 Directory of  A:\

COMMAND  COM     37557    12-19-88   12:00a
EXPER    MNT        25    06-15-91   10:54a
UTIL         <DIR>        06-29-91    5:52p
        3 File(s)    1104384 bytes free

A:\UTIL>    ←Shows that UTIL is still the logged subdirectory
```

A path name must not contain more than 63 characters, including the reverse slashes. Therefore, using short subdirectory names will allow you to have longer path names without exceeding the 63-character limit. Using the period and double period entries can also save character space in long path names.

CHDIR—CHANGE DIRECTORY The CHDIR, or CD, command allows you to change the current directory. Once you have changed to a new subdirectory, you can work with any file within that subdirectory.

The standard syntax is CHDIR or CD followed by the subdirectory name. If no subdirectory name is specified, the command will display the name of the current subdirectory. The following display illustrates the CD command in action.

```
A:\      ←Currently in the root directory
A:\>CD
A:\      ←Display of current path

A:\>CHDIR UTIL    ←Change to the UTIL subdirectory.

A:\UTIL>CD
A:\UTIL    ←Display of current path. Note how use of the PROMPT
            $p$g command makes using CD unnecessary.

A:\UTIL>
```

If the current directory is not the root directory, using CD is a little more complicated. Refer back to Figure 3-4 to see the hierarchical tree that is used in the following discussion. Assume that you are in the root directory. To change to any first-level subdirectory, enter CD followed by any one of the first-level subdirectory names—for example, CD PRGMS.

The CD (subdirectory name) command lets you move up or down a level in the hierarchical tree. You cannot move directly from one subdirectory to another one on the same level. For example, if PRGMS is the current directory and you enter CD GRAPH, a DOS error message tells you that you have entered an invalid directory.

To move to the GRAPH subdirectory, you must move up a level and then down a level, or you must start from the root directory and proceed to the subdirectory you want. Either of the following two commands can be used to change to the GRAPH subdirectory from the PRGMS subdirectory.

CD..\GRAPH The double period changes to the parent directory, in this case the root directory. The reverse slash followed by the name GRAPH changes to the GRAPH subdirectory.

CD \GRAPH	By starting with the reverse slash, you are telling DOS to start with the root directory.

Assume that PERSN is the current directory. A: \GRAPH \PERSN is the current path. Issuing the following commands will produce the results shown.

CD BUSINESS	Produces an error message because you cannot move "sideways" in the tree.
CD.. \BUSINESS	Moves up to the parent, then down to the subdirectory.
CD \GRAPH \BUSINESS	Also changes to the BUSINESS subdirectory.
CD.. \.. \DOCMNT	Moves up two levels and then down to a first-level subdirectory.
CD \DOCMNT	Changes to the DOCMNT subdirectory by starting from the root directory.

RMDIR—REMOVE DIRECTORY The RMDIR, or RD, command functions the same as the ERASE command. Instead of removing a file, however, the RMDIR command removes a subdirectory from the disk. DOS provides one restriction in the use of RMDIR. The command will not function if the subdirectory being removed contains any files or other subdirectories. The period and double period directories are not included in this restriction. If you attempt to remove a subdirectory that contains a file, DOS displays an error message. The following display shows the message that occurs if you try to remove a subdirectory containing a file. For this example, assume that you are in the root directory, which is one level above UTIL.

```
A:\>COPY B:TEST.TXT A:\UTIL     ←This puts a new file in \UTIL.
        1 File(s) copied

A:\>DIR \UTIL

 Volume in drive A is FIRST DISK
 Volume Serial Number is 144D-0EF1
 Directory of  A:\UTIL
```

```
.            <DIR>       06-29-91    5:52p
..           <DIR>       06-29-91    5:52p
TEST     TXT         25  06-15-91   10:54a
         3 File(s)    1103872 bytes free

A:\>RD \UTIL
Invalid path, not directory,     ←You cannot remove UTIL because
or directory not empty             it contains a file.

A:\>
```

If you want to remove a subdirectory and you discover that it contains files, you must erase these files before you can remove the subdirectory itself. Make the subdirectory current and list its directory. Inspect the file names to see if there are any you wish to save. If there are, you should copy these files into another subdirectory or onto another disk.

After you have confirmed that you do not want to save any of the files in the subdirectory, use ERASE *.*. This is a dangerous command; you must be certain that the subdirectory is the current directory. After you have erased all of the files within the subdirectory, change to its parent (use CD ..). Then use the RD command to remove the subdirectory.

Easier Subdirectory Management

It is easy to use these commands to work with your subdirectories. Some computer users prefer, however, to use menus rather than key-entered commands. Menu-style batch files provide one way of switching between subdirectories by making menu choices. In Chapter 5, you will learn how to create batch files that will perform this task for you.

A second choice for the menu-oriented user is the use of front-end "shell" programs. These are commercial programs written to manage subdirectory tasks. In most cases, these shell programs provide more than subdirectory control. Usually they contain menu choices for executing almost all of the other common DOS commands. They provide additional convenience and efficiency for those who prefer not to key-enter commands. DOSSHELL is such a program.

HANDS-ON EXERCISE

In this exercise, you will create a disk containing files to help manage files and disks. You will create several subdirectories and copy DOS files into them. After you have created the disk and have copied the appropriate files into their subdirectories, you will see how the hierarchical subdirectory tree works in action. This exercise assumes that you have two 5¼″ floppy disk drives. Instructions are provided if you do not have this configuration.

First, create the disk.

1. Start the computer if it is not already on. Use your DOS disk or your start-up disk. Make sure your DOS disk is in drive A before beginning the next step.
2. Key-enter the command PROMPT pg. (Do not enter the period.)
3. Create a start-up disk by key-entering FORMAT B: /V /S. Insert a new disk in drive B and press ENTER.
4. After the format process is complete, DOS will ask you for a volume name. Type SECOND DISK and press ENTER.
5. Be sure your DOS working copy is in drive A and your SECOND DISK is in drive B. You will create a disk organized with numerous subdirectories.

   NOTE: If your computer has a 5¼″ drive A and a 3½″ drive B, you will have to temporarily copy files onto a formatted 3½″ disk in drive B and then copy those files back onto the SECOND DISK, which you place in drive A. If you have a single drive, you can issue the command COPY (filename) B: and DOS will allow you to change the disk in drive A. If your computer has a B drive, entering this command will make DOS copy the file to drive B. You cannot enter the command COPY (filename) A: because if you do DOS will issue an error message preventing a file from being copied onto itself.

Next, make the subdirectory tree and copy files into it.

6. Make drive B the current drive.
7. Create the following subdirectories on SECOND DISK using the MD (MKDIR) command: DISKS, FILES, UTIL. For example, to create the first subdirectory, key-enter MD \DISKS. (Do not key-enter the period.) Key-enter MD \FILES. Key-enter MD \UTIL.
8. Create a second-level subdirectory named ARCHIVE in the DISKS subdirectory. Key-enter MD \DISKS \ARCHIVE. Do not key-enter a space before the second reverse slash. You can also log into the DISKS subdirectory (use CD \DISKS), then key-enter MD ARCHIVE.

9. Create a second-level subdirectory named PROG in the UTIL subdirectory. Your subdirectories should be organized like this:

```
A:                    ← Root directory
+—DISKS               ← First-level subdirectory
|  +—ARCHIVE          ← Second-level subdirectory
+—FILES
+—UTIL
   +—PROG
```

10. Make drive A the current drive. Copy files from the DOS disk in drive A onto the disk in drive B. The copies should be made into the subdirectories according to the following list. For example, to copy EDLIN.COM, use the following command: A> COPY EDLIN.COM B:\UTIL. You may also change to the appropriate subdirectory on drive B and then copy the files from drive A into that subdirectory. For example, log onto drive B, key-enter CD \UTIL. The prompt will indicate B: \UTIL>. Key-enter COPY A: \EDLIN.COM and press ENTER.

NOTE: If your disk contains GWBASIC instead of BASIC, copy the GWBASIC file at the appropriate time. If you are not using PC-DOS Version 3.1 or above or MS-DOS Version 3.2 or above, some of the file names may be different. You may need to modify this exercise slightly.

Root directory (\)

COMMAND COM

\DISKS subdirectory

CHKDSK COM
DISKCOPY COM
LABEL COM
XCOPY EXE

\DISKS \ARCHIVE subdirectory

RESTORE COM
BACKUP COM

\FILES subdirectory

XCOPY EXE (second copy)
TREE EXE
FIND EXE

\UTIL subdirectory

MORE COM
SORT EXE

EDLIN	COM
MEM	EXE

\UTIL \PROG subdirectory

BASIC	COM
or	
GWBASIC	COM

11. Make drive A the current drive. Remove the DOS disk from drive A and replace it with the SECOND DISK from drive B. If you have a single 5¼″ drive, insert SECOND DISK in drive A.
12. List the root directory with DIR.
13. List the directories of several of the subdirectories. For example, enter DIR \FILES or DIR \DISKS. The command prompt should tell you that you are still in the root directory.
14. Make the FILES subdirectory current using the CD command.
15. List this subdirectory.
16. From the FILES subdirectory, list the root directory. Use the double period designation by keying DIR .. and then pressing ENTER.
17. From the FILES subdirectory, run the TREE program. Key-enter TREE. This will list all subdirectories and any subdirectories they contain.
18. Make the UTIL subdirectory current. List the UTIL directory using DIR to be sure you are in the current directory. This step is not necessary if you have issued the PROMPT pg command at the start of the session.
19. Key-enter BASIC to run the BASIC.COM program. If your BASIC program is named GWBASIC, key-enter GWBASIC. You should see an error message on the screen.
20. Key-enter the PATH command PATH=\UTIL \PROG;\FILES. Do not include the period at the end, but be certain to include the semicolons as shown. Do not include any spaces in the path name.
21. You should still be in the DISKS subdirectory. Repeat the instructions in step 19. (Key-enter BASIC or GWBASIC, depending on the BASIC file name on your disk.) This time, the BASIC program will run because the PATH command tells DOS to search the DISKS and UTIL subdirectories if it does not find the requested program in the current directory.
22. After you are in the BASIC program, key-enter the word SYSTEM to return to the system prompt.

23. Run TREE again. Because you added the FILES subdirectory to the search path (in step 20), the TREE program should run without your changing the current subdirectory.
24. Experiment with key-entering other PATH commands and running other programs.

Summary

1. An organized file system saves time, conserves disk space, and promotes greater computer effectiveness.
2. The hardware arrangement, especially the type of drives available, influences file organization. Floppy disks have less storage room than hard disks, requiring the user to change disks more frequently.
3. Hard disks are usually organized with subdirectories that act like separate floppy disks. Subdirectories can be organized by project, work topic, or application.
4. Subdirectories are special files containing the names of other files. Subdirectories can be listed, and their files can be copied, run, or used as though they were on separate floppy disks.
5. Directory and subdirectory names follow the same conventions as file names. No spaces or special DOS characters are allowed; extensions may be used; eight or fewer characters are allowed.
6. The path is the list of subdirectory names leading to the specific file. In the path name, subdirectory names are separated by reverse slashes beginning with the first-level subdirectory after the root directory.
7. The PATH command tells DOS which subdirectories to search if the specified executable file is not in the current directory. The APPEND command tells DOS to search subdirectories for nonexecutable files.
8. Three subdirectory handling commands are used to create, change, and delete subdirectories. These are MKDIR, to make a subdirectory, CHDIR, to change from one subdirectory to another, and RMDIR, to remove a subdirectory. These three commands may also be abbreviated as MD, CD, and RD, respectively.

Exercises

1. You begin to use someone else's computer and find over 100 files in the root directory. Some are duplicates. What problems do you see immediately because the files are not organized?

2. You have been given a word processing program. The manual says that the program files will take up 1050K of disk space. A high-density 5¼″ floppy disk holds 1200K. Your computer has two high-density 5¼″ disk drives. How will you use this word processing program?

3. You use an outline program, a word processor, and a drawing program. You write magazine articles which you outline, write, and illustrate. Your computer has a 50M hard drive and two 3½″ floppies. Describe how you would organize the program and data files for this situation. What would be your answer if you needed to work on computers in two different locations?

4. Refer to exercise 1 above, in which you have found over 100 files in the root directory. Describe how subdirectories would help.

5. "Where is the Bigalow spreadsheet file?" you ask. "It is in the 1991 subdirectory under small companies (SMALL). 1990 and 1991 subdirectories are in the SHEET main subdirectory." is the answer. What is the path to the file?

6. There are two main subdirectories named SCIENCE and MATH. Each of these subdirectories contains five subdirectories named MON, TUE, WED, THR, and FRI. Describe the double period file. You are in the SCIENCE \FRI subdirectory and want to list the file names in the MATH \WED subdirectory. Describe the command you would issue using the double period file.

7. Enter the PATH command that will allow DOS to find any file in any of the subdirectories in the MATH subdirectory. Assume all of these subdirectories are on drive C.

8. How can you create a subdirectory? You must add a MISC subdirectory to the SCIENCE subdirectory. Describe two ways to issue this command. Assume that the root directory is the current directory.

9. If you are in the new MISC subdirectory you just entered, how do you make the MATH \WED subdirectory current?

10. What command would you use to remove the MISC subdirectory? MATH \WED is the current directory.

11. Why would you receive the following message as you attempt to remove a subdirectory: "Invalid path, not directory, or directory not empty"?

Chapter 4

Hard Disk Operations

Objectives

After completing this chapter, you should be able to:

1. Use a hard disk.
2. Protect files on a hard disk.
3. Back up and restore files on a hard disk using the BACKUP and RESTORE commands.
4. Use the TREE command.
5. Use the SORT command.

Terms

hard disk	parking the heads	shell program
platter	application subdirectory	background
recording head	data subdirectory	back up
formatting	AUTOEXEC.BAT	
sector	batch file	

Overview

The hard disk provides more data storage space than floppy disks provide. The hard disk is also faster and easier to use. To use the hard disk effectively, you must properly set up and configure your system. DOS commands are used to move among the hard disk files, and several commands make it easier to manage your directory structure. Because it is possible for files to be lost or damaged on the hard disk, DOS provides commands that make it easy to back up your files.

THE HARD DISK

Except for a few removable models, your computer's **hard disk** is designed to remain inside the computer. The hard disk holds more data than floppy disks hold. The hard disk drive operates faster than a floppy drive and uses more precise mechanisms. These characteristics require the hard disk to be sealed in its own cabinet where it is isolated from jars or bumps.

What Is a Hard Disk?

The previous chapter introduced hard disks and described their general features. Although it is not necessary for you to know the details of how a hard disk works, you will find it useful to know about some aspects of its internal operation. This will help you operate your system with more confidence and greater effectiveness.

A hard disk is mounted inside the computer and comes in two basic styles. Fixed, or built-in, hard disks are permanently mounted in the computer cabinet, sealed, and removed only for repair. Hard disks on a card are removable and smaller, but they operate the same as fixed hard disks. Card, or board, hard disks are inserted into one of the slots in the back part of the computer. Although hard disk cards are removable, the hard disk hardware itself is sealed in a small enclosure mounted on the card surface. Removable hard disk drives have recently been developed. Figure 4-1 shows both an internal disk and a disk on a board.

How Does a Hard Disk Differ from a Floppy Disk?

A hard disk is made up of one or more rigid **platters** that are highly polished and coated with magnetic material. Although similar to the surfaces of floppy disks, hard disk platters will not bend. In addition, these rigid platters spin at much higher speeds than do floppy disks. Because of their higher speed, greater rigidity, and multiple platters, hard disks operate faster and hold more data than floppy disks. Figure 4-2 illustrates these internal platters.

A floppy disk drive contains one or two **recording heads** that are moved by a mechanical arm over the disk surface. The recording heads either record data onto the disk or read data from the disk into the computer. The hard disk's heads move more quickly than the floppy disk's heads so they can move to the proper position and begin work sooner.

The hard disk is formatted the same as a floppy disk. As described in Chapter 2, **formatting** records a pattern of magnetic signals in the shape of circular tracks and pie-shaped **sectors**. These sectors become holding places

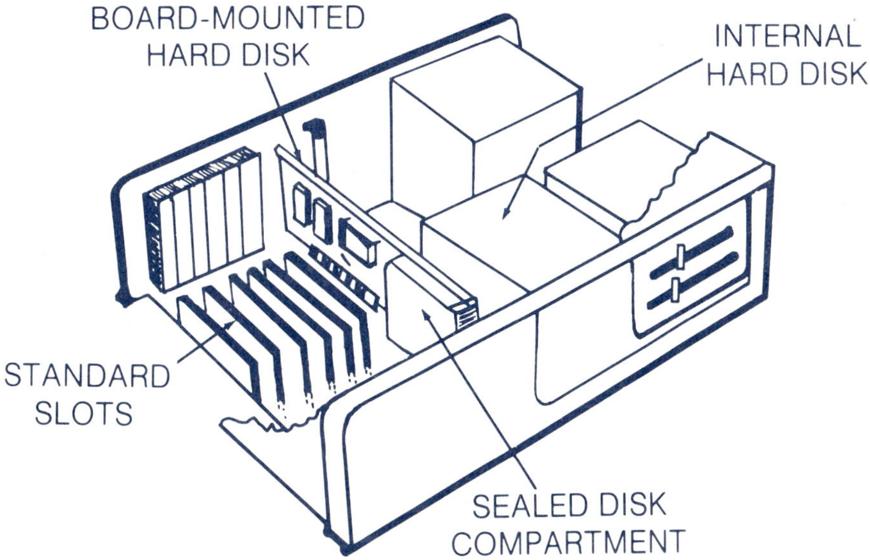

Figure 4-1.
Internal and board-mounted hard disks.

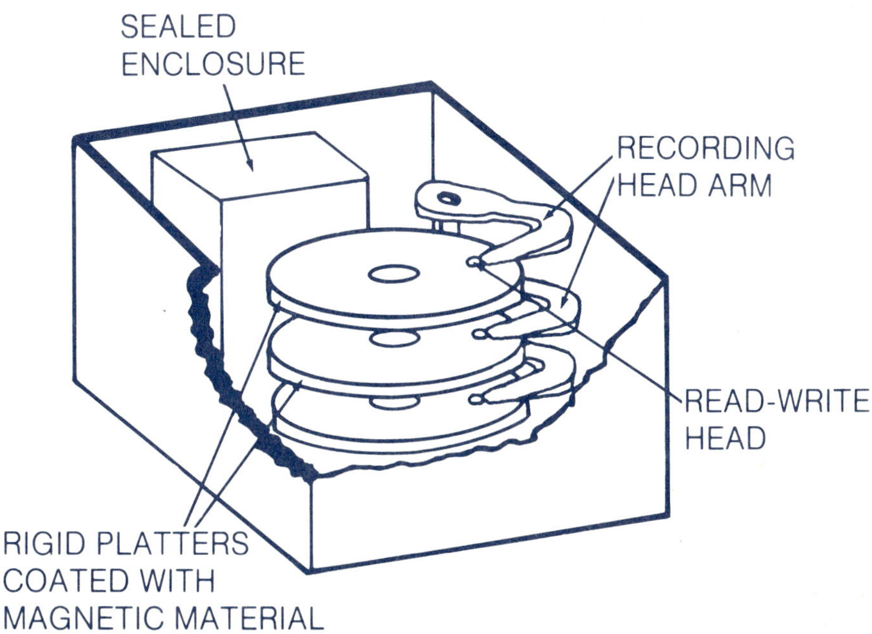

Figure 4-2.
The platters in a hard disk.

for data. The pattern is similar on both hard disks and floppy disks. The hard disk has room for more circular tracks, called cylinders, and it creates more pie-shaped sectors on each track. Data is stored in these sectors in the same way on hard disks or floppy disks. The hard disk can simply hold more.

The hard disk you are using probably has already been formatted. If your system is new and must be formatted, refer to the hardware instructions. Never attempt to format a hard disk that is in use and contains programs and data. Formatting erases the disk, and all of the work it contains is lost. Remember that formatting is the most dangerous operation you can perform. As you learned in Chapter 2, be very cautious when using the FORMAT command. DOS Version 5 provides the UNFORMAT command which will attempt to undo the changes caused by formatting of a hard disk containing data.

Special Precautions

New hard disks are more rugged than their predecessors, and are able to withstand some jarring when being moved. Laptop computers contain hard disks that undergo daily moving and bumping. Nonetheless, you should treat any hard disk as a delicate instrument. Even today's hard disks may suffer problems and data loss from too much shock. If you are using an older hard disk, the risk from mishandling is even higher.

The damage results from the heads being forced to bounce off the highly polished platter surface. This can leave a mark that is very small but that can present a significant problem when the head is trying to read data from the disk surface. If the computer cannot read the data, an error results. The data in that part of the disk surface may not be recoverable.

Most recent hard disks will automatically "park" the heads when not in use. **Parking the heads** means to position the heads over a portion of the hard disk where no damage can occur. Older hard disks require a short software program to park the heads. If you have such a machine, develop the habit of parking the heads before moving the computer.

ORGANIZING THE HARD DISK

You were introduced to hierarchical directory trees in Chapter 2, and several concepts for organizing files were discussed. If these concepts were not completely clear, return to Chapter 3 and review them now. The following section discusses ways to organize the hard disk for maximum advantage.

Two major considerations in hard disk organization will be discussed. The first involves the approach to organizing data files. The second involves the number of regular users of the hard disk.

Organizing Data Files

Each application program produces its own data files. Word processors create document files. Spreadsheet programs create spreadsheet or worksheet files. Database programs create data or record files. Graphics programs or drawing programs create picture files. These files contain the work you do on the computer.

It is usually inefficient to allow data files to accumulate in the same subdirectory as the application program. If you generate a small number of files, this can be manageable. If, however, the number of files is large, it is time-consuming to find files after they have been created.

A better way to organize files is to create at least one data subdirectory within the application subdirectory. For example, the path name to document file File1.DOC could be C:\WP\DATA\File1.DOC. The **application subdirectory** is \WP whereas the **data subdirectory** is \WP\DATA. Most application programs allow you to specify the default data subdirectory. In this case, the word processing program can be told to save or retrieve data files from the \WP\DATA subdirectory.

As the types and number of files increase, having them all in one subdirectory becomes increasingly inefficient. Finding personal letters scattered among business reports becomes more time-consuming. At this time, you could consider several data file subdirectories. You could have personal data files in a \PERSDATA subdirectory. Business files could be in the \BUSDAT subdirectory, and report files could be in the \REPRTDAT subdirectory. Notice in Figure 4-3 that all of these subdirectories are second-level ones contained within the main application subdirectory.

Organizing by the Number of Users

When a number of people use the same hard disk, efficient file organization is very important in saving time and avoiding mistakes. Security may also be a consideration. It would not be economical to have multiple copies of the same applications on the hard disk. This would waste disk space.

In this situation, having everyone's data files in one subdirectory would be confusing. This approach might cause file name conflicts and confusion due to similarly named files. An alternative system is to have separate data subdirectories for each person using the computer. This would be like each

Figure 4-3. Separate data subdirectories.

```
C:\
+— \WP
|       +— \PROGRAMS
|       +— \PERSDATA
|       |           FILE1.DOC
|       |           FILE2.DOC
|       |
|       +— \REPRTDAT
|       |           FILE3.DOC
|       |           FILE4.DOC
|       |
|       +— \BUSDAT
|
+— \SS

C:\>
```

person having his or her own data file folder in which to save new work or from which to retrieve existing information.

The individual subdirectories can be located within the application's subdirectory or on the same level as the application subdirectory. Figure 4-4 illustrates the former approach and Figure 4-5 illustrates the latter approach.

◆ HANDS-ON EXERCISE ◆

Complete this exercise without using the computer. You will need paper and pencil to design a hierarchical directory tree. You will design this directory structure for a school computer. This computer is the only computer in the data processing lab, and it has a hard disk.

Three classes will use the computer: a programming class, a graphic arts class, and a word processing class. The instructor, who manages all three classes, will use the computer for record keeping and lesson planning.

Three separate application programs have been purchased, one program for each class. SPCLBAS.EXE will be used in the programming class, GRAPHART.COM in the graphic arts class, and WORDPROC.EXE in the word processing class. Mr. Danley uses RECORD.COM to maintain records for all the students.

In addition, Mr. Danley uses a special program that requires the user to enter a password before gaining access to any directory or subdirectory. Thus, users can use only those

Figure 4-4. Individuals' data subdirectories within the application.

```
C:\
+—\WP
|     +—\PROGRAMS
|     |
|     +—\SAMS
|     |     +—\PERSDATA
|     |     |        FILE1.DOC
|     |     |        FILE2.DOC
|     |     | +—\REPRTDAT
|     |              FILE1.DOC
|     |              FILE2.DOC
|     |
|     +—\BARBS
|     |     +  —\PERSDATA
|     |     |        FILE1.DOC
|     |     |        FILE2.DOC
|     |     | +—\REPRTDAT
|     |              FILE1.DOC
|     |              FILE2.DOC
|     |
|     To other users' subdirectories
|
To other application subdirectories
```

subdirectories accessible by entering their password. The program does allow access to the parent of a subdirectory once access to the subdirectory is obtained. Access to a subdirectory on the same level requires another password.

You will draw a hierarchical tree for the system. Following is a list of the students enrolled in each class.

Programming: Jim, Nancy, Mary, Martha

Graphic arts: Sally, Pablo, Wanda, Frank

Word processing: Mei-ling, Fred, Penny, Chris, Elizabeth

1. Create four subdirectories, one for each class and one for Mr. Danley. Invent your own subdirectory names and file names. Leave space to add to your directory tree.
2. Place the programs in the appropriate subdirectories by drawing the program names on the tree. Do not consider the special program that requires password entry to move from subdirectory to subdirectory.

Figure 4-5. First-level data subdirectories.

```
C:\
+—\WP
|        +— \PROGRAMS
|
+—\SAMS
|        +— \PERSDATA
|        |        FILE1.DOC
|        |        FILE2.DOC
|        +— \REPRTDAT
|                 FILE1.DOC
|                 FILE2.DOC
|
+—\BARBS
|        +— \PERSDATA
|        |        FILE1.DOC
|        |        FILE2.DOC
|        +— \REPRTDAT
|                 FILE1DOC
|                 FILE2.DOC
|
```

To both other users' data subdirectories and other application subdirectories.

3. Create a subdirectory for each student. Place these appropriately in the directory tree. Design the subdirectories so that each student's files are isolated from the other students' files.
4. Write the commands that Mr. Danley would enter to run his record keeping program. Make up a password any time you think one is needed.
5. Write the commands that Fred would use to start the word processing program. Assume that Fred should be in his own data subdirectory before running the word processing application program.
6. Write down the commands that Nancy would use to begin programming.

USING THE HARD DISK

In this section, you will learn more about using the hard disk. If you do not have a hard disk, you will still benefit from the material in the next several sections. The previous chapter described the hard disk as being similar to floppy disks but with more available storage. Most of the commands that you use to operate your computer system are the same regardless of the type of disk storage you use. Some, however, can be used to promote efficiency with hard disks.

Starting the Computer

In Chapter 1, you learned to start the computer and enter the TIME and DATE commands when prompted. This is the simplest and most basic start-up necessary to prepare the computer to work for you. You do not even have to enter an actual time and date. Pressing ENTER without keying anything will complete the command. You cannot, however, skip these commands; DOS will prompt you for input.

The DOS program can provide two kinds of start-up. The first is a standard start-up, which includes a minimum number of standard steps to prepare the computer for work. The second is a custom or automatic start-up. This can provide any number of standard and customized steps that you select. You choose these in order to use features particular to your computer and software configuration.

STANDARD START-UP The computer hardware contains a small program to start drive A after the power switch is turned on. Assuming there is a start-up disk in drive A, the computer's next step is to look for a short program in the first disk sector. This boot program will cause DOS to be loaded. Then DOS directs the remaining steps of the start-up process.

A data disk has no boot program in the first sector. If drive A contains a data disk, the computer will detect the disk, but it will not be able to find a boot program. It issues an error message and stops and waits for you to correct the situation. If this happens to you, replace the data disk with a bootable, or start-up, disk. You may also find that you have placed a start-up disk in the drive but have forgotten to close the latch. Close the latch and press any key to tell the computer to try to start again.

A start-up disk is a floppy disk containing the DOS programs. As described in Chapter 2, such a disk is formatted with the /S command, or the SYS command is used to copy the DOS files onto a newly formatted disk. A hard disk, formatted and set up with the DOS-supplied FDISK program, contains the DOS start-up programs. The FDISK program is discussed in Appendix D.

If the computer determines that drive A is empty, it will try drive C. If it does not find the DOS programs in any drive, it will stop. Standard start-up, then, means making sure that the DOS start-up programs are in one of the computer system's drives.

After start-up, you have to key-enter the time and date, or you may just press ENTER, which completes the command but does not establish a new date or time. In contrast to a standard start-up, an automatic start-up allows initialization or start-up commands to be processed automatically.

AUTOMATIC START-UP DOS contains instructions that direct the computer to search for two special files. The first file is CONFIG.SYS, and its job is to load special programs that add features to the operation of the computer. For example, CONFIG.SYS can tell the computer to use a mouse (pointing device) or to set aside extra memory for an electronic disk drive. Setting up your own CONFIG.SYS file is described in Chapter 6.

The second special file is named **AUTOEXEC.BAT**. If this file does not exist, DOS proceeds with a standard start-up. If an AUTOEXEC.BAT file is found, the computer executes this file first.

AUTOEXEC.BAT is a batch file. A **batch file** is a file containing command statements. Each statement is on a separate line ending with a carriage return. DOS reads the first command from the file and executes the command as if it had been key-entered. After the first command is completed, DOS checks for the next line in the file. If one exists, it is executed. Each additional command line is executed in turn until DOS comes to the end of the file.

You will learn more about batch files and how to use and create them in Chapter 5. For now, you need to know about the special batch file named AUTOEXEC.BAT. The following display shows the contents of a typical, simple AUTOEXEC.BAT file.

```
A>TYPE AUTOEXEC.BAT    ←This lists the AUTOEXEC.BAT contents.
DATE   ←Standard command
TIME   ←Standard command
CLS   ←This clears the screen.
EDITOR   ←This runs a program named EDITOR.

A>
```

AUTOEXEC.BAT can make it easy to start the computer and run your programs. It is especially useful when you go through the same steps every time you start the computer. AUTOEXEC.BAT can do this repetitive task for you. For now, use any existing AUTOEXEC.BAT file that your disks contain, or just use a standard start-up procedure. You will learn how to create and modify AUTOEXEC.BAT and other batch files in the next chapter.

Running Applications

Assuming that your computer performs a standard start-up, you will need to run an application in order to begin work. A standard start-up will leave you in the root or main directory. You may not have any application programs in the root directory.

The first step is to change to the application subdirectory using the change directory command. This subdirectory becomes the current directory. The next step is to key-enter the file name of the application program, without the extension. When you exit from the application program, you will still be in the subdirectory. Use the change directory command again to move to another subdirectory, where you can run a different application. The following display shows how to start a word processing application named ED.

```
C>           ←Waiting in the root directory for a command

C>CD WP      ←Changes to the WP subdirectory

C:\WP>ED     ←Runs a word processing program named ED
```

Menu Systems

A menu can make a hard disk or a floppy-based system easier to use. Many application programs use menu systems. Unfortunately, DOS does not have a built-in menu system. Instead, DOS is command driven, which means that an action is executed by entering a command at the system prompt. DOS will execute valid commands and will display error messages if it does not recognize the entry.

Two popular alternatives to command entry are batch file menu systems and commercial menu systems. This section introduces these techniques. Chapter 5 discusses batch files in more detail.

BATCH FILE CONTROL DOS will execute the commands in batch files, as described previously. You run a batch file by entering its file name on the command line. You are not required to enter the BAT extension. The following display illustrates some typical batch file names and the associated commands you would enter to run each of them.

```
A>GO    ←Runs the GO.BAT file

A>1     ←Runs the 1.BAT file

A>MENU  ←Runs the MENU.BAT file
```

A typical batch file menu system is composed of several standard batch files. The main menu batch file typically runs first. Its job is to clear the screen and display the list of menu choices. The display below shows the commands in a batch file called MENU.BAT.

```
CLS
TYPE MENU.DAT
```

The file MENU.DAT would show the menu choices. The following display shows a sample main menu that might be displayed.

```
MENU SYSTEM


1. Run Spreadsheet

2. Run Word Processor

3. Run Graphics

Enter choice:
```

The remaining files in the menu system correspond to the menu choices. Each menu choice in the main menu file would run a separate batch file.

Because your choices are 1, 2, and 3, the batch files must have these names. Specifically, the files 1.BAT, 2.BAT, and 3.BAT will reside in the same directory as the main menu system file. When you key-enter 1, you run 1.BAT. The following commands are those that 1.BAT might contain in order to run the LOTUS 1-2-3 spreadsheet program.

```
CLS      ←Clears the screen
CD\123   ←Changes to the LOTUS 1-2-3 subdirectory
LOTUS    ←Runs the LOTUS 1-2-3 program
CD\      ←Changes back to the root directory after exiting LOTUS 1-2-3
CLS      ←Clears the screen again
MENU     ←Runs MENU.BAT to again type the menu on the screen
```

A separate batch file would run each menu choice. The batch file 2.BAT runs the word processing program, and 3.BAT runs the graphics program. Each batch file is similar to 1.BAT. Each batch file changes to the appropriate subdirectory and runs the correct program. The MENU command is last in each file.

This example shows several batch file properties. First, batch file names can begin with any legal character, making it easy to name files with the same character used to make the menu selection. Second, DOS will process commands to the end of the batch file, even if one of the commands runs an application program. For example, in 1.BAT, the batch file runs the LOTUS 1-2-3 spreadsheet program. When you exit from the program, DOS remembers that it must complete any additional batch file commands. It continues with the change directory command and runs the menu program. This ability to continue processing batch file commands, even after a long session with a commercial program, allows batch menu programs to function.

COMMERCIAL SHELL PROGRAMS It is very common to use a set of batch files as your own DOS menu system. However, this set of files can grow fairly large and complicated if you wish to control many operations and commands. Commercial programs make this job easier. They are also more versatile than batch file menu systems. They are often called menu programs or DOS **shell programs**.

Some shell programs operate in the background and appear whenever you end one program and are ready to use another. Operating in the **background** means that they automatically appear when you exit from one of your commercial programs. Other shell programs perform their functions and then are removed from memory. The shell program may appear after you start your computer to help you select the first program. One of the main benefits of using shell programs is that you do not have to set up a series of batch files to carry out each command you wish to execute. Standard DOS commands are usually built into the shell program, and you simply make a menu choice to execute such commands as COPY, ERASE, RENAME, and TYPE. Shell programs range from the moderately simple to the complex. Some have many features beyond those you need to help you with DOS commands.

To run your particular application programs, you tell the shell program which commands to use. The shell program contains a procedure by which you enter your applications and their commands. You do this when you start the shell program, and your commands become a part of the shell program until it is changed.

DOS Version 4 provided the first shell program for the DOS environment, called DOSSHELL. DOS Version 5 improved on the features and screen layout of the original DOS Shell program.

OTHER HARD DISK OPERATIONS

Once you begin using a hard disk, you will generate files and subdirectories. The application programs that you use will save your data in work files. It is important to manage these files effectively. Several important hard disk operations help you to accomplish this.

First, you should frequently **back up** your files on the hard disk. Otherwise, you risk losing your work if there is a computer disk malfunction. Second, you will want to be able to easily manage the many files on the hard disk. Directory control commands help you do this.

File Protection

New computer users are always told to back up their work. You should form this habit as soon as you start using your computer and applications. Backing up your files can prevent you from losing work that may have taken a long time to create.

A general rule is to back up any work that would be difficult to re-create. The amount of backing up that satisfies this rule varies from individual to individual, but the idea is clear. You use the computer to save time, and if you need to refer to this computer-generated work in the future, you should avoid having to redo it. You can avoid redoing your work if you back it up at regular intervals.

The data that you save on a floppy disk or a hard disk may be lost for several reasons. First, a power outage while you are working on a long letter or spreadsheet will destroy hours of effort. The computer's memory is erased when the power goes out and its contents are lost. At times, the power outage can damage the data on a disk.

Second, entering the wrong command may erase a disk or cause an unexpected problem with the disk directory. If this occurs, you will not be able to load your files from the disk into the computer.

Finally, your disk may become damaged. Dropping an object or spilling liquid on it can render it unreadable. A power surge can alter the sectors on a hard disk that allow access to the files. These are common ways that files can be lost or made unavailable. None will cause you real trouble if you have consistently created backups of all of your work. When and if a problem occurs, the backup copy can be loaded into the computer and your work can proceed. You avoid having to duplicate everything you have done. At worst, you have to re-create whatever you have generated since the last backup.

You should be cautious about immediately using your backup copy when a problem occurs with a file. Sometimes, hardware malfunctions will affect certain disk operations. The equipment problem can actually erase a file that you have instructed the computer to read or load. If you use your backup without understanding and solving the difficulty, the malfunctioning computer may damage the backup copy also.

For example, assume that you save your word processing documents on floppy disks. One day, you enter the command to load a document you had previously saved and backed up. Your computer unexpectedly displays an error message indicating that your document is not on the disk. After concluding that you cannot load the file from the main disk, you reach for your backup copy. If the hardware is at fault and you enter the load command again, the computer may damage the backup copy as well.

In rare instances, a malfunction of a computer chip may cause the computer to erase or damage the directory when a command is entered. By immediately using the backup copy, without understanding why the error message was displayed, you may lose the backup also. Uncovering the cause of the problem can be very difficult. Note any problems you have with the disk drives. Also notice if the computer drive sounds or acts unusual during operation. As you gain computer experience, you will begin to notice how long certain operations take and how the disk drive sounds during operation. Deviations from normal operation should catch your attention. Finally, it is a good idea to keep two sets of backup copies of very important files.

MAKING BACKUPS The typical way to back up a file is to copy the original. You may copy a single file or several files. You may also copy the entire disk. Several approaches are convenient and may be used regularly.

First, by using the COPY command, you can copy files one at a time from your floppy or hard disk onto another floppy disk devoted exclusively to holding backup files. By using wild-card characters, you can copy more than one file with a single command. Second, you can copy an entire floppy disk onto another floppy disk. The DISKCOPY command makes it easy to produce an image of a floppy data disk. DISKCOPY will not work, however, with your hard disk. Here, you can rely only on the COPY command. Because you will probably be copying numerous files from hard disk to floppy, you will encounter one of the COPY command's limitations. If the target floppy disk becomes full in the middle of copying a file, that entire file is erased from the backup copy and the command stops.

To avoid this problem and to facilitate the process of backing up large numbers of files, DOS provides the BACKUP command. The BACKUP command lets you copy files from your hard disk onto one or more floppy disks. In addition, XCOPY, described in Chapter 2, provides some of the benefits of both COPY and BACKUP. XCOPY will let you copy files from multiple subdirectories, and will identify files that have been copied so that only uncopied or updated files are duplicated. The copies you make with XCOPY are usable on the destination disk. BACKUP produces files that must be translated by the RESTORE command before they can be reused.

Copying files one by one or in small groups works well if you work with only a few files. It also works well if you back up your files immediately after creating them. You will find this approach more difficult to use correctly if you make backup copies only once per week or once per month. You will not be able to remember reliably which files should be copied and which should not.

The XCOPY and BACKUP commands have features that help you with this situation. BACKUP will prompt you for additional disks until all files have been processed, whereas XCOPY will stop when the destination disk is full. You then have to repeat the command, using a switch to copy those files which have not been processed. As such, XCOPY is useful for backup purposes if you have only a few files, or only enough files to fill a few disks.

BACKUP AND RESTORE The BACKUP command automatically copies all files in the directories you specify onto a disk in a destination drive. Usually, this is drive A or drive B. In addition, BACKUP allows you to copy only those files that have been changed or added since you last performed a backup. As a further convenience, BACKUP allows you to copy files created after a specified date. The proper form of the command and some of the available options are shown in the display that follows.

```
C>BACKUP C:\REPORTS A: /M
```

←*Backs up all files in the REPORTS subdirectory that have been created or updated since the last backup. Drive A is the target drive. /M tells DOS to copy only new or updated files.*

```
C>BACKUP C:\ B: /S /D04-12-91 /A
```

- /A — *Adds the backup files to previous backup files*
- /D04-12-91 — *Backs up only files created or updated since 04-12-91*
- /S — *Includes all files in all subdirectories*
- B: — *Specifies drive B as the target drive*
- C:\ — *Backs up the root directory*

The BACKUP command allows you to create copies of any file, group of files, subdirectory, or directory. /S selects all subdirectories in the specified directory. /M selects only files created or updated since the last backup. /D selects files created or updated on or after a specified date. /A adds the backups to already existing backup files; otherwise, disks containing backup files will be erased. On a network, you can back up any files to which you have access.

Prior to DOS Version 3.3, you were required to use formatted disks for backup purposes. Version 3.3 allows you to use disks that have not been formatted. Use /F to tell the BACKUP command to format the destination disk. If you use /F, you must also have the subdirectory with FORMAT.COM named in your PATH command.

BACKUP creates two files named BACKUP.001 and CONTROL.001, both of which are unusable by themselves. Individual files cannot be loaded and run from these files. Instead, the RESTORE command must be used to put the copies back on the hard disk. When this has been done, the restored copies will work the same as the originals.

To use the RESTORE command, specify a source drive and a target drive. The backup copies will usually be on floppy disks in drive A. Drive C is the typical target drive. Enter the path name and the name of the file to be restored. You may also add /S, /P, and other options to the RESTORE command. If you add /S, all files in the specified directory and its subdirectories will be restored. If you add /P, a prompt will ask permission to restore any file that has been updated since the last backup.

BACKUP UTILITIES DOS provides the BACKUP, RESTORE, and XCOPY commands to make it easy to back up the many files on a hard disk. These commands, handy as they are, are not as versatile as some commercial programs designed solely for backup purposes. If your backup requirements are extensive, consider using a commercial program.

Commercial programs can provide more versatility, flexibility, and speed than the DOS commands. For example, most commercial backup programs let you specify your requirements in several ways: you can answer menu-like questions, input instructions via a command line, or create a command file that runs like a batch file. In addition, commercial utilities are faster, and some show progress information on the screen as the backup process proceeds.

Directory Control

Chapter 3 introduced you to the importance of directory organization in saving time and improving accuracy. As your files grow, you will spend more time with file maintenance and directory control. Making backup copies and other file manipulations will take more of your time.

You also will spend more time searching for files you need. Because DOS limits file names to eight characters plus an extension, it may be difficult to adequately describe the file in the file name. The best way to minimize the time spent in finding old files is to group them in appropriate subdirectories. You may still need to search through file names that are hard to decipher, but you will limit the area of your search.

TREE, SORT, and COPY are three commands that can help you manage your files. The TREE command displays a list of your subdirectories and the files they contain. SORT makes it easy to arrange a list of your file names. COPY is used to move files from one directory to another. Whereas commercial programs have a MOVE command, DOS does not supply one. The DOS Shell program allows you to move a file by combining the COPY and DEL commands.

TREE TREE is an external DOS command that will display a list of all directories and their subdirectories. Using the /F switch with the TREE command lists all files in the subdirectories. TREE is not available in all versions of DOS. The following display shows how to enter the TREE command. The second sample command in this display sends the listing to the printer. Output is redirected from the display screen to the printer by the addition of >PRN. Redirection will be explained in Chapter 6.

```
A>TREE C:     ←The disk in drive A contains TREE.COM. The drive C
                directory will be analyzed and displayed.

A>\SYSTEM\TREE D: /F >PRN    ←This runs TREE from the SYSTEM
                               subdirectory in drive A. The directory
                               in drive D will be listed. /F will list
                               all files. The output will be redirected
                               to the printer.

C>TREE /F     ←From the directory containing TREE.COM, this
                command lists all files and subdirectories.
```

In DOS versions prior to Version 3.2, TREE.COM lists subdirectories and their files in a list format, as shown in the next screen display.

```
B>TREE /F:

Directory PATH Listing for TEST__DISK

Files:              COMMAND .BAT

PATH: \WP

Subdirectories:     PROGRAMS

Subdirectories:     PERSDATA

Files:              FILE1    .DOC
                    FILE2    .DOC


Etc.
```

Newer versions of TREE.COM use a more graphical approach, as illustrated below.

```
B:\>TREE /F
Directory PATH listing for Volume TEST__DISK
Volume Serial Number is 2654-1AFC
B:.
|    COMMAND.BAT
|
+--\WP
|     +-- PROGRAMS
|     +--\PERSDATA
|     |         FILE1.DOC
|     |         FILE2.DOC
|     |
|     +--\REPRTDAT
|     |         FILE3.DOC
|     |         FILE4.DOC
|     |
|     +--\BUSDAT
|
+--SS

B:\>
```

SORT SORT is an external DOS command. It will arrange a text list in ascending or descending order and can be used to alphabetize your directory listings. With SORT, you can produce directory listings by file size, file date, or extension. It can also alphabetize text files used in databases. This use is described in Chapter 6.

As you save a file, its directory information is placed in the next available directory position. When you delete a file, its directory position becomes vacant. The next file saved will then be placed in the first open directory position. The new file name will not be placed in the last position in the directory list unless the last position is the first open spot in the directory. This results in a directory listing that appears random. It is difficult to find a particular file in such a list, especially if it is a long one.

SORT can rearrange your directory listings in the order you want. This helps with directory control and management. SORT can produce a file of sorted directory names. Assume that the directory entries in the following display are on your disk.

```
A>DIR

 Volume in drive A is DATA DISK 9
 Directory of  A:\LET

.            <DIR>      5-02-91  11:09a
..           <DIR>      5-02-91  11:09a
PERSON   LET        345 5-02-91  12:10p
ADVERT   LET       1254 6-09-91  02:32p
SALES    EST        455 9-12-91  08:45a
         5 File(s)  1127808 bytes free
```

You would like a sorted list in alphabetical order. The display below shows the command you would use and the results. The vertical bar in the command tells DOS to "pipe" the output of DIR to the SORT command. (The vertical bar is often on the same key as the backslash.) Piping will be discussed in Chapter 6.

```
A>DIR | C:SORT   ←This tells DOS to use SORT on drive C to list the
                   directory on drive A.

         5 File(s)  1127808 bytes free
 Volume in drive A is DATA DISK 9
 Directory of  A:\LET
.            <DIR>      5-02-91  11:09a
..           <DIR>      5-02-91  11:09a
ADVERT   LET       1254 6-09-91  02:32p
PERSON   LET        345 5-02-91  12:10p
SALES    EST        455 9-12-91  08:45a
```

The additional lines produced by the directory command are sorted along with the file names. They are placed first because the first column contains a blank space, which the computer places before other characters. Periods are placed before letters. To create a list without these lines requires some editing with a word processing program or with the EDLIN program on the DOS disk (see Appendix C). DOS Version 5 provides the new EDIT command to make editing of text files easier than with EDLIN.

The directory list can be sorted in other ways, such as by date or file size. Add the /+*x* switch to sort on data whose first character is in the *x* column. Listing of the date usually begins in the 25th column; thus, to sort by date, issue the command SORT¦ /+25.

A list can be sorted in reverse order by adding /R to the command line. For example, the file names in the previous example can be listed in reverse alphabetical order. Also, the files could be arranged from largest to smallest by using /R and sorting on the column containing the file sizes.

DOS Version 5 makes it much easier to produce sorted directories. Switches have been added to the DIR command to allow files and subdirectories to be easily sorted by file name, date, size, file extension, and even file type. Enter DIR /ON to sort by file name, DIR /OE to sort by extension, DIR /OD to sort by date and time, DIR /OS to sort by size, and DIR /OG to group subdirectories before files. Adding a minus sign (–) before any code reverses the effect. For example, DIR /ON sorts files by name whereas DIR /O–N sorts the file names in reverse order. Other switches permit sorting by file type—for example, subdirectories only, or even the files in all subdirectories within a subdirectory.

COPY You have already used COPY in previous chapters. It is used in directory control to move files from one subdirectory to another. DOS does not have a MOVE command. If you need to change a file's location, you must first copy the file to the new location and then erase it from the old location.

If you have set up a comprehensive set of directories, you probably have most of your files in the correct directory. However, many users have saved files in illogical places, where they are hard to find. As you periodically review your files, you should delete obsolete files, and you may want to move files to other directories.

HANDS-ON EXERCISE

1. Start your computer if it is not already on.
2. Insert your SECOND DISK in drive A.
3. List the contents of the root directory.
4. Change to the \SYSTEM subdirectory.
5. List the \SYSTEM subdirectory to confirm that TREE.COM is there.
6. Run the TREE.COM program. Key-enter TREE A: to list all of the subdirectories on the disk in drive A.

7. Key-enter TREE A: /F to list all of the files on the disk.

8. Move TREE.COM to the \UTIL subdirectory. Use the COPY command to copy TREE.COM from the \SYSTEM subdirectory to the \UTIL subdirectory. Then use the ERASE command to erase TREE.COM from the SYSTEM subdirectory.

9. Sort the \DISK subdirectory in reverse alphabetical order. From the root directory, key-enter DIR \DISK ¦ \UTIL\SORT /R to do this.

Summary

1. Fixed hard disks and hard disks on a board or card are the two styles prevalent today. Both store large amounts of computer data and both can find and load specific files very rapidly.

2. Hard disks hold more data than floppy disks hold, and they load and save data faster. Both are formatted the same, but hard disks have more sectors per platter.

3. Parking the heads on a hard disk moves them to a special place over the disk where no data is stored. Special programs park the heads, which should be done every time the computer is to be moved.

4. Subdirectories may be organized so that each application program contains its own data subdirectory. Another approach arranges separate data subdirectories for separate users.

5. A standard start-up requires DOS files to be located in one of the drives. A hard disk, once properly formatted, contains the DOS start-up files. These files will start the computer if the floppy drives are empty when power is applied.

6. DOS will run an AUTOEXEC.BAT file if one is present when the computer is turned on. This special batch file provides the commands that help the computer start up automatically. You enter the commands in the AUTOEXEC.BAT batch file with a word processor, after which they are executed every time the computer is started. In addition, DOS executes special commands in CONFIG.SYS, a file that helps set up the operation of the hardware and software.

7. Menu systems make computer operation easier, especially for inexperienced users. DOS does not have a built-in menu system, but one can be made using batch files. The new DOS Shell program or commercial shell programs can also provide this capability.

8. Creating a backup copy of your hard disk file will prevent you from having to re-create your work if the hard disk file becomes erased or unreadable. COPY, DISKCOPY, XCOPY, and BACKUP are four DOS commands you can use to back up your hard disk files. RESTORE must be used before files created by BACKUP can be loaded and run.

9. The TREE command is used to list your directory tree. The SORT command is used to arrange a text file listing or a directory listing in a specified order. Files are moved from subdirectory to subdirectory using the COPY and ERASE commands, because DOS does not have a MOVE command.

◆ *Exercises*

1. Assume that your disk contains a program named DATEBOOK. The disk also has an AUTOEXEC.BAT file. Write the commands that should be in the file to display the date and time and allow the user to change them. Then write the commands to clear the screen, run the DATEBOOK program, clear the screen again, and type the AUTOEXEC.BAT file on the screen. The DATEBOOK program is named DATEBOOK.EXE.
2. What is the difference between subdirectories organized by application and organized by user? How would you use this information in designing a network hard disk to serve four persons, Saul, Janice, Thomas, and Will?
3. List five legal batch file names as they would appear in the DOS directory and show the command that you would key-enter to run the batch file. Make these names the ones you would put in a menu to run (a) a game; (b) a statistical analysis program; (c) a command to clear the screen; (d) a spelling check program; and (e) a drawing program.
4. You are told that a computer is supposed to start up and run a spreadsheet program, but that it does not. You observe the start-up and see the date displayed, followed by a request to enter the correct date. Is this a standard start-up or an automatic one, and what should you see according to what you have been told?
5. How would you convince your boss to spend money to buy a shell program? Right now, she expects you to use DOS commands to run the computer. What arguments might you offer in defense of your recommendation?
6. As the computer lab supervisor responsible for data analysis, you learn that a computer will not start after an electrical storm. What is the first question you will ask the lab personnel when you see them the next day?
7. You want to transfer files from your computer at the lab to one you have at home. Why is XCOPY a better choice than COPY?
8. You have just used BACKUP to make copies of files from your lab computer. When you arrive home, you place the disk in the drive and attempt to load a data file. The computer responds with the "File not found" error message. Why did you receive this message, and what do you need to do next?

9. You are following the rule to back up your data every week. You use BACKUP to create these backup copies. After several weeks, you notice that you have only created two new files since the last backup. What is a command switch that you can use with BACKUP to save you time?

10. With 14 subdirectories, you are having a hard time keeping track of your files. You have named these subdirectories SUB1, SUB2, SUB3, and so forth. How can the TREE command help you? What does it do, and how can it help you save time in finding files?

11. You have received a request for a list of files on your computer that were created between February and July of 1991. How would you create this list using the computer? What is the command you would use to sort such a list?

Part 3

Advanced DOS

OVERVIEW OF PART 3

Part 3 introduces some of the more advanced DOS features. With the foundation in DOS operations provided by Parts 1 and 2, you are now ready to round out your operating system knowledge. Chapter 5 provides in-depth training with one of the most useful DOS features—batch files. Earlier chapters hinted at what batch files can do, but Chapter 5 will give you a thorough understanding of basic batch file techniques. Chapter 6 discusses several important, advanced DOS features. Subjects include devices and how to use them, how to configure your system, redirection and its ability to aid file manipulation, techniques for improving DOS efficiency, and common problems and how to avoid them.

Chapter 5

All about Batch Files

Objectives

After completing this chapter, you should be able to:

1. Create and use batch files.
2. Improve DOS efficiency by using batch files.
3. Design a menu system with batch files.

Terms

batch file	screen editor	batch subcommand
execution flow	EDLIN	smart batch file
ASCII file	AUTOEXEC.BAT	label
CON	parameter	loop
end-of-file marker	parameter passing	string
line editor	parameter marker	null string

Overview

The DOS batch file feature allows you to execute several commands with a single entry. When you enter the batch file name on the command line, the commands contained in the file are executed one by one, as if you had entered each from the keyboard. Batch files can save you time and provide convenience and accuracy, especially for repetitive tasks. Knowing how batch files are created and used will make you a more effective DOS user. This chapter demonstrates many batch files that you can use to improve your computer proficiency and accomplish more useful work.

INTRODUCING BATCH FILES

Batch files are simple in concept once their operation is understood. Less-experienced computer users do not appreciate the time and effort batch files can save. Once computer users become more comfortable with DOS commands, these commands become a familiar and integral part of everyday computer use. Computer users then usually wish to find ways to accomplish tasks with fewer keystrokes.

This first section defines and illustrates a basic batch file. It presents several examples of how batch files work. Once you understand these examples, you will be ready to create and use your own batch files for various computer operations.

A Batch File Definition

A **batch file** is a collection of commands saved on disk. When you enter the name of a batch file, DOS executes the commands contained in the file until the last command is completed or the batch file is stopped. As with other executable files, you enter only the basic file name (without the extension), sometimes called the root name. For example, if your file is named GO.BAT, you simply key-enter GO.

In simple batch files, the commands are executed one by one, from the beginning of the file to the end. This is the basic **execution flow.** In more complex batch files, the execution flow can be altered with special batch file subcommands. These subcommands may cause execution to jump from the beginning to a section at the end, or to "loop back" from the middle to the beginning. The batch file subcommands let you build in logic to accomplish a specific purpose. The specific logic may cause the execution flow to be nonsequential.

A batch file may contain any legitimate command. As long as DOS will accept the command from the keyboard, it will accept it from a batch file. In addition, you can build commands into a batch file that you cannot use from the DOS command line. Batch files may contain the file names of commercial programs. These programs can be run from a batch file in the same way as a DOS command. Commercial programs follow the same rules and act the same as any file from your DOS disk.

For example, assume that you are using a disk or subdirectory containing LOTUS 1-2-3. You can use a batch file to automatically enter the command LOTUS, and the LOTUS 1-2-3 start-up screen will appear. You may then proceed to use the program. While you are using it, DOS remembers that the program was started from a batch file. When you exit from the program, DOS looks to see if the batch file contains any other unexecuted commands. If it does, DOS continues processing those remaining commands. If there are no other commands, the batch file operation is finished and the system prompt reappears.

DOS will execute each batch file command until it completes the last command or until you cancel the batch file operation by pressing CTRL-C (or CTRL-BREAK). Pressing CTRL-C will reveal a DOS message asking you to confirm that you want to terminate the batch job. If you press Y, the batch file will stop and the system prompt will reappear.

Batch File Examples

One of the best ways to understand batch files is to see examples. Another way is to create batch files for solving your own kinds of problems. Before learning how to create batch files, you will gain additional appreciation of how batch files work from the following examples.

Assume that you have a batch file named SHOW.BAT. This file will display the contents of specific text or ASCII files on your screen. **ASCII files** are those composed only of alphanumeric characters. The following display shows the contents of the SHOW.BAT file.

```
A>TYPE SHOW.BAT
TYPE DOS_SUMM      ←This lists the contents of DOS__SUMM.
                     (You created DOS__SUMM in Chapter 2
                     and saved it on your FIRST DISK.)
A>
```

The SHOW.BAT file contains a command to type the contents of DOS__SUMM, which you saved on your FIRST DISK. The following display shows the results of running SHOW.BAT. Key-enter SHOW to run SHOW.BAT. DOS__SUMM must be on the same disk or in the same subdirectory as SHOW.BAT or an error message will be displayed.

```
A>SHOW

A>TYPE DOS_SUMM    ←DOS repeats the batch file command.
DIR: Lists the directory    ←This is the first line in DOS__SUMM.
DISKCOPY: Duplicates an entire disk
COPY: Creates a duplicate file
```

```
TYPE: Lists a file's contents on the screen
ERASE: Removes a file from the directory
RENAME: Changes a file's name

A>
```

A simple way to see the directories of either drive A or drive B is to have two batch files on drive C that are named A.BAT and B.BAT. A.BAT contains the following commands.

```
A:
DIR
```

B.BAT contains these commands.

```
B:
DIR
```

The contents of both files are similar. In the first, the batch file makes drive A the logged drive and then displays the directory. The second batch file does the same for drive B. Both files change the logged drive from C to the given floppy drive and display the directory in that drive.

You can alter these files so that they will automatically return to drive C. If you want A.BAT to automatically return to drive C, change the contents as follows.

```
A:
DIR
C:
```

The third line logs back into drive C after the drive A directory has been displayed. The batch file for listing the directory of drive B is not shown, but it would have the same third line.

CREATING BATCH FILES

There are two methods of creating batch files. The first method creates a file by copying keystrokes from the keyboard into a named file. This method can be used only to create a new file. The second method uses a text processor or line editor to create the lines of the batch file. This method allows you to create a new file or to modify an existing file.

Modifying an existing batch file requires a word processor or line editor with the capability to add, delete, or otherwise modify text lines. The DOS EDLIN editor is included on the DOS disk. EDLIN provides a way to create and modify the lines in your batch files. If you do not know how to use the EDLIN line editor, refer to Appendix C.

DOS Version 5 also provides EDIT, a new full screen text editor. Compared with EDLIN, which works only with full lines, EDIT can enter and change text anywhere on the screen. It operates more like a standard word processor than does EDLIN.

Key-Entering Commands Using COPY CON

The COPY CON approach uses the COPY command with an extra command designator. **CON** instructs DOS to capture keystrokes from the keyboard (the Console) and direct them to a file. The correct syntax for the command is as follows.

- COPY CON <filename>

After you key-enter this command, the cursor will move down one line and wait for your keyboard entries. The lines you type will be captured and recorded, one line at a time, into a file with the name you have specified. Because the command copies full lines, you can backspace and correct within the line you are typing. However, you cannot move back to a previous line to change it. To do this, you need a line editor or word processor.

When you have completed your command line entries, tell DOS that you are finished by pressing the F6 function key. This generates a CTRL-Z (shown on the screen as ^Z), which is known to DOS as an **end-of-file marker**. This signals that you are finished, and DOS records all of the lines on the disk using the file name you specified when you started the command. The following display illustrates the creation of the A.BAT batch file.

```
C>COPY CON A.BAT     ←Key this and press ENTER.
A:    ←Pressing ENTER places the cursor on the next line.
DIR
C:
^Z    ←This indicates that F6 was pressed.
        1 File(s) copied.

C>
```

Using EDLIN to Create a Batch File

The second method of creating a batch file is to use a word processor or line editor. A **line editor** is a program that allows you to modify lines of text in a file. Each line must end with a carriage return. Pressing ENTER inserts a carriage return. To modify the entire file, the line editor operates on lines of characters. Lines are inserted, deleted, and copied. However, you cannot work with more or less than a line at a time.

A word processor is similar to a screen editor. A **screen editor** displays text continuously on the screen. If the screen editor does not have a feature called "word wrap," a series of characters longer than the screen width will disappear to the right. If the editor has word wrap, the series of characters will break at the first space, and the remaining characters will appear on the line or lines below. In addition, the cursor in a screen editor may be moved to any location on the screen, where you may insert, delete, or change the text.

EDLIN is a line editor, and it is included on your DOS disk. Appendix C describes some of the EDLIN commands. The following examples show how to create a batch file using EDLIN. EDLIN must be on the current disk or in the current subdirectory, or the PATH command must have specified the EDLIN subdirectory. To use EDLIN, key-enter EDLIN <filename>. You must key-enter the file name on the command line. If the file name does not exist on the disk, a message tells you that it is a new file.

```
C>EDLIN B.BAT
New File
*I    ←The * prompt is displayed. Key-enter I to go to Insert mode.
        1:*B:    ←Key-enter each line; EDLIN prints the *.
        2:*DIR
        3:*C:
        4:*^C    ←Press CTRL-C to stop inserting.
*E    ←Key-enter E to end the session and save the file.
        B.BAT will now be on your disk.
C>
```

If the file exists, EDLIN will take you to the end of it and display a message showing the end of the file list. To view the whole file, key-enter an L (for List) next to the * prompt and press RETURN.

The AUTOEXEC.BAT File

The **AUTOEXEC.BAT** file is a useful and common batch file. As mentioned earlier, if you have a batch file named AUTOEXEC.BAT on your floppy disk or in the root directory of your hard disk, DOS will automatically run it after the computer is booted. It can contain any number of start-up commands that you normally run each time you start the computer.

For example, you should always log in the current date and time when you start a session on your computer. You must respond to the DATE and TIME commands to enter the current date and time unless you have a clock card that automatically supplies DOS with this information.

Unless you have an early-style IBM XT computer, the time and date are maintained automatically. If your disk contains an AUTOEXEC.BAT file, you will not see the DATE and TIME commands displayed. Rather, the commands in the AUTOEXEC.BAT file will be executed. However, if the DATE and TIME commands are in your AUTOEXEC.BAT file, or if you do not have such a file on your start-up disk, they will be automatically called to the screen for appropriate entry. After the date and time have been key-entered, the AUTOEXEC.BAT file can run your most-used program. Later, you will learn how the AUTOEXEC.BAT file can start another batch file to run a series of menus enabling you to run all of your important programs.

Assuming you have the LOTUS 1-2-3 program, the following commands could be included in your AUTOEXEC.BAT file. They would log in the date and time and then run the LOTUS 1-2-3 start-up program. If you have a different spreadsheet program, substitute its start-up command for the LOTUS command.

```
DATE
TIME
LOTUS
```

Because the batch file remains in control until you press CTRL-C or until it processes the last command, it can execute additional commands after you exit from a program. To expand the previous example, use the batch file to print a reminder on the screen about backing up files. There are two ways to do this.

The first way adds the appropriate commands to the end of the batch file. It might appear as follows.

```
DATE
TIME
LOTUS
CLS
ECHO Remember to copy your file.
```

The last two lines of this batch file are executed after you exit from the LOTUS 1-2-3 program. These commands clear the screen (CLS) and then display the message reminding you to copy your data file.

The ECHO command, followed by a message, will print the message on the screen. ECHO OFF, by itself, tells DOS to suppress printing any commands on the screen. In addition, the ECHO command may be entered from the command line as well as from within a batch file.

Entering ECHO OFF from the command line will eliminate the prompt, but not the blinking cursor. Enter ECHO ON to make the DOS prompt reappear. ECHO OFF within a batch file suppresses the printing of DOS commands on the screen, except the first ECHO OFF command. To suppress even this command, enter @ECHO OFF.

The second method of printing a reminder message requires you to create a second batch file. The second batch file could, for example, be named REMIND.BAT, and it could contain the following commands.

```
CLS
ECHO Remember to copy your file.
```

Running this second batch file requires a different command to be added to the end of the first batch file. Modify the original batch file so that it appears as follows.

```
DATE
TIME
LOTUS
REMIND
```

Because DOS treats commands in a batch file as if they had been key-entered, it can run other batch files. This batch file feature will be used later in building a menu system. The advantage of using a second batch file named REMIND is that you can display the copy file reminder message at any time by entering the REMIND batch file name.

However, the REMIND command must be the last command in the batch file, because DOS will not return to the batch file. If the batch file contained the commands DATE, TIME, LOTUS, REMIND, and EDITOR, then EDITOR would not be run because DOS would run REMIND and not return.

With DOS Version 3.3, the batch command CALL was added. This allows DOS to return to the original batch file after running another. In the previous example, if the batch file contained

```
DATE
TIME
LOTUS
CALL REMIND
EDITOR
```

then all commands would be processed. DOS would return to execute the command following the CALL command.

HANDS-ON EXERCISE

In this exercise, you will create a new batch file to run BASIC after simulating the booting of the computer. If directed by your instructor, you can make this batch file into an AUTOEXEC.BAT file and actually start your computer with it. Otherwise, create only the AUTO.BAT file described below.

1. Turn on your computer if it is not already on. Place your SECOND DISK in drive A.
2. You will create a batch file called AUTO.BAT using the COPY CON command. Begin by keying COPY CON AUTO.BAT. Press ENTER.
3. Key the following commands, pressing ENTER at the end of each line. Be sure that BASIC is in your \PROG subdirectory. If BASIC is in your root directory or in another subdirectory, you must adjust the PATH command accordingly. Also, you may need to run GWBASIC if that is the name of your BASIC program.

```
PATH=\UTIL\PROG
CLS
DATE
TIME
PAUSE
BASIC
```

4. Press F6 after you have entered the last command. A ^Z will appear on the screen as an end-of-file marker.
5. Press ENTER to save the file to your disk.
6. Run this batch file by keying AUTO and pressing ENTER. The screen will clear, and you will be asked to enter the date. Assuming that you did this when the computer was first started, simply press ENTER to accept the displayed date.
7. You will be asked to enter the time. Press ENTER to accept the displayed time.
8. The screen will display PAUSE, and a message will prompt you to strike a key when you are ready to continue. This simulates running of some other application programs. Press a key and your BASIC program will run. The prompt for BASIC is Ok. When you see the Ok prompt, this indicates that BASIC is awaiting your next command. Do not key-enter any BASIC commands or press any of the function keys unless you understand BASIC programming.
9. Return to DOS by keying SYSTEM (in either uppercase or lowercase) and pressing ENTER. The DOS prompt will reappear.

Notice that each command was printed on the screen before DOS executed it. You saw the DATE and TIME commands as well as the PAUSE command printed on the screen. In the following steps, you will use the EDLIN editor to modify your AUTO.BAT file so that the commands will not be displayed. If you are not familiar with EDLIN, turn to Appendix C and learn the main commands.

10. Edit the AUTO.BAT file using the EDLIN editor. Add ECHO OFF as the second line in the batch file. After this change, the batch file should appear as follows.

```
PATH=\UTIL\PROG
ECHO OFF
CLS
DATE
TIME
PAUSE
BASIC
```

11. Finally, add two lines to the end of the AUTO.BAT file to clear the screen and indicate that you have just completed working with BASIC. Key-enter the command CLS and then key-enter the line ECHO You have just completed BASIC. Your batch file should appear as follows when you are finished editing.

```
PATH=\UTIL\PROG
ECHO OFF
CLS
DATE
TIME
PAUSE
BASIC
CLS
ECHO You have just completed BASIC.
```

12. Save this edited file, and run it. Repeat steps 6 through 9 and observe how the screen is different. Remember to key-enter SYSTEM to exit BASIC and return to the DOS prompt.

Passing Parameters

Batch files can perform many other tasks in addition to accepting dates and times and printing messages on the screen. Information can be transferred to a batch file to allow it to work on different problems. In addition, as you will see in later sections, batch subcommands allow you to create very flexible, "smart" batch files.

A **parameter** is data that is entered on the DOS command line after the batch file name. The program that the command runs must be set up to accept parameters. The parameter data is transferred to the program: this is called **parameter passing.** The following example shows the principle of parameter passing. After you understand this concept, you can use it to expand the REMIND.BAT example to help ensure that you create backup copies of new data files.

For example, a file called GREETING.BAT shows how parameters are passed to a batch file. GREETING.BAT contains the following command lines.

```
ECHO OFF
ECHO This is the start of a computer career for %1
ECHO Good luck, %1
```

The %1 at the end of the second and third lines is known as a parameter marker. A **parameter marker** tells DOS where to use the parameter from the command line. DOS allows as many as ten markers, %0 to %9, to be used within the batch file. Ten different words or groups of characters may be added to the batch command line; they must be separated by delimiters such as spaces, commas, or semicolons.

In this example, DOS will replace the %1 marker with whatever follows the batch command. The following display illustrates what you see when you run GREETING.BAT without adding a parameter to the command line. In this case, no entry is placed into the marker's position.

```
A>GREETING

A>ECHO OFF
This is the start of a computer career for
Good luck,

A>
```

Adding a parameter after the command expands the usefulness of the batch file. The following display shows the results of passing the parameter JOHN__SMITH to GREETING.BAT.

```
A>GREETING JOHN_SMITH

A>ECHO OFF
This is the start of a computer career for JOHN_SMITH
Good luck, JOHN_SMITH

A>
```

JOHN__SMITH was the parameter passed to the batch file. The name was substituted for every occurrence of the marker %1. The %1 represents the first parameter. In this example, John Smith's name was entered with an underline character connecting the first and last names. If we had entered John's name with a space delimiter, DOS would have assumed that SMITH was the second parameter. The batch file did not contain any %2 markers, so the second name would not have been used. The following GREETING batch file could handle first and last names.

```
ECHO This is the start of a computer career for %1 %2
ECHO Good luck, %1
```

With this use of %1 and %2, John's full name, JOHN SMITH, will appear on the second line, but only his first name will appear on the third line. Using two parameters and key-entering GREETING ALICIA MENENDEZ produces the following.

```
This is the start of a computer career for ALICIA MENENDEZ
Good luck, ALICIA
```

Key-entering GREETING ANDREW FULMER produces the following.

```
This is the start of a computer career for ANDREW FULMER
Good luck, ANDREW
```

Passing parameters lets you use the same batch file to do similar but not identical tasks. The batch files will accept different data, so the batch file commands can be used with different data in a variety of situations.

You can add several commands to the reminder file, REMIND.BAT, so that it can help make the backup copies instead of just issuing a message. You can take advantage of passing parameters to let the batch file work in a variety of situations. The REMIND.BAT file contains the following lines.

```
CLS
ECHO Remember to copy your file.
```

Modify the batch file so that it asks if the file has been backed up. If the answer is yes, a congratulatory message will appear and the batch file will be done. If the answer is no, the batch file will issue instructions for naming the file to make the backup and then will enter the correct copy commands. Several short batch files will accomplish this.

First, modify the REMIND.BAT file. REMIND.BAT will now ask whether you have made a copy. If you type Y for Yes, you receive a congratulatory message. If you type N for No, the batch file runs N.BAT to copy your file. REMIND.BAT will then appear as follows.

```
ECHO OFF
ECHO Did you copy your file?
ECHO Type Y for Yes or N for No.
```

Now create two more batch files. One will be named Y.BAT, and it will run when you answer Y (Yes) to the question asked by REMIND.BAT. The second batch file to be created will be named N.BAT. N.BAT will run if you answer N to the question in REMIND.BAT. The commands in Y.BAT are as follows.

```
ECHO OFF
ECHO Good, you are protected if problems happen.
```

The commands in N.BAT are as follows.

```
ECHO OFF
ECHO A backup file will be created with the same root name.
ECHO and a BAK extension.
ECHO Key-enter C and the name of the file to copy.
ECHO The name of the file should show the root name and extension.
ECHO Do not place a period between the root name and extension.
```

Finally, create C.BAT. C.BAT will copy the new file to a backup file having a BAK extension. You may have created or modified a number of files. You can use the one batch command to make backup copies of all files rather than key-entering the COPY command numerous times. The commands in C.BAT are as follows.

```
ECHO OFF
COPY %1.%2 %1.BAK
```

When N.BAT prompts you to key-enter the command to run C.BAT, you must key-enter the following: C FILENAME EXT. Do not key-enter a period between the root name and the extension, but do leave a space between them.

If you have tried these examples, you will now have a series of batch files on your disk. REMIND.BAT is the main batch file, followed by Y.BAT, N.BAT, and C.BAT. These batch files will work together to remind you to back up any data files you have just created. The batch file system will create the backup copies for you.

Your Own Batch Files

Batch files can be used in many ways to save time. Batch files can save time by automating those keystrokes you use frequently. Batch files can also help you avoid making critical mistakes. In this section, you will create several helpful batch files. From this practice, and from the examples provided above, you should be able to make additional batch files to meet your specific needs.

Key-enter the examples in the following table, which show several short but useful batch files. Use the COPY CON command or the EDLIN line editor to create your batch files. (See Appendix C for instructions on using EDLIN.) You may want to modify the text instructions to make the batch file operate according to your own specifications. The listed file names are only suggested names, because you can enter any name. The listed commands will accomplish the batch file purpose; you may add to these as you wish.

Suggested File Name	Commands	Purpose
DW.BAT	CLS DIR /W	←DW.BAT clears the screen and lists a wide directory.
DR.BAT	CLS DIR *.%1	←DR.BAT lists all files with the entered extension.
KILLBAK.BAT	ECHO OFF CLS DIR *.BAK ECHO These BAK files will be deleted. ECHO To abort, press CTRL-C NOW. To delete, PAUSE DEL *.BAK	←KILLBAK.BAT deletes all files with a BAK extension from the current directory.

In the file named KILLBAK.BAT, the subcommand PAUSE is used. PAUSE is a batch subcommand that stops execution of the batch file and displays a message requiring a key to be pressed. When this key is pressed, the program continues. If no BAK files are in the directory, a no file message will be displayed, but the batch file will not stop.

CHSUB.BAT is a more complicated batch file. CHSUB.BAT and its auxiliary files make it easy to change to another subdirectory. CHSUB.BAT requires two additional files in order to work. The first additional file is SUBS.DOC. SUBS.DOC contains a list of the subdirectories on the disk. It is created in the same way as a batch file. SUBS.DOC will not be updated automatically if new subdirectories are added. The second additional file is CH.BAT. CH.BAT must be in the same subdirectory as CHSUB.BAT and SUBS.DOC. When you key-enter CH followed by the subdirectory name, CH.BAT will then change to the subdirectory you have chosen.

You can place CH.BAT in each of your subdirectories so that you can change to another subdirectory by entering CH followed by that subdirectory's name. You could also include the PATH command in the directory in which CH.BAT resides. The following table shows the commands in CHSUB.BAT and CH.BAT and the list of file names that you should key-enter into the SUBS.DOC file. You can key-enter these batch files on your SECOND DISK.

Suggested File Name	Commands	Purpose
CHSUB.BAT	CLS ECHO OFF TYPE SUBS.DOC ECHO Change to one of ECHO these subdirectories ECHO by entering CH followed ECHO by the subdirectory name.	←This batch file works with CH.BAT to change to another subdirectory. It types SUBS.DOC to show the available subdirectories.
CH.BAT	ECHO OFF CD \%1 ECHO You are in this subdirectory: CD	←This changes to and displays the new subdirectory.
SUBS.DOC	PROG DISK FILE UTIL SYSTEM	←These are the first-level subdirectories on SECOND DISK.

You can also use CH.BAT to change subdirectories from another subdirectory with the following entry: A:\CH <subdirectory name>. You must add the drive designator, a colon, and a reverse slash to run the CH batch file in the root directory.

SMART BATCH FILES

Batch files can accomplish much more difficult tasks than those shown in the previous examples. They can do this because DOS contains batch subcommands. **Batch subcommands** are key words that DOS recognizes within a batch file. These subcommands allow batch files to be more versatile and manage more complex situations. More versatile batch files are more complicated batch files. Creating them requires planning, effort, and some programming skill.

A batch file that can change its operation depending on conditions present when it is running is called a **smart batch file**. Several comparison commands or parameter passing features allow the smart batch file to react differently depending on conditions and the outcomes of comparisons. Creating smart batch files does not require great programming expertise. The applications in which these subcommands are used range from relatively simple to very complex. In this section, you will gain an appreciation of some of the batch subcommands and will use them to create additional, more versatile batch files.

Batch Subcommands

Batch subcommands are one-word instructions. Several of them are also recognized as system commands and may be entered at the command prompt. Batch subcommands provide additional control for batch files.

In the following section, you will learn about batch subcommands and use them in several batch file examples. You should practice the text examples and create your own applications of these commands. Many of these commands will be used later to build a menu system for your use.

ECHO The ECHO subcommand can be used at both the system command level and within batch files. Used alone and followed by OFF or ON, ECHO turns off or on the screen display of commands. Enter ECHO OFF in your batch file to suppress the display of subcommand messages normally displayed after completion of the command. Enter ECHO ON to restore the normal message display. If you enter ECHO OFF on the DOS command line, neither DOS messages nor the normal DOS prompt will be displayed. The blinking cursor will be visible. Enter @ECHO OFF to suppress even the first ECHO command.

ECHO <message> may be entered on a batch file line and the message contents will be displayed, or echoed, to the screen as the line is executed. This provides a convenient way to display messages for the batch file user.

REM The REM (remark) subcommand provides a way to place explanatory notes (remarks) within the batch file. These notes will not affect running of the batch file. The value of this lies in helping others understand what your batch file does or in reminding yourself about its operation. It is easy to forget how your batch file works if you have not looked at it for a long time.

REM <message> will display the message on the screen when ECHO is on, but not when ECHO is off. In contrast, ECHO <message> will always display the message on the screen.

You may have a situation in which you want to display one message if a condition exists and another message if the condition does not exist. This is easy to do using several additional batch subcommands, such as IF or GOTO, which you will learn about shortly. The following portion of a batch file is shown as an example. This batch file is used to install data files into subdirectories. The first four remarks inform the user of the process that is occurring. The last two remarks are not displayed. If the user wishes to modify the batch file in the future, these last two remarks will serve as a reminder of what the batch file is doing next.

```
ECHO ON
REM This batch file will install data files created at
REM the field offices into the correct subdirectories.
REM It also correctly renames the existing data files
REM before copying in the new data files.
ECHO OFF
REM Use the COPY command to install      ←Not displayed
REM, etc., etc.....                      ←Not displayed
```

PAUSE The PAUSE subcommand tells DOS to stop executing the batch file and wait until a key is pressed before continuing. It also automatically displays a message on the screen telling you to press a key to continue. You used this command in the KILLBAK batch file created in the previous section.

GOTO The GOTO subcommand causes the batch file execution order to jump to the line after the GOTO command label. When batch file execution reaches the GOTO command, the next line processed follows the line containing the command label. The command syntax is as follows.

- GOTO <label>

The **label** may be any character or group of characters. The label must be preceded by a colon, and it must be the first entry on the line. It may be located in the batch file before or after the GOTO command. A label on the first line does not affect batch file operation.

The GOTO command allows batch file sections to be bypassed if they are not needed. However, you must provide a way to get to these sections when they are needed. Accomplishing this requires another batch subcommand called the IF command. The IF command evaluates a condition you define. If the condition is true, IF jumps to the label; if the condition is false, IF proceeds without going to the label. Defining the condition allows you to select one batch file section at times and skip it at other times. The IF command will be explained in detail later in this section.

In the following example, the GOTO command is used alone. In this case, several lines are never executed because the batch file always jumps past them under control of the GOTO command.

```
ECHO ON
ECHO The batch file begins now.
GOTO SKIP
ECHO These lines will never be printed on the screen
ECHO because the batch file always skips over them.
:SKIP
ECHO This line is printed because the GOTO command
ECHO sends batch file control to the line following
ECHO the GOTO label.
```

SHIFT The SHIFT subcommand provides a way to enter up to ten parameters on the batch command line. The batch file then processes these parameters. DOS keeps track of the parameters you enter by their positions on the command line. Markers within the batch file act as place holders for each parameter and substitute the parameters in the batch file commands. DOS moves or shifts each of the parameters to the left by one position. For example, assume that you enter the following batch file command.

```
A>TAG FILE1 FILE2 FILE3
```

FILE1 is in the second position; the %1 marker will substitute FILE1 in the batch file. Note that TAG is in the zero position, which is the first position on the command line and is represented by the %0 place marker. Similarly, FILE2 is in the third position, and FILE3 is in the fourth position. After the SHIFT command is processed once, FILE1 is moved to the zero position, and the other parameters are shifted one position to the left. TAG.BAT, listed below, demonstrates how SHIFT works.

```
ECHO OFF
:CONTINUE
ECHO %1 is ready to tag...
SHIFT
PAUSE
GOTO CONTINUE
```

The second line (:CONTINUE) is a label. When the GOTO command is encountered, execution will continue with the line after the label. The third line will echo the first position file name, FILE1, to the screen. You have used the PAUSE command before; it merely stops execution and displays a message telling you to press any key to continue. The last command directs execution back to the second line. Note that you will have to press CTRL-C to stop the batch file. As it is written now, it runs in an endless loop until a break stops it. A **loop** is a condition in which the batch file executes the same commands over and over. The batch file does not contain a natural way to terminate itself. Later you will learn to use other batch subcommands to avoid endless loops.

The SHIFT command moves all of the parameters one position to the left. FILE1, which starts in the %1 position, moves into the %0 position. The name in the second position, FILE2, shifts into the %1 position. The %3 position, first occupied by FILE3, becomes empty after the first time SHIFT is used.

The same effects could be achieved without the SHIFT or GOTO command. Such a file would appear as follows.

```
ECHO OFF
ECHO %1 is ready to tag...
PAUSE
ECHO %2 is ready to tag...
PAUSE
ECHO %3 is ready to tag...
PAUSE
```

Although this short example is not much longer than the version with the SHIFT command, imagine the keystrokes you could save by using SHIFT in a much longer file. Also, there is no provision in this example for more than three files to tag. In the example that used the SHIFT command, the same batch file will work with as many as nine different file names or as few as one. In other words, it is a much more versatile file structure.

IF The IF subcommand tests for a condition. If the condition is satisfied, IF executes another subcommand. If the condition is not satisfied, IF "drops down" to the next line. In other words, this command makes a comparison and goes one way or the other depending on the outcome. The IF command syntax is as follows.

◆ IF condition subcommand

If the condition is true, DOS stays on the same line and executes the subcommand; otherwise it drops down to the next line without doing anything else. The IF subcommand can test for three different types of conditions: (1) a string comparison, (2) the existence of a file, and (3) an error condition or error level.

A **string** is a group of text characters. The IF subcommand can compare two strings. If the two strings are exactly the same, the command will be executed. If the two strings are not the same, control drops to the next line.

If you refer to the TAG.BAT example described earlier, you will see that the parameters have been shifted so that none remain, but the batch file continues to loop. As it is now written, it has no way to know when there are no more file name parameters to process. We can use the IF statement to provide a way to automatically stop this batch file. The current command lines for TAG.BAT are as follows.

```
1: ECHO OFF
2: :CONTINUE
3: ECHO %1 is ready to tag...
4: SHIFT
5: PAUSE
6: GOTO CONTINUE
```

We can change the batch file so that it will not loop endlessly. Line 6 should be changed as follows.

```
IF NOT %1 == STOP GOTO CONTINUE
```

The batch file will then compare the first parameter with the string STOP. As long as the comparison is not equal, the GOTO command will be processed and control will return to line 2. When STOP has been shifted into the %1 position, the strings will be equal, and the batch file will end. To use the revised batch file, you would key-enter the command as follows.

```
A>TAG FILE1 FILE2 FILE3 FILE4 STOP
```

Four files will be processed, and the batch file will stop when it encounters the string STOP. In this case, you must be precise about using uppercase or lowercase characters. The comparison is done with exact characters, so the following will not work correctly.

```
A>TAG FILE1 FILE2 FILE3 FILE4 Stop
```

Because the computer codes for uppercase and lowercase letters are different, the comparison Stop == STOP is not satisfied. Therefore, the batch file would process Stop as if it were another file name. After the next SHIFT, the batch file would stop anyway because the IF command will not work with "null" strings.

A **null string** is a string containing "nothing." It contains no visible or hidden characters. The IF subcommand will not work with null strings. If either string in the comparison part of the command is null, the command stops with a syntax error message. In our example, we get a null string when the fifth string, Stop, is shifted out of the %1 position. When the string Stop is shifted into %0, the IF comparison encounters a null string and issues its error message.

You can use a technique that avoids problems with null string comparisons. To illustrate this technique, we will use TAG.BAT again. The file contents are listed as follows.

```
ECHO OFF
:CONTINUE
ECHO %1 is ready to tag...
SHIFT
PAUSE
IF NOT %1 == STOP GOTO CONTINUE
```

The following listing is a modified version of TAG.BAT. It merely adds an ECHO line at the end to indicate when tagging is complete.

```
ECHO OFF
:CONTINUE
ECHO %1 is ready to tag...
SHIFT
PAUSE
IF NOT %1 == STOP GOTO CONTINUE
ECHO Tagging is complete.
```

If you key-enter TAG FILE1 FILE2 STOP, the following will be displayed.

```
ECHO OFF
FILE1 is ready to tag...
Strike a key when ready...
FILE2 is ready to tag...
Strike a key when ready...
Tagging is complete.
```

If, however, you enter Stop instead of STOP, the following will result.

```
ECHO OFF
FILE1 is ready to tag...
Strike a key when ready...
FILE2 is ready to tag...
Strike a key when ready...
Stop is ready to tag...
Strike a key when ready...
Syntax error
Tagging is complete.
```

Your batch file thinks that Stop is a file name, and it suggests that Stop is ready to tag when it is only the command to stop the batch file. This can be avoided by modifying the string comparison statements in the batch file.

TAG.BAT can be modified so that it will automatically know when all parameters have been used. Then, it will not be necessary to include an entry to force the batch file to stop. The following example shows the necessary modification.

```
ECHO OFF
:CONTINUE
ECHO %1 is ready to tag...
SHIFT
PAUSE
IF %1 . == . GOTO END
GOTO CONTINUE
:END
ECHO Tagging is complete.
```

The sixth line contains the trick for handling null strings. As long as a complete string is in the %1 position, indicating a file to tag, the string comparison in the sixth line will not be true and the flow will never go to the END label. Instead, flow will return to the CONTINUE label so that another file name can be processed. When there are no more file names to process, %1 will be a null string. At this point, DOS will evaluate the sixth line as follows.

```
IF %1 . == . GOTO END
```

Because %1 is nothing, the string comparison "." == "." (quotation marks added for emphasis) is true and the flow goes to the END label. Key-enter a space before and after each period so that each string will be exactly the same. The batch file then stops with the message that Tagging is complete. If you key-enter TAG FILE1 FILE2, the following screen output will be produced.

```
ECHO OFF
FILE1 is ready to tag...
Strike a key when ready...
FILE2 is ready to tag...
Strike a key when ready...
Tagging is complete.
```

Another test condition for an IF subcommand is the EXIST <filename> comparison. This test condition will be true if the listed file name is in the current disk drive or directory or if the file is in the specified path. If the EXIST condition tests true, the IF statement command will be processed.

This capability allows a batch file to test for a specific file name. The following batch file is CHECK.BAT. It will test to see if the file name you enter following the batch file name is on the drive or in the directory. Use COPY CON or EDLIN to create the following batch file on your disk.

```
ECHO OFF
IF EXIST %1 GOTO FOUND
ECHO Sorry, %1 is not on this drive.
GOTO END
:FOUND
ECHO %1 is on this drive.
:END
```

To use the file, key-enter a command such as CHECK KILLBAK.BAT. If you are using the disk that contains KILLBAK.BAT, you should get a response confirming that KILLBAK.BAT is on the drive. If you key-enter the command without the file extension, CHECK KILLBAK, you will be told that the file is not on the drive because the file name you entered did not include the extension. You must key-enter the extension with this CHECK.BAT program.

Notice the use of the GOTO commands in the previous batch file, CHECK.BAT. The command GOTO END is especially important. If this command were not present and the file name entered were not on the drive, the first message would be echoed correctly. However, control in a batch file passes from one line to the next line unless directed differently by a GOTO or IF subcommand. Thus, the batch file would next echo the statement indicating that the file was on the drive. Thus, the GOTO END command routes control around the incorrect choice.

The other type of condition that an IF subcommand can test for is the ERRORLEVEL. The syntax is IF ERRORLEVEL X, where X is the code number of the error. This allows the IF subcommand to check for successful completion of program processing. For example, when a program begins to run, the program can set the ERRORLEVEL. At the end of processing, the program sets the ERRORLEVEL to another number. When control returns to the batch file, the IF subcommand would then test for the current ERRORLEVEL. If the ERRORLEVEL indicates that the program did not complete processing, the IF subcommand can cause a message to be displayed.

FOR..IN..DO The last major batch subcommand to discuss is known as the FOR command, or more completely, the FOR..IN..DO command. The FOR command makes it possible to automatically repeat a subcommand using one or more variables from a special list. This command has the following structure.

- FOR variable IN (set) DO command

When DOS interprets this command, it sets the variable to each value in the set of values and completes the command. With each cycle, DOS uses another value of the variable from the set. The set can include a single item, a pair, or a long list. The set often includes a list of files on a floppy disk or in a subdirectory. The variable is entered with two percent symbols. For example, if the variable is named A, it would be entered as %%A. If you use %%A as the variable, key-enter %%A rather than %%a if you use this variable again. In this case, you must be consistent with the use of uppercase or lowercase. The following example will read each file from a disk and print its file name on the screen.

```
FOR %%A IN (*.*) DO ECHO This file's name is %%A
```

You may also key-enter the FOR command from the DOS command line; however, instead of using a double percent sign in front of the variable, you must use a single percent sign or DOS will issue a syntax error message. The following shows the previous command key-entered from the DOS command line.

```
A>FOR %A IN (*.*) DO ECHO This file's name is %A
```

The subcommand will continue to cycle as long as the directory contains another file name. With each repetition of the cycle, the variable %%A will assume the file name and DOS will repeat the command to echo the message to the screen. The file name that is held in variable %%A is echoed to the screen. The following shows a modification of this subcommand.

```
FOR %%A IN (*.BAT) DO ECHO This file's name is %%A
```

This FOR subcommand will list only the batch files in the current subdirectory. This same command can be modified further to take on a parameter entered with the batch file command. For example, suppose that the batch file LIST.BAT contained the following line.

```
FOR %%A IN (*.%1) DO ECHO This file's name is %%A
```

Key-enter LIST BAT to run the file. The names of all batch files on the disk or in the subdirectory will be listed. Key-entering LIST COM will list all COM files on the disk.

The FOR batch subcommand can also be used to repeat a command with changing names. If you must copy a number of files with similar names to the same disk, you could repeat the command the required number of times. For example, you might key-enter the following copy commands.

```
COPY ALL.DOC B:
COPY NONE.DOC B:
COPY GREEN.DOC B:
COPY SALES.DOC B:
```

You can use the FOR command to do this same task. For example, you could key-enter the following on the DOS command line.

```
A>FOR %F IN (ALL,NONE,GREEN,SALES) DO COPY %F.DOC B:
```

Each item in the set is assigned to the variable %F and the COPY command after the DO is executed. A more general expression would be the following example, which could be contained in a batch file called CPY.BAT.

```
FOR %%F IN (%1,%2,%3,%4) DO COPY %%F.DOC B:
```

To run CPY.BAT and copy ALL.DOC, NONE.DOC, GREEN.DOC, and SALES.DOC, key-enter the following command: CPY ALL,NONE, GREEN,SALES. If there are more than nine files to be copied, you can use the SHIFT command as illustrated earlier.

The FOR subcommand can be used to check that the proper entry has been made. For instance, in the TAG example, the batch file would cease to operate when it encountered the word STOP as the last item in the list. If, however, the spelling of this word did not match the spelling within the batch file command, the file would continue for at least one additional loop. The FOR subcommand can be used to check for the correct entry among multiple entries, as shown in the following example. This is a modification of the TAG.BAT file we created earlier.

```
ECHO OFF
:CONTINUE
ECHO %1 is ready to tag . . .
SHIFT
PAUSE
FOR %%A IN (STOP,Stop,stop,sTOP) DO IF %1 == %%A GOTO END
GOTO CONTINUE
:END
ECHO Tagging is complete.
```

The sixth line is different from the earlier example: it includes the FOR..IN..DO subcommand. If the shifted variable does not include one of the four versions of the word "stop," the batch file will continue to loop. It stops when the shifted variable in the %1 position matches one of the four spellings. If you key-enter a different character rather than a different uppercase or lowercase pattern, the test will fail.

Batch File Applications

The previous sections of this chapter have introduced the basic batch commands, including subcommands used within batch files. The examples have been relatively easy in order to demonstrate the command principles. Batch files will save time even with short applications and problems. You should always look for opportunities to assign a repetitive task to a batch file.

Batch files can be used for more difficult applications than those already shown. Batch files can perform many complicated tasks. For example, the installation disks of the larger commercial programs usually contain batch files. Many of the installation procedures are controlled by a complicated batch file. If you have an installation disk available, list the directory. Look for files such as INSTALL.BAT, SETUP.BAT, and other batch files. If you type these batch files, you may see some of the more complicated jobs a batch file can do.

Batch files can also be used to build a menu system. For example, you could build a menu system for the DOS commands. This menu system would save you time, and might improve your accuracy, by reducing the number of keystrokes needed to complete an operation.

HANDS-ON EXERCISE

In this exercise, you will build a DOS command menu system. The Main Menu contains options for three types of activities: disk control, file management, and applications activities. Disk control activities involve listing the directories of each of the three drives. If your computer does not have three drives, you can modify the batch files and their menu choices to fit your system. File management activities allow you to type files automatically. You will also be able to determine the free space left on a disk in any drive. The third type of activity involves applications. You must set up this menu to fit the applications you use. Because the batch file is in control, the menu will reappear when you exit from the application program.

This menu system can be expanded. You will probably see many ways you can add to the basic menu structure in order to automate your common DOS operations. After you practice using batch files with this application, expand your batch file skills by adding to the DOS command menu system.

The structure of the batch file menu system is given, and the commands of the batch files are listed. You should follow all of these instructions in order to start the system. Depending on directions from your instructor, you may add to or customize the DOS command menu system.

1. Start your computer if it is not already on. Place either a copy of the DOS master disk or your FIRST DISK in drive A.

   NOTE: *If you use your SECOND DISK with the subdirectories, you must use the PATH command so that DOS will search the appropriate subdirectories for the command files. Do not change the path name unless this is acceptable to your instructor. If it is acceptable, key-enter the following PATH command* *so that DOS will look in all first-level subdirectories: PATH= \UTIL; \DISKS; \FILES. You may wish to use only the DISKS subdirectory in the PATH command, because the only external DOS command used in this menu system is CHKDSK, which is in the DISKS subdirectory.*

2. The menu system consists of two menu levels. These menu levels are similar to the directory trees discussed in previous chapters. The second-level menus include a command to return you to the Main Menu. The Main Menu includes a command to exit to DOS. The following table lists the menu names and their choices. Suggested command entries for each menu choice are also shown. These command entries are the names of the associated command batch files. For example, when you key-enter MM from the Disk Control Menu or the File Management Menu, the batch file used to run MM.BAT will display the Main Menu again. The Applications Menu is not shown because you must tailor it to meet your specific needs.

Main Menu

1. Disk Control	(SK)
2. File Management	(FM)
3. Applications	(AP)
4. Exit to DOS	(E)

Disk Control Menu

1. Directory Drive A	(DA)
2. Directory Drive B	(DB)
3. Directory Drive C	(DC)
4. Return to Main Menu	(MM)

File Management Menu

1. TYPE files	(TY)
2. Find free space	(FS)
3. Return to Main Menu	(MM)

3. Each menu will be displayed on the screen by typing the menu data file that you have prepared. (Another approach, which is not used in this exercise, is to include ECHO statements within the batch file.) The following table shows you the contents of MMENU.DAT, which is the Main Menu.

   NOTE: *When you prepare MMENU.DAT (using COPY CON or EDLIN), begin with four carriage returns so that the menu is not located at the top of the screen.*

Main Menu

1. Disk Control	(SK)
2. File Management	(FM)
3. Applications	(AP)
4. Exit to DOS	(E)
Enter your choice:	

4. Create the other menus patterned after the Main Menu shown in step 3. It will look better if you use consistent spacing for the top and side margins. When you change from one menu to another, the menus will seem to switch instantly if they are all positioned on the screen in the same location.

   NOTE: *For now, name the Disk Control Menu file SK.DAT, and name the File Management Menu file FM.DAT. For the Applications Menu, and for any other menus that you add independently, you may use your own naming conventions.*

5. Complete the batch files that display the menus. Allow them to clear the screen, and then print, or type, the appropriate data file. The batch file that displays the Main Menu is called MM.BAT. MM.BAT contains the following commands. You may wish to add ECHO OFF at the beginning of each batch file.

   ```
   CLS
   TYPE MMENU.DAT
   ```

   The Return to Main Menu option on each of the three activities menus calls this batch file.

6. The batch file used to display the Disk Control Menu is called SK.BAT. It contains the following commands.

   ```
   CLS
   TYPE SK.DAT
   ```

7. The batch file used to display the File Management Menu is called FM.BAT. It contains the following commands.

   ```
   CLS
   TYPE FM.DAT
   ```

8. You are now ready to enter specific batch files for each of the commands offered by each menu. Start with the directory command in the Disk Control Menu. This command will list the directory of the disk in drive A. You may key-enter an extension with the command, and it will list only those files with that extension. For example, to list all batch files, key-enter DA BAT. To list only COM files, key-enter DA COM. To list all files, simply key-enter DA. To list files on drive B, substitute DB for DA. The following is a suggested structure for DA.BAT. Key-enter these commands and save them in the file DA.BAT.

   ```
   CLS
   IF %1 . == . GOTO ALL
   DIR A:*.%1 /P
   PAUSE
   GOTO END
   :ALL
   DIR A:*.* /P
   PAUSE
   ```

```
:END
SK
```

9. Key-enter commands for DB.BAT and DC.BAT, which will perform the same actions as DA.BAT but on drives B and C, respectively. When you have completed this step, you will have the following files on your disk.

    - MMENU.DAT
    - SK.DAT
    - FM.DAT
    - SK.BAT
    - FM.BAT
    - MM.BAT
    - DA.BAT
    - DB.BAT
    - DC.BAT

10. TY.BAT will type a series of files to the screen automatically. For now, design the batch file to type only BAT files. Later, you may modify it to type other kinds of text files. Text files, also known as ASCII files, contain only alphanumeric characters.

    TY.BAT will check that you have key-entered the extension. TY.BAT will check for four ways in which you might key-enter the letters B, A, and T. If the extension has been key-entered in one of the four acceptable ways, TY.BAT will clear the screen, remind you that you must press CTRL-S to stop scrolling, and type all batch files, and then return to the File Management Menu when it is complete. The following commands will meet these specifications. Key-enter them into TY.BAT. To run TY.BAT, key-enter TY bat, TY Bat, TY BAT, or TY bAT, and all files with these extensions will be typed.

```
CLS
FOR %%B IN (bat,Bat,BAT,bAT) DO IF %1 == %%B GOTO CONTINUE
GOTO ERROR
:CONTINUE
ECHO Press CTRL-S to stop and start scrolling.
PAUSE
FOR %%A IN (*.BAT) DO TYPE %%A
PAUSE
GOTO END
:ERROR
ECHO Can only type BAT files for now.
PAUSE
:END
FM
```

11. Now add FS.BAT. FS.BAT will find the free space remaining on the disk in the drive you specify. You will also see the memory status of the computer. FS.BAT will use the CHKDSK.COM program, which is on your DOS disk and your FIRST DISK. You should key-enter the following commands into FS.BAT.

    ```
    CLS
    TYPE FS.DAT
    CHKDSK %1
    PAUSE
    FM
    ```

    Notice FS.DAT on the second line. This file will provide a message on the screen reminding you that DOS is determining the free space on the disk. Type the following lines into FS.DAT. Place several carriage returns before the message so that it will not appear at the top of the screen.

    ```
    Please wait.
    Now checking for the remaining space on this disk.
    ```

    When you run FS.BAT, the CHKDSK statistics will be displayed after the above informational message. After you press a key, DOS returns to the File Management Menu.

12. The file name E.BAT should contain the CLS command to clear the screen and return to the DOS prompt.

13. You now have the basic structure for a DOS command system. Begin the system by key-entering MM. Choose options by key-entering the appropriate letters shown in the parentheses. Add your own commands for the Applications Menu. Modify the system by adding other commands you use frequently.

Summary

1. A batch file is a collection of DOS commands and statements saved in a text file. Key-entering the batch file name, without the extension, informs DOS to execute each command until the last command is completed or the batch file is stopped.

2. Batch files can control many operations—both simple and complex. They use command logic and can become long and complicated.

3. Batch files may be created by using the COPY CON command from the DOS command line or by using a text or line editor. EDLIN.COM is a line editor included on the DOS disk. EDLIN.COM can create or modify batch files.

4. AUTOEXEC.BAT is a batch file used to issue start-up commands each time the computer is booted.

5. Batch files can significantly reduce repetitive work. Various batch files can call a common file, which can reduce duplicate command lines.
6. Parameter passing allows different data to be introduced into the batch file every time it is run. Such data is included on the command line following the batch file name. Up to nine parameters, separated by spaces, commas, or other delimiters, may be transferred into the batch file.
7. Batch subcommands are key words that control special actions within batch files. Subcommands give batch files added versatility and allow comparisons, repetitive cycles, and branching to different parts of the batch file.
8. Comparisons are made using the IF command. Conditions are tested, and a DOS command is executed if the comparison is true. Tests for error codes, string comparisons, and checks for file names are three conditions supported by the IF command.
9. Batch files can be used to build menu systems to make it easier and faster to execute different programs or DOS operations. Because batch files cannot accept keyboard input while they are running, all intermediate files must finish and leave you at the DOS prompt. The system is then ready for you to input the next command, which is the name of another batch file in the menu system.

◆ *Exercises*

1. You receive requests for sales literature and use a simple word processor to list names and addresses in text files named JAN02.DAT, JAN03.DAT, and so forth. You need to refer to the lists. Answer the following questions.
   a. Why can you not just enter JAN02.DAT on the DOS command line and see the contents of this file?
   b. How would you use the TYPE command to view the contents of the JAN02.DAT file?
   c. How would a batch file help you view these files? What command would such a batch file contain?
   d. How would you create this batch file?
2. The batch file you have created does not perform the steps you want. How do you view the contents of this file, and how can you change it?
3. EDLIN is a line editor, whereas the DOS Version 5.0 EDIT command is a screen editor. What is the difference between EDLIN and EDIT?
4. How does the AUTOEXEC.BAT file differ from other batch files?
5. What is a parameter, and how does a batch file use one?
6. What is a smart batch file?

7. What is a batch subcommand, and how are batch subcommands used to make a batch file perform useful work?
8. How would you use a batch file to test for the presence of a specific file in a directory? Which batch subcommand is most critical in making this work?
9. What does the GOTO subcommand do? What must follow it in a batch file?
10. What is a string? How is one used within a batch file?
11. Explain what a null string is and illustrate how you would make a batch file work with one.
12. Explain what the FOR..IN..DO subcommand permits you to accomplish in a batch file.
13. What is a batch file menu system? How many batch files would be needed for a menu system with four choices?

Chapter 6

Advanced DOS Features

Objectives

After completing this chapter, you should be able to:

1. Use redirection and the DOS filters MORE, SORT, and FIND.
2. Use the ASSIGN, SUBST, and JOIN commands.
3. Understand memory management, including RAM drives.
4. Use common configuration commands.
5. Avoid or recover from common problems.

Terms

device	display standard	device driver
peripheral	monochrome	ANSI.SYS
console	port	buffer
laptop computer	redirection	RAM disk
monitor	appending	memory-resident programs
screen resolution	filter	TSRs
scan rate	piping	alias
bandwidth	configuring the system	file recovery

Overview

In this chapter, you will learn about additional advanced features of DOS. These features can help expand your operating system use. You will learn about system configuration and how to use file redirection, filters, and RAM disks. In addition, you will learn about some of the problems that you may encounter in using DOS and what you can do about them.

DEVICES

Each computer subsystem is known as a **device**, and devices may be connected together to perform different tasks. You learned about computer devices in earlier chapters. DOS is designed to help you handle other pieces of equipment that can be hooked into the computer system.

Some devices are essential to operation of the computer, whereas others are optional. Optional pieces of computer equipment are called **peripherals** or accessories. They are designed to enhance the work you can do with the computer system. In some cases, peripherals allow you to accomplish tasks that are impossible with any other approach. In addition, as computer systems have grown more complex and technology has advanced, the numbers and types of computer peripherals have expanded rapidly. You will probably use a computer system that has several peripherals.

This section will discuss some of the parts of a computer system that are not covered in detail in other parts of this book. This exposure is designed to give you some awareness about these devices and about what DOS needs to make them a part of the operating system.

Console

Console is another name for the keyboard. The term "console" was used in the early days of computers to mean the integrated cabinet holding the keyboard and the computer electronics.

Most keyboards are now separate from the computer cabinet that houses the electronics, except for **laptop computers**. Laptops contain the keyboard, display, and disk drives in one small cabinet.

Display

The screen on which the text and graphics appear is known as the **monitor**. The monitor has become a complex device and can display color or monochrome characters and graphics with different degrees of detail.

Monitors are characterized by screen resolution, scan rates, and bandwidth. **Screen resolution** is the number of dots that can fit within the width or height of the display screen. **Scan rate** is the fraction of a second it takes for the full screen to be covered with the moving electronic beam that illuminates some of the screen dots. **Bandwidth** is an electronics term used to indicate the speed of the signal being sent from the computer to the monitor.

The combination of these monitor characteristics is called the **display standard** or protocol. Today there are several display standards. These standards are supported by products such as the Color Graphics Adapter (CGA), the Enhanced Graphics Adapter (EGA), the Video Graphics Array (VGA), and the Multi Color Graphics Array (MCGA).

The earliest monitors were supported by the **monochrome** standard and used a single color. Hercules Computer Technology developed a way to display monochrome in high resolution. **High resolution** means that many dots will fit across and up and down the screen. The image on a computer monitor is created by a beam of electrons that sweeps across the screen. Each horizontal sweep creates a **scan line.** "Resolution" refers to the number of scan lines on one screen. The closer together the lines are, the higher the resolution and the clearer the detail.

Each scan line is composed of a series of dots, and the closer together the dots are, the higher the resolution. Display standards, then, are defined most simply by the amount of resolution they offer. The number of dots per line and the number of lines per screen describe this resolution. For example, if a screen is 320 × 200, it contains 320 dots per line and 200 lines per screen.

With advances in technology, monitors offer greater resolution and more color choices. Some of today's monitors offer resolutions of 800 × 600 or even 1200 × 1048 and a maximum of 256 on-screen colors. These monitors are used for graphics applications.

Laptop computers use a display called an LCD, or liquid crystal display. These flat panels generate images by turning on voltage to millions of intersecting connections. Today's LCDs can create high-density single-color displays. Color LCDs are also being introduced.

Ports

A **port** is a connection through which data passes from the computer to an external device. The device can be physically connected to the computer but must be electrically separate from it.

For example, a printer is a separate device hooked to the computer through the printer port. However, a modem, which is a device for sending computer signals over a telephone line, may be external or internal. An external modem is outside the computer and is connected to the communications port. An internal modem resides inside the computer cabinet and is hooked into the slots provided for attaching peripheral cards. At the same time, an internal modem must be connected to the communications port if it is to work properly.

There are two types of ports: parallel and serial. A **parallel port** sends groups of signals by means of multiple (usually eight) connections that permit these groups of signals to be sent at the same time. Parallel ports are commonly connected to a printer and are typically labeled LPT1, LPT2, or LPT3.

A **serial port** has several connections, but it passes signals one at a time (serially). A serial port may also receive signals for processing if a device such as a mouse, light pen, or pressure pad is attached. A **mouse** is a device that moves a pointer or mark on the screen as you slide it across the table. A **light pen** looks like a pen and is connected to the computer; when you touch the tip of the light pen to the surface of the monitor, the computer can sense the exact point on the screen that you have touched. A **pressure pad** responds when a special surface is touched with a stylus or finger.

Serial ports can be labeled COM1 or COM2 and usually are connected to devices other than printers. Modems and mouse pointing devices are the most common. Other serial devices include peripherals such as digitizing pads, scanners, and trackballs.

The video signal is sent to the monitor or display over the **video port.** This connection is typically a part of an entire graphics card that contains the circuitry for displaying characters and graphics on the monitor's screen.

Device Names

DOS keeps track of special devices by means of special abbreviations. These abbreviations, or names, are reserved for DOS use. Reserved words cannot be used for file names. Figure 6-1 lists some of these device names, showing whether they are used only for output or for both input and output.

REDIRECTION

Your computer system is versatile because of the many DOS commands available. However, DOS has a limited number of features in order to keep its size reasonable. Fortunately, it has commands that allow you to customize many of the ways it works. Redirection of data flow paths is one of the DOS capabilities which lets you select the method that best fits your needs at the moment.

Redirection—a Definition

You have learned how the DOS commands can give you information about your computer system. In doing this, DOS causes data to move from one part of the system to another. The path for this data movement is set by DOS, but you can change it by redirecting it.

Figure 6-1.
Device names.

Reserved Name	Input/ Output	Comments
CON	Both	Represents the display for output. Represents the keyboard for input.
COM1	Both	Communications port.
COM2	Both	Second communications port.
PRN	Output	Represents the printer. Normally assigned to LPT1.
LPT1	Output	First parallel printer port.
LPT2	Output	Second parallel printer port.
AUX	Both	Represents first communications port. Normally assigned to COM1.
NUL	Both	Used for testing or eliminating unwanted output. When used for input, it generates an immediate end-of-file marker. When it is used for output, all output disappears.

For example, the DIR command will list file names on the monitor. As you have used it, the DIR command tells DOS to read the file names from the disk directory and display them on the screen. The data flow path is from the disk to the monitor's screen. Figure 6-2 indicates this data flow path.

Redirection means a change in the normal data flow path. Redirection changes the built-in data flow path and sends the data to a device other than its typical destination. For example, you can tell DOS to redirect the DIR output to the printer instead of the monitor. A printed list of names would result instead of a screen display. Figure 6-3 shows the flow path for this redirected data. Also, instead of being redirected to the printer, the list of file names could be redirected to a disk file. Figure 6-4 shows how redirection sends the data from the disk back to the disk.

Redirection Commands

DOS provides two approaches to redirection. First, data can be sent from the computer to another device or from the device to the computer. This is known as data input/output. Second, data can be added to other data. This is known as **appending** of data.

Figure 6-2.
Normal data flow path for DIR.

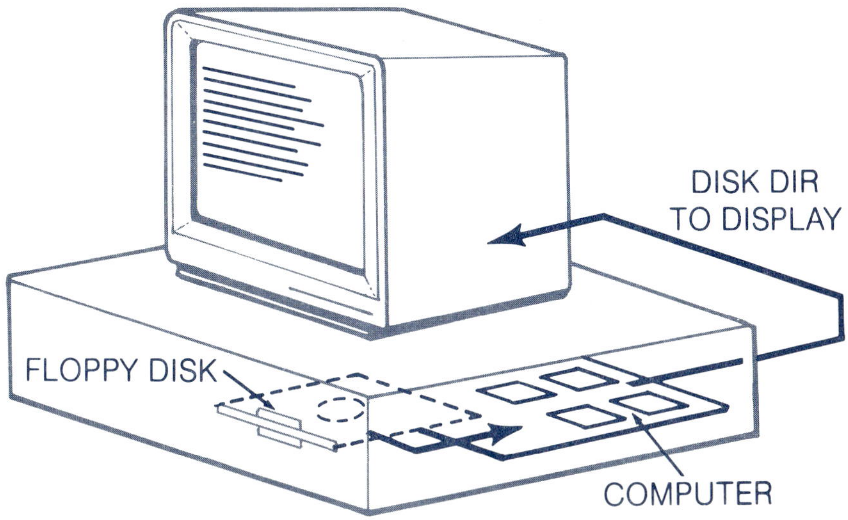

Figure 6-3.
Redirection of data to the printer.

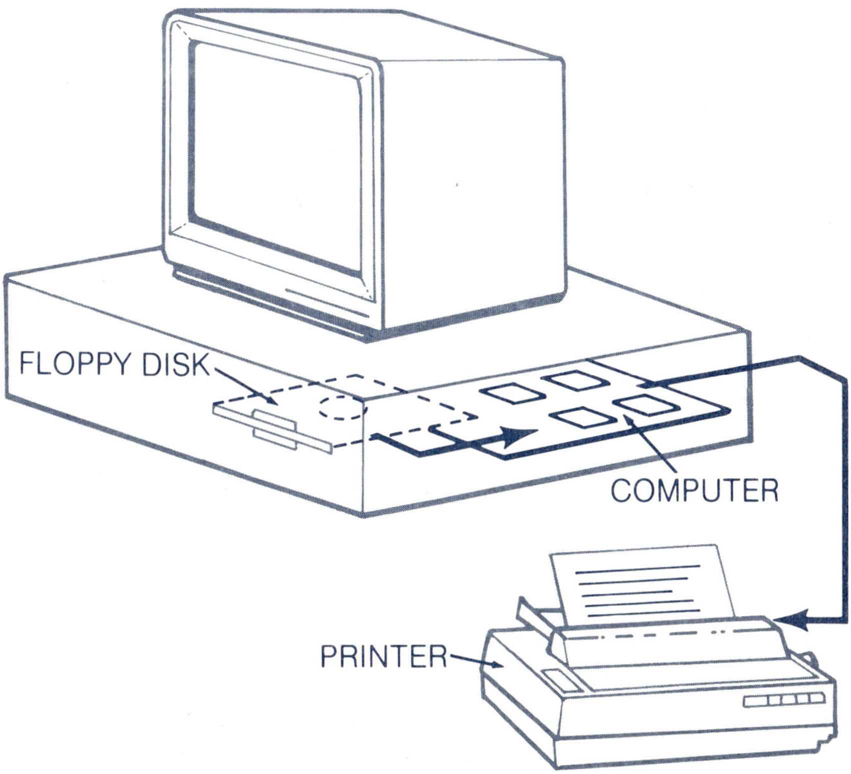

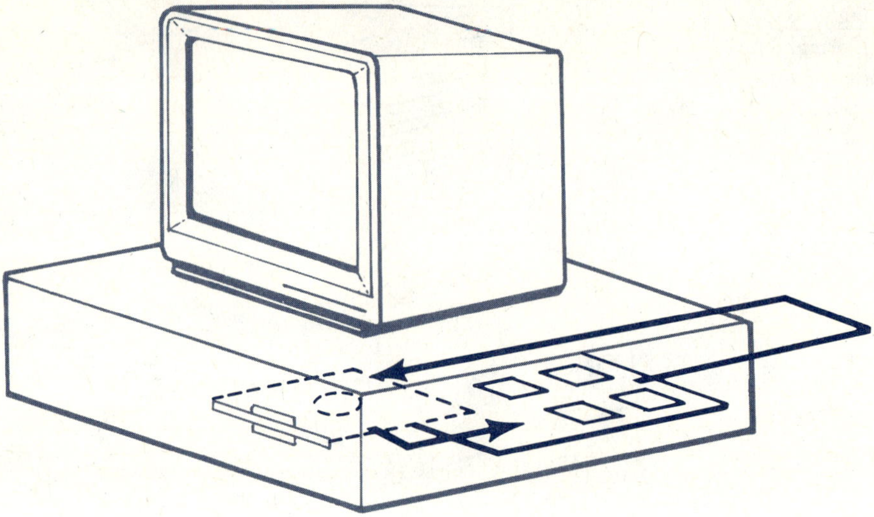

Figure 6-4. Redirection of data to a disk file.

OUTPUT AND INPUT The "greater-than" and "less-than" symbols tell DOS to redirect data. The greater-than (>) symbol sends data from the first-named device to the second-named device. The proper syntax is as follows: first device > second device.

To send the directory listing to a printer instead of to the screen, key-enter the following command on the DOS command line.

```
A>DIR > PRN
```

This routes the output from the DIR command to the printer instead of to the screen. Nothing is visible on the screen because the data is being sent to the printer.

Output can also be sent to a disk file. The following command will send the DIR output to a file named DIRLIST.TXT.

```
A>DIR > DIRLIST.TXT
```

Drive designators and path names also can be used with redirection. In the following examples, the first line shows how to redirect the DIR command output to a disk file in another drive. The second line uses a path name.

```
A>DIR C: > B:DIRLIST.TXT
C>DIR C:\WORD\PROJ1\*.DOC > A:PROJECT.SUM
```

Data can also be redirected to a device as input by using the less-than (<) symbol. For example, the contents of a file can be used instead of keyboard entry to satisfy a request or complete a command. The less-than symbol directs data from the second-named device as input into the first-named device. The proper syntax is as follows: first device < second device.

ADDING TO FILES Output from one or more DOS commands can be redirected to a file. Output can also be added to the end of an existing file. The command used to add output to a file is a double set of greater-than signs (>>). This tells DOS to append the data to the existing file without writing over it.

This capability could be used, for example, to create a single file holding the directories of several subdirectories on your disk. The directory listing for each subdirectory can be appended as shown in the following display.

`C>DIR C:\SALES\RGN1 > REGIONS.LST`	←*This creates the file containing Region 1 file names.*
`C>DIR C:\SALES\RGN2 >> REGIONS.LST`	←*This appends RGN2 to the end of the file. The file now contains Region 1 followed by Region 2 file names.*

After these two operations, REGIONS.LST contains the directory listing of the files in the RGN1 and RGN2 subdirectories. Listing this file will display all of these entries in a single file.

Redirection Problems

Redirection is a useful feature for saving time with a variety of computer tasks. It also improves the accuracy with which these chores are accomplished. Care is needed, however, because some commands can lock up your computer and cause loss of work performed since the last time you saved data.

First, do not redirect output to a nonexistent device. Although this is an obvious rule, it is easy to redirect a directory listing to your printer when it is off-line or unconnected. If this happens, the computer may lock up and become unresponsive to any key. Usually a warm reboot (pressing CTRL-ALT-DEL) is all that is needed to get going. Occasionally a cold reboot (turning the power switch off and on again) is needed.

Second, redirecting input from a device can put the system on hold, waiting for input, while you are unable to provide any input via the keyboard.

For example, if you redirect input from the AUX device to your modem, you would expect input from a phone connection. If any problems occur with the connection, you are helpless as your computer waits for input that cannot come.

A similar problem can occur when you redirect input from a disk file. Depending on the program or command that is awaiting the input, you may not get sufficient input from the file. This is sometimes called a "short input file," and it does not provide enough data to satisfy the running program. The result is that the program sits and waits, and you have no way to intervene.

Another common problem has a result less drastic than hanging up your computer but can cause confusion. When you redirect output and append it to an existing file that contains an end-of-file marker, such as CTRL-Z, it may be difficult to list all of the new file. The TYPE command will list a file up to the end-of-file marker. If more data exists beyond this marker, the appended data cannot be listed on the screen. This problem occurs with certain application programs that end the file with a CTRL-Z. [Creating a batch file with COPY CON and ending it with F6 (CTRL-Z) will not append the control character to the file.]

Redirection Applications

The following redirection applications are included here for two reasons. First, they provide additional instruction on redirection techniques. Second, they provide hands-on experience if you turn on your computer and follow the explanations provided.

SEND DIR TO PRN Creating a printed list of directory files is a common redirection technique and is easy to do. Earlier discussion showed how to send a directory listing to the printer. The following example shows a batch file with directions for sending a directory listing to the printer. Be sure that your printer is ready before you run this batch file. To create FF, the NUL character, press the ALT key and then key-enter 255 using the numeric keypad. The NUL character is shown as <FF> in the example below. This will insert two blank lines into your display when the batch file runs. This batch file is named PDIR.BAT.

```
ECHO OFF
REM
REM PDIR.BAT sends the current directory to the printer.
REM
ECHO Is the printer turned on?
ECHO If not, turn it on.
```

```
ECHO <FF>   ←Create the NUL character (FF) by pressing ALT
ECHO <FF>     and then 255 on the numeric keypad.
ECHO Press CTRL-C or CTRL-BREAK if you wish to terminate,
ECHO Otherwise, when you are ready,
PAUSE
DIR > PRN
```

SEND DIR TO DISKFILE.TXT Another common redirection technique, which you also learned about in an earlier discussion, is sending a directory listing to a disk file. This has several advantages. First, it creates a permanent record of the directory. Even if later additions and deletions alter the directory, the disk file maintains the file arrangement that existed on the date it was created. Such a capability could be important if an auditing requirement demanded accurate records of disk files and their sizes. The following example, FDIR.BAT, shows a batch file used to keep records of disk files for auditing and backup purposes.

```
ECHO OFF
REM FDIR.BAT creates or adds to a file of
REM the current directory.
REM A new file, DIRLIST, is created if one
REM does not exist in the directory.
IF NOT EXIST DIRLIST GOTO CREATE
ECHO ------------------------
DIR >> DIRLIST
GOTO END
:CREATE
DIR > DIRLIST
:END
```

SEND LOG-IN TIMES TO LOG.RPT This redirection application is one that can be used to maintain a regular log-in procedure. Assume that the individuals in your office use computers for a variety of tasks. You need to see that records are kept on the times that work begins on different subjects. A log-in batch file will work in this situation.

Because cumulative records are being generated, redirection will enable you to add information each time you begin work without losing the previously created data. Redirection with addition to a file can maintain the necessary log.

The following batch file is named LOG.BAT. It will maintain a weekly log report for each individual for all work topics. LOG.BAT uses two other files. You will have to create these files in order for LOG.BAT to work properly. First, create LOG.BAT by entering the command lines shown below. Use COPY CON, EDLIN, or your word processor.

```
REM  LOG.BAT
REM
ECHO OFF
ECHO Appending to LOG.RPT.....
TYPE LINE >> LOG.RPT
ECHO.
DATE < CONT.NUE >> LOG.RPT
TIME < CONT.NUE >> LOG.RPT
TYPE CONT.NUE >> LOG.RPT
ECHO Type the subject, press ENTER, press F6, press ENTER.
ECHO.
COPY CON SUBJ.TMP
ECHO SUBJECT: >> LOG.RPT
TYPE SUBJ.TMP >> LOG.RPT
ERASE SUBJ.TMP
ECHO LOG IN COMPLETE
```

Now create the following files, LINE and CONT.NUE, before attempting to test LOG.BAT. These files must be in the same subdirectory as LOG.BAT in order for LOG.BAT to work properly. LINE is composed solely of a single line of dashes. Use COPY CON, press ENTER, enter the dashes, press ENTER, press F6, and press ENTER. LINE appears as follows.

```
------------------------
```

CONT.NUE contains a single carriage return. Use COPY CON, press ENTER, press ENTER again, press F6, and press ENTER again. Do not type <Enter> as shown in the example. CONT.NUE appears as follows.

```
<Enter>
```

Notice these features of LOG.BAT. The LINE file is used to place a separation mark between different log-in times. ECHO immediately followed by a period (.) with no space is used to create a blank line on the screen. In some versions of DOS, ECHO followed by spaces will cause DOS to indicate the status of the ECHO command. Therefore, the period is needed.

CONT.NUE is used to supply a carriage return and line feed character. When CONT.NUE is redirected as input to the DATE and TIME commands, it provides an automatic answer to the request to supply a new date or time. When it is appended to the LOG.RPT file, it merely provides a blank line in the report file. Run LOG.BAT; then type LOG.RPT to see your report.

Some versions of DOS will only place the current date and time in LOG.RPT. Other versions will also add a prompt to enter new data, which will be included in the batch file log. There is no simple way to eliminate this additional message from the file if your version of DOS creates it. Including the COPY CON command within a batch file provides a way to get your input while a batch file is running. While COPY CON is in effect, you are typing an entry. To terminate the command and return to the batch file, you must enter the end-of-file marker with F6. Once you do this, the batch file continues and the message you entered into the temporary file (SUBJ.TMP) is redirected and added to the LOG file. The temporary file is erased before the batch file ends. To suppress the DOS message "1 File(s) copied," which is displayed on your screen, you may try to send the COPY CON command to the NUL device. Your line will appear as follows.

```
COPY CON SUBJ.TMP > NUL
```

When output is redirected to NUL, screen messages that DOS normally displays are suppressed. The rest of the command operates normally. For example, if you enter the following command, the screen prompt will reappear immediately following some disk activity.

```
COPY File1 File2 > NUL
```

The "1 File(s) copied" message will not be displayed. However, sending COPY CON to the NUL device causes some versions of DOS to hang up. Experiment with your system to see if COPY CON SUBJ.TMP > NUL works. If it does, the screen display will be a little neater and more readable.

DOS Filters

In the previous section, you learned that output from one DOS operation can be redirected to a device other than the default, or normal, device. A DOS **filter** is a program to which you redirect a command's output before sending it to either the default or the new device. The DOS filter through which the output passes performs some useful work. The filter may make the screen display pause so that it is easier to read, or it may perform some operation on the output and change its appearance. The following section describes three common DOS filters.

MORE MORE.COM is a command file on your DOS disk. Its purpose is to process the stream of data from another source and stop the display when 23 lines of data are on the screen. It displays the message "---More---" on the last line and waits for a key press before displaying additional lines. After another 23 lines are displayed, the screen pauses again.

The typical way to use the MORE filter is to pipe the output of another command to it. **Piping** means to send the output of one command through another program. The second program alters the data coming to it. It "filters" this data before sending it on. To better understand this, consider the following example using redirection.

```
A>DIR > MORE.TXT
```

The directory contents will be saved in a new file called MORE.TXT. Now, however, use the piping command symbol " ¦ " (broken vertical bar). (The broken vertical bar may be on the same key as the backslash.) The piping command appears as follows.

```
A>DIR ¦ MORE
```

Now the directory will be listed on the screen in normal fashion. The first entries listed will not scroll off the top of the screen. After 23 lines, the listing will stop and display "More" on the last line of the screen. MORE.COM will wait for you to press any key before it resumes listing the directory contents. It will stop again after 23 entries have been listed on the screen.

A handy time to pipe to MORE.COM is when you want to type a long text file. You normally have to press CTRL-S to stop the display and then press it again to begin scrolling. MORE.COM will stop automatically after a screen display of lines is listed. Pressing any key will display the next group of lines.

SORT SORT.EXE is another filter that will arrange the lines of a file into ASCII character order. If only alphabetic characters are involved, this is alphabetical order. When numbers are involved, you may see 111 and 123 before 2 or 24. This happens because the command is looking at the character codes for 1 or 2 or 3; it is not treating them as numbers with numeric value. The piping command used to sort a DIR listing is as follows.

```
C>DIR ¦ SORT
```

This form of the command will sort the directory on the first character of each line. SORT permits you to use switches to sort in reverse order or on a specified column. When you wish to sort according to a specified column, you must enter a plus (+) sign before the column. The following display shows the switches you can use with SORT.

`C>DIR ¦ SORT` ←*Sorts the current directory.*

`C>DIR ¦ SORT /R` ←*Sorts the current directory in reverse ASCII order.*

```
C>DIR | SORT /+14        ←Sorts the current directory on the contents of
                          column 14. The file size starts in column 14,
                          so all entries will be arranged from the smallest
                          to the largest.

C>DIR | SORT /R /+24     ←Sorts the current directory in reverse date
                          order.

C>DIR | SORT /R /+14 | MORE   ←This command shows double piping.
                               The directory listing will be reverse
                               sorted by file size and will stop after
                               every 23 entries.
```

SORT can arrange the contents of text files as well as those of directories. Arranging a simple text file of names and departments will illustrate the SORT command's features. Assume that you have a text file called NAMES on your disk and that it contains the following entries. Note that the text file must consist of single lines each ending with a carriage return. The department begins in the 25th column.

```
Williams, Barry         Marketing
Fennwick, Susan         Finance
Cardin, Tom             Marketing
Smith, Harry            Marketing
Lopez, Juan             Marketing
Davis, Fran             Finance
Adams, Donald           Finance
Roberts, Nancy          Finance
Tefler, Edward          Marketing
```

To use SORT, you must redirect the file to make SORT read the NAMES file and arrange it, as shown below. Both SORT and the NAMES file are in the root directory on drive A.

```
A>SORT < NAMES      ←The < symbol causes SORT to read the contents
                      of NAMES.

Adams, Donald       Finance
Cardin, Tom         Marketing
Davis, Fran         Finance
Fennwick, Susan     Finance
Lopez, Juan         Marketing
Roberts, Nancy      Finance
Smith, Harry        Marketing
Tefler, Edward      Marketing
Williams, Barry     Marketing
```

In the following example, SORT arranges the list by department. In this case, SORT arranges the list according to the 25th column, which contains the first character of the department name.

```
A>SORT /+25 < NAMES    ←The +25 tells SORT to arrange on the contents
                         of the 25th column.

Fennwick, Susan        Finance
Davis, Fran            Finance
Adams, Donald          Finance
Roberts, Nancy         Finance
Williams, Barry        Marketing
Cardin, Tom            Marketing
Smith, Harry           Marketing
Lopez, Juan            Marketing
Tefler, Edward         Marketing
```

FIND FIND is a command that will locate a text string within one or more files and list the line in which the specified string occurs. Switches allow some variation in how this command works. The FIND command is used to locate files that contain specific text, words, or phrases which identify the file. FIND uses the following syntax.

```
FIND /C /N /V "string" <file to search>
```

The switches must come before the string in this DOS command. /C counts the number of "string" occurrences. /N displays the line numbers and lines containing "string." /V displays all lines that do not contain "string." "String" must be in quotation marks, and the precise use of uppercase and lowercase is critical—i.e., "the" is different from "The." The file to be searched must be entered after the other parts of the command. More than one file name may be entered on the command line; however, wild-card characters will not work.

The following example will demonstrate how FIND can be used. Assume that you must locate all correspondence with reference to the Waterloo Project. Your company works on many projects, and many letters and reports exist, but only some relate to the Waterloo Project. Use FIND, shown as follows, to solve this problem.

```
C>FIND "Waterloo" CORRES1.DOC CORRES2.DOC CORRES3.DOC

---------- CORRES1.DOC
and we find that the Waterloo Project will be completed on time and

---------- CORRES2.DOC

---------- CORRES3.DOC
believe that costs for the Waterloo Project will be slightly over
Waterloo Project personnel include:
```

The command will print each file that it searches and will list each line containing the search string. If the search string is not found, as shown in the middle file in the previous example, the title is still printed followed by blank lines.

The following example shows the results of using the /C switch. This switch counts the number of lines containing the "string" but does not print the lines.

```
C>FIND /C "Waterloo" CORRES1.DOC CORRES2.DOC CORRES3.DOC

---------- CORRES1.DOC 1
```

```
---------- CORRES2.DOC 0

---------- CORRES3.DOC 2
```

If there are many correspondence files, entering each file can consume a lot of time. FIND does not allow wild-card characters to be inserted on the command line. Therefore, you must use the FOR..IN..DO batch subcommand (see Chapter 5) to repeat the FIND command using different file names. The following example illustrates this.

```
C>FOR %A IN (CORRES*.DOC) DO FIND /C "Waterloo" %A >> FOUND.LOG
```

```
C>TYPE FOUND.LOG

---------- CORRES1.DOC 1

---------- CORRES2.DOC 0

---------- CORRES3.DOC 2

---------- CORRES4.DOC 5

---------- CORRES5.DOC 0

---------- CORRES6.DOC 0

---------- CORRES7.DOC 2
.
.
.
```

The command line in the previous example illustrates redirection while using the FOR..IN..DO command structure. The output of the entire search is captured in FOUND.LOG. Note that the APPEND redirection command (>>) must be used, or each cycle of the FOR command will overwrite the previous entry. If the APPEND command were not used, the file would never have more than a single line item. By appending, we capture the results from all files.

HANDS-ON EXERCISE

1. Start the computer if it is not already on. Place a copy of the DOS master disk or your FIRST DISK in drive A.

   NOTE: *If you use your SECOND DISK, you must key-enter the PATH command. Do not change the path on the computer you are using without asking your instructor. If it is acceptable to change the path, key-enter the command to search all of the first-level subdirectories on your SECOND DISK. You can also copy some of the command files used in this exercise into your root directory.*

2. Perform the DIR command in the typical manner. Press CTRL-S to freeze the display so that you can read all the file names.

3. Pipe the DIR output through MORE.COM. If you are using your SECOND DISK, but you did not change the path, you can key-enter the following command: DIR | A: \UTIL\MORE. If you used the PATH command earlier or if MORE.COM is in the root directory, key-enter DIR | MORE.

4. Sort the directory to a holding file. Key-enter the following command.

   ```
   DIR | SORT > DIR.LST
   ```

   Then view this file with the following command.

   ```
   TYPE DIR.LST | MORE
   ```

5. Repeat step 4, but sort the file names on the extension. Determine which column contains the first character of the extension and enter this in the command with the /+ switch.

6. Use the disk that contains the batch files you key-entered in Chapter 5. Find out which batch files contain the following strings: "%1," "IF," and "GOTO." Use the FOR..IN..DO batch subcommand. For example, the first time key-enter the following command.

   ```
   FOR %A IN (*.BAT) DO FIND "%1" %A
   ```

   Press CTRL-S to stop the display as needed to see what is being found. In this case, it does no good to pipe the command output through MORE.COM. Each cycle of the FOR subcommand starts the line count over; MORE never sees more than a couple of lines, and the long display will scroll off the top of the screen.

IMPROVING DOS EFFICIENCY

DOS makes it easy to accomplish useful work on the computer. When you first start to use the computer, everything seems to happen very quickly.

Even though the computer's speed makes short work of most tasks, it is amazing how inefficient some steps can be.

Repetitive operations are time-consuming. One step may require only a few minutes but the cumulative time may be long. DOS provides a number of commands and features to help you improve efficiency.

System Configuration

DOS is designed to work with many systems and satisfy the needs of millions of users. DOS provides configuration commands to set the way the computer system works. **Configuring the system** means changing the standard or default settings built into DOS to ones that better meet your particular needs. You can change the configuration features to fit your system components and the ways in which you want them to work.

DOS contains fundamental or default settings that will often work the best in a majority of situations. Many times, you will not notice that some programs run more slowly than necessary. The default settings can be changed to increase speed and efficiency.

Sometimes, however, a new program will not work at all or will be noticeably slower. A new program manual may instruct you to change a configuration setting to achieve optimum performance. Use the CONFIG.SYS and AUTOEXEC.BAT files to change your configuration.

DOS looks for the CONFIG.SYS file when you boot your computer. It then executes the commands in CONFIG.SYS. Configuration commands are placed in the CONFIG.SYS file. DOS then looks for the AUTOEXEC.BAT file and executes other configuration files that you have placed there.

Earlier versions of DOS did not permit as much configuration of the computer system as Version 3 does. Version 5.0 permits the most configuration of any DOS version. This added capability makes the computer system more flexible and thus more productive. The following example lists a complicated CONFIG.SYS file.

```
C>TYPE CONFIG.SYS
DEVICE=C:\HIMEM.SYS
DEVICE=C:\ATIVGA\MOUSE.SYS
DEVICE=C:\DOS\ANSI.SYS
DEVICE=C:\WIN3\SMARTDRV.SYS 1024 256
DEVICE=ANSI.SYS
DEVICE=RAMDRIVE.SYS 64 128 64 /E:512
```

```
INSTALL=C:\DOS\FASTOPEN.EXE C:=(50,25)
SHELL=C:\DOS\COMMAND.COM /P /E:256
COUNTRY=001
FILES=20
BUFFERS=20
LASTDRIVE=E


C>
```

Configuration commands can be set to change three main aspects of the computer's operation. You can affect the devices that operate with the computer, disk access, and memory management. You affect these operations by issuing commands from the command prompt or from the AUTOEXEC.BAT file, or by commands you insert in the CONFIG.SYS file.

DEVICE The DEVICE command provides additional flexibility for your hardware and software. It allows you to plug in boards and use unusual software. Without the DEVICE command, many computer products could not work with the majority of machines and would not be commercially successful. The command directs the computer to a specific file. The correct syntax is as follows.

```
DEVICE = PATHNAME\FILENAME.EXT
```

FILENAME.EXT is the device driver. A **device driver** is a special program written to tell the computer how to work with the special device, or peripheral, connected to it. In general, the computer is equipped to work with the hardware pieces that come with the unit, such as the keyboard, disk drive, or monitor. Many systems are constructed using hardware from various manufacturers. Printers, plotters, mouse systems, and modems are examples of peripherals that are usually added later.

The device driver tells DOS how to control the added piece of hardware. The DEVICE command tells DOS where to look for instructions about the peripheral being connected. During the booting process, the CONFIG.SYS file tells DOS how to locate the software and load it for use.

ANSI.SYS is one of the most common device driver files, and it is supplied on your DOS disk. Its purpose is to control the way DOS handles the video screen and the keyboard. Normally you would not change the standard method by which DOS is set to use the keyboard and monitor. However, an application program may require you to change either of these, or your personal preferences may dictate a change. Technical reference manuals can tell you how to modify the ANSI.SYS file to suit your requirements. After you modify the ANSI.SYS file according to a vendor's instructions, you would use your modification by adding the following line to your CONFIG.SYS file.

```
DEVICE=ANSI.SYS
```

The CONFIG.SYS file shown in the last screen display above contains device drivers for memory management (HIMEM.SYS), a mouse (MOUSE.SYS), a disk cache (SMARTDRV.SYS), and a ram drive (RAMDRIVE.SYS). Each of these improves DOS efficiency or versatility.

DISK ACCESS A second way to improve the operation of a computer system is to fine tune the way DOS accesses the disk drives, especially the hard disk drives. Speed improvements will most often be noticed with improved hard disk access. As programs, and the amounts of data used or generated, grow larger, the time required to read from or write to the hard disk becomes critical.

One of the most simple actions you can take to minimize disk access time is to defragment your hard disk. Over time, the data or program code gets segmented all over the hard disk. The disk heads need to jump around to read all of the information. Compress programs will automatically rearrange the hard disk so that all the data or program code is adjacent. No data is removed, but the heads will not need to move to read all of the information. Speed improvements can be substantial.

The other major speed-up activity is to add a disk cache. This is a program that uses extra memory to store commonly used information from the hard disk. This puts the information in memory where it can be retrieved more quickly than from the disk the next time it is needed.

Still another speed improvement program is FASTOPEN.EXE, a program available on the DOS disk. This program keeps a list of the disk addresses of the last ten to 999 programs you access in the current session. This allows DOS to go right to the disk location for specific information instead of taking time to find this information in the disk directory. The effect is to speed up the disk access.

Finally, disk access can be improved by using the BUFFERS command. A **buffer** is a reserved area in RAM that DOS sets aside to aid in transferring files to and from disks. A buffer contains a limited number of bytes, and DOS adds data to the buffer until it is full. When the buffer is full, DOS sends the data to the disk drive for recording on the disk.

Enough data to fill a buffer is read each time from a disk. The buffer is loaded and the data is transferred to other parts of memory for use by your programs. Obviously, having only one buffer would slow down the process. Therefore, DOS normally reserves two buffers (or three for some computers).

The BUFFERS command allows you to specify more than two or three buffers. Some systems run best with ten buffers, whereas others run faster with 20 buffers or more. You can experiment with the number of buffers to find the optimum level. Because each additional buffer takes memory, the amount of memory available for the application program data is reduced. Therefore, if too many buffers are specified, the system will actually slow down rather than run faster. Twenty buffers have been reserved in the CONFIG.SYS file shown above.

MEMORY MANAGEMENT Early computers contained a maximum of 640K of memory, but today's computers come equipped with 1M or more. However, DOS is restricted to allowing programs to use only the "lower" 640K. Therefore, elaborate switching systems have evolved to allow storage in the memory above 640K, while programs operate within this active memory.

These evolving systems make it necessary to optimize memory management. Even with DOS Version 5.0, you must experiment to find ways to maximize operating memory. Some of the disk access and device commands will install program codes within the 640K memory area. These can easily add up and prevent an application from running. Most large programs today will indicate an error and not run if they find insufficient base memory.

Memory between 640K and 1M is known as "upper memory" or "high memory," and there are special programs that allow its limited use. In general, it is used for video and special code storage tasks, and is beyond the user's control. Memory above 1M is called either extended memory or expanded memory, depending on the way it is to be used. Simply, extended memory is storage space for programs that are switched into 640K active memory or for data storage. Expanded memory is also storage space, but it is used in 16K chunks that are switched into use as needed. The effects are most often the same: large programs or multiple programs can run at the same time. Unseen by you, the computer is manipulating the program and data into and out of the main 640K area and either extended or expanded memory.

Memory managers are programs you install with the CONFIG.SYS program using an INSTALL= or DEVICE= statement. Depending on the memory manager you install, your extra memory may be either extended or expanded. Most programs look for and use expanded memory. Windows works with either but does best with extended memory. Specific hands-on practice with memory managers is left to individual systems and programs.

RAM Disk

A RAM disk can save a lot of time, especially with programs requiring numerous disk accesses. A **RAM disk** is a section of memory set aside to act just like a disk drive. This memory will hold programs and data the same way a floppy disk or hard disk will. A RAM disk will have a directory and will hold as many files as a regular disk, depending on the memory you reserve for it.

The RAM disk must be defined by the CONFIG.SYS file at start-up. This is accomplished by key-entering the following command on a line in your CONFIG.SYS file: DEVICE=VDISK.SYS or DEVICE=RAMDRIVE.SYS. You can adjust the size of the ram drive by changing parameters in the DEVICE= command.

VDISK.SYS is a file included in PC-DOS Version 3.0 and above. (In some versions of MS-DOS, this program is called RAMDRIVE.SYS, and it is available in Version 3.2 and above.) The file name, VDISK.SYS, indicates that VDISK is a virtual disk or virtually a disk drive. The RAM disk characteristics are set by default parameters unless you enter different ones. You can define the memory size devoted to the RAM disk, the sector size it will use, and the number of directory entries it will hold. If you have extended memory, the /E extended memory switch tells VDISK to set itself up in extended memory.

A RAM disk is even faster than a hard disk. Once it has been defined and required files have been loaded, it functions faster than any other configuration you can install. Programs requiring a lot of disk accesses, such as some database management programs, operate much faster with a RAM disk. Your time savings can be substantial.

Files are initially loaded onto the RAM disk by copying them from a floppy or hard disk. You can define your own batch file to copy the necessary files during start-up. Once they have been loaded, application programs using the RAM disk must be set so that the RAM disk is the default drive rather than one of the regular drives. After this, using the RAM disk is exactly the same as using another drive.

The data in a RAM disk can be lost if a power failure occurs or if you turn your computer off before copying the RAM disk files. To preserve the data files that accumulate on the RAM disk, you must copy them onto a floppy or hard disk. Again, another batch file can be defined to make this task easy, but you must run the batch file before it can do its job.

If you have only 640K of RAM memory, you can use some of it for a RAM disk. However, if you make the RAM disk only as large as a floppy disk (for example, 360K), you will not have much memory left for your program and data. RAM disks of any great size are more practical only if you have extended memory.

HANDS-ON EXERCISE

1. Place your DOS disk in drive A and turn on your computer if it is not already on.
2. Create a start-up disk by entering FORMAT /V /S. If your computer has two drives, enter FORMAT B: /V /S. Insert a new disk in the proper disk drive and press ENTER.
3. After the format process is complete, DOS will ask you for a volume name. Type THIRD DISK and press ENTER.
4. Copy VDISK.SYS (or RAMDRIVE.SYS) from the DOS disk onto your THIRD DISK.
5. Place your THIRD DISK in drive A. Create a CONFIG.SYS file by entering COPY CON CONFIG.SYS.
6. Key-enter the following lines (press ENTER at the end of each line).

```
BUFFERS=20
FILES=15
DEVICE=VDISK.SYS
DEVICE=VDISK.SYS
```

NOTE: *Type the DEVICE=VDISK.SYS line twice. This will set up two RAM disks, each with the same default characteristics. Doing this will use about 128K of your basic RAM memory. This will not, however, hurt anything for this practice session. You will have to determine if having one or two RAM disks present while you run other applications is possible. See the next section for more on memory usage.*

7. Insert your new start-up disk in drive A and press CTRL-ALT-DEL. This restarts your computer and installs two RAM disks.
8. After the A> prompt is displayed, make drive D the current drive.
9. Display the directory as follows.

```
D> DIR

 Volume in drive D is VDISK V2.0
 Directory of D:\

File not found
```

10. Key-enter COPY CON FIRST.FIL. Then key THIS IS THE FIRST LINE. Press ENTER, press F6, and press ENTER again.

11. List the directory of drive D. You will see FIRST.FIL listed as the only file in the directory. Notice the remaining space.

12. To experience the speed of a RAM disk, repeat the steps in several of the previous hands-on exercises. This requires you to copy the batch files from your FIRST DISK and your SECOND DISK onto your RAM disk. Use the FOR..IN..DO command to accomplish this. Key-enter the following command.

```
FOR %A IN (A:*.BAT) DO COPY %A D:
```

This command will copy all batch files on drive A to drive D. To check that all have been copied, do a directory listing of drive D.

13. Copy FIND.EXE and MORE.COM from drive A to drive D.

14. Perform the FIND operation from step 6 of the previous hands-on exercise. The command is as follows.

```
FOR %A IN (*.BAT) DO FIND "%1" %A
```

Notice how much faster the command is completed because all disk reading is speeded up by using the RAM disk.

15. To further practice using RAM disks, create several subdirectories on each RAM drive. Use the regular DOS commands for this, but log in to drive D or E. Copy files from one directory to another and from one RAM disk drive to another.

Memory-Resident Programs (TSRs)

Memory-resident programs are used for many tasks and with many programs. They are loaded into memory and stay there even when other programs are running. These programs are also called terminate-and-stay-resident programs (TSRs), because the program is not erased from memory when you exit from it.

To use a TSR, just press a particular key combination that the program recognizes, called a "hot key." The regular program you are running suspends itself and the memory-resident program "pops" into view, ready to run. After it does its job, it disappears from the screen (but not from memory), and the original application program reappears ready to run again.

TSR programs are popular because of the time savings they create. Another task can be completed while you are running an application program by simply switching to the other task. There is no need to exit from the first program and then return to it after the new task is done.

To further aid efficiency, more than one TSR program can be in memory at the same time. Several can be loaded at start-up time, and all will wait for you to call them.

Some of these programs allow "cutting-and-pasting," or taking data from one program and transferring it directly to another. Others, called "desk-top organizers," help organize your work. They may provide appointment management, note taking, phone list management, phone dialing, and "index card" systems for database management.

One problem with TSRs involves memory conflicts. Because each TSR is written by a different company, they tend to fight over the same memory space or the use of the same hot keys. "RAM cram" is a phrase used to describe the situation that results when you try to load too many memory-resident programs and these programs conflict with each other. DOS Version 5.0 provides ways to load TSR programs in "high memory" above the 640K limit. This allows them to work and not take up valuable operating memory.

Some memory-resident programs may also be incompatible with some application programs. You may use a powerful word processing program that is helplessly locked up when you try to run it with a particular TSR. The TSR itself may not work with one or more application programs. If you decide to use two TSR programs at once, you may need to test their use with your favorite programs. Many times, manufacturers of TSRs will advertise the applications with which their programs work. Application programs may also advertise their compatibilities. You can read magazine reviews or talk with other users before buying, but the best test is to try the programs together yourself.

Advanced Commands

Several advanced commands make it easier to use the computer's disk drives. These commands temporarily modify what DOS knows about the disk drives connected to the computer. Their purpose is to make certain repetitive tasks happen more quickly and more easily. ASSIGN is one of these commands. SUBST (substitute) and JOIN are two other commands that can speed up certain disk-related activities.

ASSIGN Older versions of some application programs were not designed to use drive C. Until hard disks became more affordable, many computer systems had only two drives, A and B. If you are using an older program, it may be necessary to tell that program to use the hard disk instead of the floppy drives. Use the ASSIGN command if you have a 5¼″ drive A and a 3½″ drive B and you use programs on 3½″ disks that expect to use drive A.

When you use ASSIGN, DOS thinks that one physical disk is another. The command syntax is as follows.

```
ASSIGN A=C
```

A drive designator, if needed, should be entered before the command itself. The drives to be assigned are entered without colons. The drive to be assigned is entered first, and the drive to be used is entered after the equals sign. In the above case, DOS will think drive C is drive A, and any commands intended for A will operate on C.

Another way to use ASSIGN is with a RAM disk. As mentioned previously, a RAM disk is a portion of memory set up to act like a disk drive. It operates much faster than a disk drive. If you call your RAM disk drive D and issue the command ASSIGN A=D, any operations that would normally involve drive A will use the much faster drive D. After the work has been completed, cancel the assignment by entering ASSIGN without any drive assignments. Then copy the files in RAM drive D onto a real disk in drive A.

SUBST To improve on the versatility offered by ASSIGN, DOS Version 3 added the SUBST and JOIN commands. SUBST (substitute) allows drive letters to be substituted for path names. JOIN allows two drives to act as one. Both commands, if used carefully, can save time and increase efficiency. If you use them carelessly, you may lose valuable work on one or more disks.

SUBST allows a path name to be represented by a drive letter designation. The letter selected cannot represent an existing floppy or hard drive or RAM disk. Once defined, the SUBST command saves much key-entering. The proper syntax for SUBST is as follows.

```
SUBST ALIAS: DRIVE:\PATHNAME
```

Alias becomes the drive designator that substitutes for the drive letter and path name. For example, you may use a long path name repetitively in your work. This means a lot of typing. Assume that you use the following path name.

```
C:\FINANCE\ACCOUNTS\MAY\SALES.REC
```

The SUBST command allows you to make the following substitution.

```
C>SUBST E: C:\FINANCE\ACCOUNTS\MAY
```

E: is the alias, and it substitutes for C: \FINANCE\ACCOUNTS\MAY. Once the SUBST command is executed, DIR E: produces the directory of C: \FINANCE \ACCOUNTS \MAY. To load the SALES.REC file, simply direct the application program you are using to E:SALES.REC.

Key-entering SUBST alone on the DOS command line will list any substitutions that have been defined. To remove a substitution, enter the alias name followed by the /D (disconnect) switch. To disconnect the SUBST command used in the above example, key-enter the following command.

```
C>SUBST E: /D
```

You must be aware of a final point before you can use SUBST. DOS will automatically set aside five drives to be used with SUBST—A through E. Even if your system contains only three physical drives, you will be able to use D and E with SUBST. If you attempt to define an alias drive above E (F, G, etc.), DOS will not recognize the drive designator. To use drive designators above E, you must include the LASTDRIVE command in your CONFIG.SYS file to define the highest letter drive you want to use. A statement such as LASTDRIVE=M will provide the drive letters from F to M for use with SUBST.

Several DOS commands should be avoided or used carefully if SUBST is in effect. CHKDSK cannot be used with the alias and will produce an error message if this is attempted. MKDIR and RMDIR actually make or remove subdirectories on the substituted path. Do not use ASSIGN, BACKUP, DISKCOPY, DISKCOMP, FDISK, FORMAT, JOIN, LABEL, or RESTORE on a substituted drive or with the alias.

JOIN JOIN makes DOS think that two drives have become one larger drive. It is available only with DOS Version 3.1 and above. The most frequent uses of this command are joining of two hard disks, C and D, and connection of a RAM disk to a real disk drive. However, a floppy drive and a hard disk, or two floppy drives, can be joined. The first drive is joined to an empty subdirectory on the second drive. For example, joining drive A to drive C would involve the following command.

```
C>JOIN A: \JOINUP
```

JOINUP is an empty subdirectory created on drive C to join the two drives. Now all commands affecting the JOINUP subdirectory will also include the entire A drive. Drive A is no longer accessible (while it is joined to C), but its contents are shown along with JOINUP's. Canceling the previous JOIN definition is accomplished as follows.

```
JOIN A: /D
```

This disconnects the joined disks and restores the system to its state before the JOIN.

You must be extremely careful not to use DOS commands that alter disks or groups of files while ASSIGN, SUBST, or JOIN is in effect! Disconnect the command if in doubt.

COMMON DOS PROBLEMS

You may encounter problems as you use DOS. It would be impossible to list all of the potential problems or offer instruction about what to do with each of them. DOS manuals often list the DOS error messages, but they may not explain the causes of the errors.

The purpose of this section is to mention several typical problems that occur so frequently that you are likely to encounter at least one of them. You may also need to refer to DOS technical manuals or, in some cases, to contact experienced DOS experts.

File Recovery

Every computer user will lose one or more important files at some time. This happens in numerous ways, and in spite of the best precautions, it even happens to experienced DOS users. If you lose a file, you can try a few **file recovery** procedures before resorting to data reconstruction or complete re-entry.

First, the best way to avoid loss of time due to file erasure is to maintain regular backup copies. Then, when a file is accidentally erased or becomes irretrievable, the work is available on the backup copy. You may lose some of the most recent additions, but the loss is far less than if no backup exists.

If you do not have a backup and your critical data is erased, there are a few steps you can take. The ability to "unerase" a file depends on the fact that deleting a file name from a disk directory is not the same as deleting the file from the disk.

When you delete a file using the ERASE (DEL) command, DOS changes the disk directory and the File Allocation Table (FAT), but it does not erase the actual file contents from the disk. This data is still present. If you can take the proper steps before anything else is saved to the disk, you have a good chance of seeing your data again.

The following list provides a series of steps you can take to recover your file. If these are not successful, your file is probably not recoverable.

1. Make a backup of the disk immediately. Use the DISKCOPY command, if the file to be recovered is on a floppy disk. Make sure your entire hard disk is backed up if the file recovery is to take place on your hard disk.
2. File recovery is easy with DOS Version 5.0 (see below). The easiest way to unerase a file with an earlier version is to use one of the commercial software utility programs available for such a job. These programs automate the steps you need to take to change the status of the directory entry from "deleted" to normal. The File Allocation Table, or FAT, is also automatically adjusted to tell the disk that the file is still in use rather than "deleted."

3. If one of these utility programs is not available, you must go through each of the steps using a sector read/write program. Another approach is to use the DOS DEBUG program. The details of these steps are involved and beyond the scope of this book. Further, if you perform one of these steps incorrectly, you could damage other file entries on your disk.
4. If the utilities mentioned above are not available, then turn to a DOS expert or look for a way to begin re-entering the data that was lost.

DOS Version 5 File Recovery

DOS Version 5.0 provides UNDELETE, UNFORMAT, and MIRROR, three commands that make it easy to recover from an unintentional erasure. UNDELETE works best if you run MIRROR when you do your work. MIRROR runs in the background and keeps a hidden file of all of the deleted files from your work station. UNDELETE uses this hidden file to bring back or recover a deleted file. It also can help recover a file if a portion of the disk is damaged or reformatted accidentally.

UNDELETE will work without MIRROR, but requires additional steps from you in determining the name of the deleted file. Also, there is a greater chance that a deleted file can be recovered after some disk activity if MIRROR is working than if it is not.

UNFORMAT is similar to UNDELETE. It allows you to recover the contents of a disk that has been accidentally formatted.

These three programs are available as commercial programs. In fact, Microsoft licenses them for inclusion in DOS Version 5. Users of earlier DOS versions can enjoy their benefits by purchasing the commercial programs from Central Point Software, authors of PC Tools, a popular utility program.

Memory-Resident Program Conflicts

Earlier in this chapter you learned about the time-saving features of memory-resident programs, or TSRs. You also learned that "RAM cram" and other problems can develop as you install more TSRs on your computer. If problems develop, you can use the following steps to try to resolve them.

1. When a problem develops, note any changes that have been made since the last time the system ran correctly. It may be obvious that the new change is the culprit.
2. The next step is to remove all TSRs from the computer. If you normally use a RAM disk, you should change the CONFIG.SYS file and reboot to remove it.

3. After all of your TSR programs have been removed, add the new program (the one with which you have had trouble), and observe whether the difficulty still exists. If it does, then it is probably not the fault of the other TSRs. Perhaps the program is not compatible with your computer or you have not followed the installation steps accurately. You should recheck these. If the problem persists, contact the software vendor. It is possible that you will not be able to use the new program.
4. If the new TSR operates as advertised with all of your other memory-resident programs removed, the next step is to determine which one is in conflict. Change the AUTOEXEC.BAT file (copy the original AUTOEXEC.BAT file to a different name, such as AUTOEXEC.ORG, so that it can be easily reinstated if this testing fails).
5. After copying the original file, alter it to load only one other TSR program. Start up the computer with both programs loaded and see if the conflict still exists. If it does not, then continue this process until you re-create the original problem. This will tell you which of your original TSRs will work with your new program and which will not.
6. At this point, you must decide which TSR you want to live without. You may talk to the manufacturer about your particular problem. Tell the vendor all the details about your system, including the results of the test you have just completed. Often, vendors will have developed small programs, called "patches," to solve your particular problem. At least, they want to know about actual conflicts that exist.

Adding Hardware to Your System

Adding hardware to your system is easy, but it sometimes causes problems. Determining how to make a piece of new hardware work is similar to determining how to make a new TSR function. You may experiment with the system to discover which other piece of hardware or program is interfering with the operation of the new piece. However, you must consider another step with a new piece of hardware: you must first configure or set up the hardware to run on your system. This is not always easy to do. If the vendor from whom you purchased the hardware does not provide setup service, you must install the equipment yourself.

Often, this requires nothing more than following a series of instructions that come with the hardware. However, if the instructions are difficult to understand, this may take a long time.

If the basic instructions provided with the hardware do not produce a working system, you might experiment with different combinations of switch settings and software commands. Many hardware boards, which are known as peripheral cards and are plugged into the slots in the computer, have switch settings that select the equipment combinations represented by your computer. Changing these settings may produce positive results.

Sometimes, a particular software program, which ran before you added the hardware, suddenly will not run. You may need to "reinstall" the program or change the configuration settings. Run the setup program that came with the software to see if such a step makes the program work again.

Finally, call the hardware vendor. Again, be prepared to document all of the steps you have taken as well as to describe your hardware and software system. Often, the vendor has heard your problem before and can suggest how to resolve the issue.

◆ *Summary*

1. Computer accessories that are connected to the computer are called devices. The common computer devices are the console, the display, the printer, and communication equipment such as modems. External devices are connected to the computer's ports.
2. Redirection is routing of data flow input or output from the normal device to another device. The greater-than (>) symbol tells DOS to direct output to another device. The less-than (<) symbol directs input from another device.
3. If a nonexistent device is specified, redirection may cause the computer to "hang up." Input from a device that does not send complete data results in the computer's waiting for the remaining data.
4. The NUL device results in data being sent "nowhere." In effect, it disappears.
5. A DOS filter is a program that processes the data from another operation. Common filters included on the DOS disk are MORE, SORT, and FIND.
6. The AUTOEXEC.BAT and CONFIG.SYS files are used to configure the system to run special device drivers or memory-resident programs, or to set memory configurations.
7. Defragmenting the hard disk or using a disk cache will speed up disk access time and improve efficiency.
8. The DOS commands SUBST, JOIN, and ASSIGN are used to combine or change the normal disk drive assignments. These changes make it easier to work with the multiple drives and complex subdirectory structures.
9. DOS uses memory above 640K to store programs and data. Extended and expanded are the two ways the extra memory can be configured.
10. A RAM disk is a portion of memory configured to work like a disk drive. The size, sector size, and number of directory entries are set with parameters and the VDISK.SYS program, all of which are included in a CONFIG.SYS line.

11. Memory-resident programs remain in memory while you run one of your main application programs. They can "pop up" for use when you press a "hot key." You return to your application when you are done with the memory-resident program. These programs are also called TSR (terminate-and-stay-resident) programs, or TSRs.

12. Problems with your computer can include accidental erasure of files, memory conflicts with memory-resident programs, and hardware conflicts between new hardware peripherals and other hardware or programs.

◆ *Exercises*

1. List three DOS devices with the DOS names for these devices.

2. You are looking at the instructions for a new laptop computer. They refer to the console. What two parts of the computer can be the console? Which part is involved with input, and which part is involved with output?

3. Your monitor has a resolution of 320 × 200. Will this monitor be able to display a lot of detail? (Defend your answer.) Define resolution.

4. Would you connect a modem to your computer's parallel port? Would you connect your printer to your computer's serial port?

5. You must have a printed list of your root directory. How can you use redirection to get this list? What is another, less direct way to get this same list?

6. While traveling with just your laptop computer, you issue the command DIR > PRN. The computer does nothing. What has happened?

7. Describe three ways in which to read a long directory listing on the screen. One way should use a filter. Name the filter and how it works.

8. You need to include a sorted directory listing in a report you are writing with your word processor. What command is used to create a file called SORTDIR.LST containing a sorted directory list?

9. What command is used to find all occurrences of "REM" comments in all batch files on drive C in the UTIL subdirectory? Explain any switches you use.

10. Your computer has a 5¼″ A drive and a 3½″ B drive. The new program you want to install is on 3½″ disks. You log onto drive B, put the install disk in drive B, and type INSTALL. A message tells you to put the disk in drive A, which cannot be done. How will the ASSIGN command help in this situation?

11. As you use a database program, you notice that you are always waiting while drive B reads and writes data. How can you create and use a RAM disk and what will be one of its advantages?

12. MIRROR is a terminate-and-stay-resident program. What does this mean, and how does such a program help you?
13. You have just deleted a file called SALES.BAK, and you discover that you have no other SALES.DAT file. Assume that you have DOS Version 5.0. What are two programs that can help in this situation, and how would you use them?
14. What habit should you develop to help you avoid losing all of your data if you accidentally erase a file?
15. After installation of a new program, your computer stops during the booting sequence. There may be conflicts among TSRs. Summarize the basic approach to finding out how to eliminate these conflicts.

Appendix A

DOS Commands, Batch Subcommands, and Configuration Commands

DOS COMMANDS

For each command explained in the text, the summary presented here briefly reviews the command's purpose, provides an example, and shows the command syntax. The summary also refers you to the appropriate chapter (or appendix) for further discussion. Additional parameters and switches are available for many of these commands. Because of the many DOS features, space does not permit exhaustive explanations.

Some of the DOS commands in this appendix are advanced commands beyond the scope of this handbook on DOS essentials. These commands are listed, with brief explanations, to let you know that they exist. You should consult your DOS manual before using any command not covered in the chapters of this text. Some commands and switches are available only in MS-DOS, and others are available only in PC-DOS.

Any parts of a command that are enclosed in brackets (in the command syntax) are optional. You do not always need to include all of the optional parts of the command.

DOS Version 5 commands are denoted by asterisks.

APPEND This command instructs DOS to search for data files that are not in the current directory. The PATH command searches only for executable files, but the APPEND command searches for data files. This command is available beginning with MS-DOS Version 3.2 and PC-DOS Version 3.3.

ASSIGN This command tells DOS to use a specified disk drive instead of the one given in a command. See Chapter 6.

Example: `ASSIGN A=C`

All requests for drive A will use drive C instead.

ASSIGN [drive1=drive2]

ATTRIB This command allows you to change a file's attribute so that it is read-only. A read-only file cannot be modified or deleted. You can later remove the read-only attribute by using the -R parameter. ATTRIB also allows the file's archive flag to be set or removed. The archive flag indicates whether a file should be copied.

BACKUP This command makes backup copies of one or more files from a disk to another disk. Several switches are available. A few are listed here. /S backs up all subdirectories. /M backs up files created or modified since your last backup. /A adds the backup files to the target disk and does not erase the existing target files. /D:DATE backs up files modified on or after the specified date. /F formats the target disk if it is not already formatted. /F is available only in DOS Version 3.3. If you use Version 3.3 to back up files, you must also use Version 3.3 to recover files. See Chapter 4.

Example: `BACKUP C:\FINAN\*.* B: /M /A`

Makes backup copies of all files in C:FINAN subdirectory that have been modified since the last backup to the disk in drive B; the backup copies are added to the files already on the disk. If you do not use /A, all files on the target disk will be erased.

BACKUP [drive:][pathname] drive: [/S][/M][/A][/D:date][/F]

BREAK This command tells DOS to check for a CTRL-BREAK or CTRL-C whenever you request. This allows you to break out of a program, such as a compiler. It also allows you to break out when your program is writing to or reading from a disk drive. DOS normally checks for the control break when reading from or writing to the printer, screen, or auxiliary port. BREAK can be turned on or off, and it can be added to a CONFIG.SYS file.

CHCP This command was introduced with DOS Version 3.3. It allows the user to choose a code page. You would change code pages if you changed the language or character set that DOS uses. You must use the NLSFUNC command before you use the CHCP command.

CHDIR The Change Directory command tells DOS to make a different directory current. If this command is issued without naming a subdirectory, DOS displays the current directory. CD is an abbreviation for CHDIR. See Chapter 3.

Example: `CD \SALES`

Changes to the sales subdirectory. If you key-enter CD, DOS displays the current directory name. To change to the parent directory, key-enter CD .. (this has no effect if entered while in the root directory).

CHDIR [drive:][path]

CHKDSK The Check Disk command shows the space allocation on the specified disk and the system's memory. It also checks for noncontiguous files and will attempt to fix them if the /F switch is on. /F attempts to fix files. /V is the verbose switch, which displays the name of each file and subdirectory as it is checked. See Chapter 2.

Example: `CHKDSK A:*.* /V`

Checks all files on the disk in drive A, listing each as it is checked.

CHKDSK [drive:][pathname] [/F][/V]

CLS This command clears the screen and places the DOS prompt in the upper left corner.

COMMAND This command lets you run a copy of COMMAND.COM and change some of its characteristics. COMMAND.COM is the DOS command processor, which displays prompts, loads and runs programs, and runs commands and batch files.

COMP This command compares files to see if they are the same. It is available in all versions of PC-DOS and in Version 3.3 of MS-DOS.

COPY This command copies a file to another file. It is used to make a duplicate of a file in another location. /V is used to verify a file. See Chapter 2.

Example: `COPY LETTER1.DOC B: /V`

Copies LETTER1.DOC from the current directory to a file of the same name on drive B and verifies that the data has been properly recorded on the target file.

COPY [drive:]source[drive:]target[/V]

COPY can also be used to combine two or more files into a single file. This will create a target file if one is specified. If a target is not specified, COPY adds the file(s) to the end of the first file. See Chapter 2.

Example: `COPY A:REGION1.DAT+B:REGION2.DAT C:EASTREGN.DAT`

Copies and adds the contents of REGION1.DAT in drive A and the contents of REGION2.DAT in drive B to the summary file EASTREGN.DAT in drive C.

COPY [drive:][path]source[+[drive:][path]source] [drive:][path]target

COPY can also be used to copy from a device to a file. The command typically copies from the keyboard (CON) to a file. See Chapter 2.

Example: `COPY CON AUTOEXEC.BAT`

Creates an AUTOEXEC.BAT file from the keyboard.

COPY source target

CTTY This command changes the character device to be used for input and output.

DATE This command allows you to change the date in the system. See Chapter 1.

Example: `DATE 10-14-89`

Changes the date to October 14, 1989.

DATE [mm-dd-yy]

DEL This command erases or deletes the specified file or group of files. ERASE can be used instead of DEL. DEL will not delete a subdirectory. Be careful, because DEL does not give you a chance to change your mind once you have pressed ENTER (unless you try to delete all files by key-entering *.*, at which point you are asked if you are sure). See Chapter 2.

Example: `DEL BUS*.*`

Deletes all files starting with BUS and having any extension.

DEL [drive:]pathname

DIR This command lists the directory of a disk or subdirectory showing the size and date of creation for each file. It also shows the number of files in the directory and the number of free bytes available on the disk. /W displays a wide directory, without size and date information. /P pauses after the screen is filled and waits for a key press. See Chapter 1.

Example: `DIR B:\STORE1`

Lists the files in the STORE1 subdirectory on drive B.

DIR [drive:][pathname][/P][/W]

DISKCOMP This command compares two diskettes. /1 compares only one side. /8 compares the first eight sectors of each track. This command is available in PC-DOS Version 1.0 and above and in MS-DOS Version 3.2. The COMPDUPE command, which was available prior to Version 3.2 in MS-DOS, would compare two diskettes after formatting and copying one diskette to another.

DISKCOPY This command copies an entire diskette to another diskette. PC-DOS formats the target disk if it has not been formatted. DISKCOPY will not copy a hard disk. Some versions of MS-DOS require the target disk to be formatted before it can be used as a target disk for DISKCOPY. /1 copies only the first side of the disk. See Chapter 2.

Example: `DISKCOPY A: B:`

Copies the floppy disk in drive A to drive B. The disk drives must be compatible to do this.

DISKCOPY [drive1:] [drive2:] [/1]

***DOSKEY** This command starts the macro program, which remembers keystrokes and which creates a macro, or automatic playback set of keystrokes.

***DOSSHELL** This is the command that invokes the newly revised command shell—a program that aids in the selection of commands and in visualizing the programs on the disk.

***EDIT** This is a new full-screen text editor for creating and modifying text files.

***EMM386** Used with 80386 processors or higher, this command will turn expanded memory on or off.

ERASE This command erases one or more files. ERASE is another name for the DEL command. See DEL. See Chapter 2.

EXE2BIN This command converts files with an EXE extension to files with a BIN extension. If the format is acceptable, the BIN file may be changed into a COM file by renaming the extension. This command may not be available on your DOS disk.

EXIT This command returns control to the primary command processor from the secondary command processor. EXIT works with COMMAND.

*EXPAND This command is used during installation of DOS Version 5. It opens or expands the compressed files provided on the installation disks.

FASTOPEN This command allows faster access of files. FASTOPEN tells DOS to keep in memory a list of those files that have been opened during the current session. Thus DOS searches in memory for the file or subdirectory before accessing the disk. This command is available beginning with DOS Version 3.3.

FC This file comparison command compares the contents of two files. This command is not available in PC-DOS.

FDISK The Fixed Disk command allows you to perform hard disk tasks such as creating and deleting DOS partitions on a fixed disk. It is available in PC-DOS Version 2.0 and above and MS-DOS Version 3.2 and above. See Appendix D.

FIND This command searches text lines in a file for a specified string. /N displays each line and line number containing the string. /C displays the number of lines containing the string. /V displays the lines that do not contain the string. See Chapter 6.

Example: `FIND /N "PROFIT" B:SALES.RPT`

Displays the line and line number containing the word "PROFIT" in the SALES.RPT file in drive B.

FIND [/V][/C][/N] "string" [drive:][path]filename

FORMAT This command creates an electronic pattern on a disk surface so that data may be recorded on the disk. It erases any data currently on the disk. Some of the available switches are as follows. /1 formats only one side. /4 creates a 360K floppy disk in a high-density drive. /8 creates a disk with eight sectors per track. /V allows you to give the disk a volume name. /S creates a system disk. See Chapter 2.

Example: `FORMAT A: /V /S`

Formats a disk in drive A, allows you to give the disk a volume label, and installs the DOS system files.

FORMAT [drive:] [/1][/4][/8][/V][/S]

GRAFTABL This command is used to display special graphics characters.

GRAPHICS This command allows DOS to produce graphics on a printer. Use of this command requires a color graphics adapter and a compatible printer.

***HELP** This command is used to display a brief description of the command entered after HELP.

Example: `HELP ERASE`

JOIN This command joins two directories into one directory by connecting a drive to a directory on another drive. See Chapter 6.

Example: `JOIN A: \BIG`

DOS treats the disk in drive A as if it were a directory named \BIG on the current drive. Cancel with JOIN A: /D.

JOIN [drive:] [\directory][/D]

KEYB-- This command changes the keyboard to support a keyboard used in another country. The country supported depends on the last two letters of the command. For example, the command to match the keyboard used in France is KEYBFR.

LABEL This command lets you assign, change, or delete the volume label of a disk. It is available in PC-DOS Version 3.0 and above and MS-DOS Version 3.1 and above. See Chapter 2.

Example: `LABEL A:MARKTDEPT`

Assigns the name MARKTDEPT to the disk in drive A. The label can be no longer than 11 characters.

LABEL [drive:][label]

MKDIR The Make Directory command creates a subdirectory. MKDIR can be abbreviated MD. See Chapter 3.

Example: `MKDIR C:\DOCUMENT\COMPLNTS.TXT`

Creates the COMPLNTS.TXT subdirectory within the DOCUMENT directory on drive C.

MD [drive:]path

***MEM** This command displays the amount of available memory and what memory is being used.

***MIRROR** A program used to keep track of deleted files.

MODE This command has several different forms. It allows you to set up specific features on your hardware configuration.

MORE This is a DOS filter that displays a full screen of lines on the screen and then pauses and waits for a key press before displaying the next screen. See Chapter 6.

Example: `DIR C:\MEDICAL | MORE`

Lists the MEDICAL directory from drive C and makes the listing pause every 23 lines. Press any key to see the next 23 lines.

MORE

NLSFUNC This national language support function command is available in DOS Version 3.3 and above. It works in conjunction with the CHCP command. This command supports data offered for countries other than the United States.

PATH This command tells DOS to look for an executable file in the specified locations if it cannot be found in the current directory. See Chapter 3.

Example: `PATH C:\;C:\UTIL;C:\DR;B:`

Tells DOS to search the root directory, the UTIL and DR subdirectories, and drive B.

PATH [[drive:][path][;[drive:][path]]]

PRINT This command allows you to print a data file on the printer and use the computer to accomplish another task at the same time.

PROMPT This command changes the DOS prompt to a string of your choice. Certain character combinations create specific responses. For example: $t=time; $d=date; $p=current directory and drive; $n=current drive; $g=the > character; $q= the = character; $__=beginning of a new line on the display.

***QBASIC** This is a new version of BASIC, the fundamental programming language supplied with DOS disks.

RAMDRIVE.SYS This command creates a virtual disk drive or RAM disk. This command is available in MS-DOS beginning with Version 3.2. PC-DOS uses VDISK.SYS.

RECOVER This command rebuilds a file if the disk has bad sectors or a damaged directory.

RENAME This command allows you to change the name of a file. It can be abbreviated REN. You can use wild-card characters with this command. See Chapter 2.

Example: `REN C:\MFG\DNTIME.RPT DNTIME2.RPT`

Renames the DNTIME.RPT file in C: \MFG to DNTIME2.RPT.

RENAME [drive:]pathname filename

REPLACE This command adds or replaces files on a disk so that a target disk may be updated with the most recent file versions from the source disk. /A transfers files that do not exist on the target disk. /P prompts for confirmation. /R allows read-only files to be overwritten. /S searches subdirectories on the target disk for matching source file names. /W waits for a key press.

RESTORE This command restores those files that were backed up using the BACKUP command. Some of the available switches are as follows. /S restores all files in the subdirectories of the specified directory. /P prompts for confirmation before restoring hidden or read-only files or files that were updated since the last backup. See Chapter 4.

Example: `RESTORE A: C:\DISTRIB\*.*`

Restores all files on drive A that were backed up from the \DISTRIB directory on drive C.

RESTORE drive1: [drive2:][pathname] [/S][/P]

RMDIR The Remove Directory command removes a subdirectory. All files must be erased from the subdirectory before it can be removed. RMDIR can be abbreviated RD. See Chapter 3.

Example: `RD C:\MFG`

Removes the MFG subdirectory from drive C.

RMDIR [drive:]path

SELECT This command places information about a country and language on a diskette.

SET This command sets a string to use in the DOS environment.

***SETVER** This command can change the DOS version that is reported to an operating program.

SHARE This command is used in file sharing.

SORT This is a filter command. It sorts lines according to alphabetical order or according to the specified column. /R sorts the lines in reverse order. /+N sorts the lines according to the column beginning at location N. See Chapters 4 and 6.

Example: `SORT < CONTACTS.DOC /+14`

Sorts the lines in CONTACTS.DOC according to the information beginning in column 14. (The file size begins in column 14.)

SORT [drive:][pathname] [/R][/+N]

SUBST This command substitutes a directory for a drive letter and accesses this directory with only the drive letter. /D cancels any previous substitution. This command is available in DOS Version 3.1 and above. See Chapter 6.

Example: `SUBST E: C:\PROD\RESRCH`

Substitutes the pathname C:\PROD\RESRCH for drive letter E. Access this pathname by key-entering drive E. For example, DIR E:*.* produces a directory listing of C:\PROD\RESRCH*.*.

SUBST [drive 1: drive2:path] [/D]

SYS The System command transfers the two hidden DOS system files from the current drive to a formatted disk in the target disk drive. See Chapter 2. COMMAND.COM must also be copied.

Example: `SYS B:`

Transfers the system files from the current drive to the disk in drive B.

SYS drive:

TIME This command allows you to set the system clock. See Chapter 1.

Example: `TIME 18:20:35`

Sets the system clock to 6:20:35 P.M. Uses the 24-hour clock.

TIME [hh:mm[:ss[.xx]]]

TREE This command displays the tree structure of a hierarchical directory. /F displays all of the files in each directory. See Chapter 4.

Example: `TREE C: /F`

Displays the names of all directories and subdirectories and their files on drive C.

TREE [drive:] [/F]

TYPE This command displays the text of an ASCII or text file. See Chapter 2.

Example: `TYPE B:\DEBT\SUMMARY.TXT`

Displays the contents of SUMMARY.TXT in the B:\DEBT directory.

TYPE [drive:]pathname

***UNDELETE** This command allows you to recover an accidentally erased file.

***UNFORMAT** This command allows you to recover the contents of an accidentally formatted disk.

VER This command displays the DOS version being used.

VERIFY This command allows you to control a switch that turns disk-write verification on or off. Verification checks for bad sectors on the target disk.

VOL This command shows the volume name of the specified disk.

XCOPY [/A/D/E/M/P/S/V/W] This command is an extended copy command. It provides very flexible copying of files, directories, and subdirectories. It is available in DOS Version 3.2 and above. /A copies files whose archive bits are on; /D copies files changed or created after a certain date; /M copies only modified files; /S copies files from a directory and all of its subdirectories.

BATCH SUBCOMMANDS

Batch subcommands are one-word instructions that provide additional control for batch files. They are discussed in Chapter 5.

CALL This subcommand allows a batch file to call another batch file. It is available in DOS Version 3.3.

ECHO This subcommand controls whether or not batch file commands are displayed as they are executed. It lets you display messages.

Example: `ECHO Stop here`

Will display the message "Stop here" on the screen.

ECHO [ON][OFF][message]

FOR This subcommand permits a DOS command to be carried out on one or more files from within a batch file.

Example: `FOR %%a IN (*.txt) DO type %%a`

Types each file in *.txt on the screen.

FOR %%var IN (set) DO command

GOTO This subcommand sends execution flow in a batch file to a label.

Example: `GOTO end`

Causes the batch file to move to the line beginning with :end (the colon is necessary to define the label).

GOTO label

IF This subcommand provides a way to make comparisons within a batch file.

Example: `IF EXIST A:GOOD.TXT GOTO CONTINUE`

If GOOD.TXT exists on the disk in drive A then go to the label CONTINUE.

IF [not] condition command

PAUSE This subcommand causes execution of a batch file to pause and await a key press.

Example: `PAUSE`

Makes the batch file pause.

PAUSE

REM This subcommand allows a remark to be placed within a batch file. The remark is displayed if ECHO is on; it is not displayed if ECHO is off.

Example: `REM This file checks for report files.`

Will display this message when the batch file is executed, if ECHO is on.

REM [message]

SHIFT This subcommand shifts the parameters one position to the left and discards the %0 parameter, thus allowing more than ten parameters to be used in the command line.

Example: `SHIFT`

Causes all replaceable parameters, if there are any, to be shifted to the next lower number.

SHIFT

CONFIGURATION COMMANDS

Configuration commands are placed in the CONFIG.SYS file rather than entered at the DOS prompt. Configuration commands are discussed in Chapter 6.

BREAK This command tells DOS how often to check for a BREAK (CTRL-C) key press.

BUFFERS This command defines the number of buffers DOS should set aside in memory for storing data while reading from or writing to disks.

Example: `BUFFERS=15`

Sets aside 15 buffers in memory for disk read/write operations.

BUFFERS=number

COUNTRY This command defines conventions for a given country.

DEVICE This command specifies a driver program that tells DOS how to use a particular peripheral. Driver programs have a SYS extension.

***DEVICEHIGH** This command loads device drivers into the upper memory above the basic 640K reserved for operating programs.

***DOS** This command tells the command processor to load the DOS program into upper memory or to maintain a link to upper memory.

DRIVPARM This command involves the system's characteristics table.

FCBS This command involves the maximum number of files that can be open at a single time using file control blocks.

FILES This command establishes the maximum number of files that can be open at one time.

LASTDRIVE This command defines the last valid drive letter. It is available only in DOS Version 3 or above.

SHELL This command defines the name and location of the file containing the command processor (default is COMMAND.COM).

STACKS This command tells DOS how much memory to set aside for its use. Some application programs require this command.

*SWITCHES This command forces an enhanced keyboard to perform like a conventional keyboard.

Appendix B

DOS Editing Keys and Special Keys

Overview

The DOS editing keys provide a way to repeat and modify DOS commands. These keys are also used for editing of lines with the EDLIN line editor (see Appendix C). They are useful for modifying repetitive DOS commands. They are not very useful if you need to key-enter a command only one time.

The DOS Version 5.0 EDIT command provides a full screen editor that works much like standard word processors. Because of the general nature of its operation, it will not be covered here.

Each editing key has a name to help you remember its function. The following sections give the key names, discuss the keys themselves, and provide simple examples of how they work. Keystrokes that you make are shown in angled brackets (<>). DOS screen responses are shown in uppercase letters. You may follow these examples on your computer. If you do, please practice them within the EDLIN program. If you enter a DOS command directly on the command line, DOS will try to execute the command, and it may not be able to do this. To avoid error messages, practice the commands and editing keys within EDLIN.

To begin, start EDLIN by key-entering the command EDLIN EDIT.PRA. Key-enter the path to EDLIN.COM if it is not in your current directory. You will see "New file" on the screen. Press I to enter the EDLIN Insert mode. "I:*" will be displayed on your screen. EDLIN is waiting for your entry. (See Appendix C for more on starting and stopping EDLIN.)

If you have to copy several similarly named files, the DOS editing keys can save time. Assume that you must copy the following files from drive A to drive B: P&LREGN1.DAT, P&LREGN2.DAT, P&LREGN3.-DAT, P&LREGN1.DOC, P&LREGN2.DOC, and P&LREGN3.DOC. One approach is to key-enter COPY P&LREGN1.DAT B: for the first file, COPY P&LREGN2.DAT B: for the second, and so on, retyping the entire command each time.

The DOS editing keys let you repeat the entire command or parts of it without rekeying. For example, after you key-enter the command the first time, you can repeat parts of it using the editing keys. The following display shows how to do the above task using the DOS editing keys. The keystrokes that you should make are shown in angled brackets. Do not enter a space before or after you press the function key unless indicated in the text.

<COPY P&LREGN1.DAT B:> ←*Key this.*

<ENTER> ←*Press the ENTER key. (Do not key the word ENTER.)*

<F2><1> ←*Press the F2 key followed by 1, without a space.*

COPY P&LREGN ←*DOS enters this much.*

<2> ←*Key the number 2.*

<F3> ←*Press the F3 key.*

COPY P&LREGN2.DAT B: ←*DOS completes the command. Press ENTER. You have pressed five keys (including ENTER) to execute the command.*

There are ten DOS editing keys, which you may use on the command line or in EDLIN, the DOS line editor. Other programs also allow you to use the DOS editing keys. Refer to their instructions to see if this is possible.

COPY-ALL KEY (F3)

F3 will repeat the entire entry. F3 is Function Key 3 on the left side of the keyboard (it may be positioned along the top of your keyboard). F3 will enter every character in the last legal DOS entry you made. To continue the previous example, key-enter the following.

<COPY P&LREGN1.DAT B:> ←*Key this.*

<ENTER> ←*Press the ENTER key.*

<F3> ←*Press the F3 key.*

COPY P&LREGN1.DAT B: ←*DOS immediately inserts the previous entry.*

<ENTER> ←*Press ENTER to move to the next line in EDLIN. The command would be executed if entered on a command line.*

CANCEL KEY (ESC)

ESC will cancel previously typed keystrokes if pressed before ENTER. It cancels the entry, moves the cursor to the next line, and awaits a new entry. It leaves a reverse slash at the end of the line to indicate that the entry has been canceled. This is illustrated below.

<F3> ←*Repeats the last command. Do not press ENTER.*

COPY P&LREGN1.DAT B: ←*DOS re-enters the command.*

<ESC> ←*Cancels the entry and leaves a \ at the end of the line. The cursor moves down one line and awaits a new entry.*

<F3> ←*Repeats the last command again.*

<ENTER> ←*Press ENTER.*

BACKSPACE (BS) OR LEFT ARROW (LA) KEY

BACKSPACE (BS) erases characters to the left of the cursor one at a time. LEFT ARROW (LA) does the same thing. Pressing BS or LA erases characters from the screen, but it does not erase them from memory. DOS saves your entry, and you may copy the rest of the line (the characters that you erased with LA or BS) using F3. Try the following exercise to see how this works.

<COPY1234> ←*Key this.*

<ENTER>

<F3> ← *Press F3 to copy all.*

COPY1234 ←*DOS copies the last entry.*

<LA><LA><LA><LA> ←*Press LEFT ARROW four times.*

COPY ←*This remains on screen.*

<F3> ← *Press F3.*

COPY1234 ←*DOS copies 1234.*

<LA><LA><LA><LA><LA><LA><LA><LA> ←*Press LEFT ARROW eight times.*

← *Nothing remains on screen.*

<F3> ← *Press F3.*

COPY1234 ←*DOS copies the entire entry. (Do not press ENTER.)*

DOS keeps an image of the entry in memory. This image is called a template. Pressing F3 displays the entire template. Pressing LEFT ARROW once removes one character from the screen but does not change the template. DOS moves an invisible "pointer" back and forth. When you pressed LEFT ARROW four times, four characters were removed from the screen, and the pointer was moved four places to the left. Pressing F3 did not display the entire entry from the beginning but only from the pointer's position. This concept of an invisible pointer may help you understand the remaining DOS editing keys.

SKIP-ONE KEY (DEL)

DEL (Del) will skip a character in the template. When you press DEL, DOS does not erase the character, but it does remove it from the screen and from the template. DEL will skip one character each time it is pressed. When you press DEL, however, the cursor will not move.

INSERT KEY (INS)

INS (Ins) permits you to add one or more characters to the template. It opens a space for the added characters and pushes the remaining template characters to the right as each new character is inserted. Press the INS key once to turn on the Insert mode. The following example allows you to practice using both DEL (Skip-One) and INS (Insert). This is a continuation of the previous example.

COPY1234 ←*DOS has copied this template.*
The cursor is just after the 4.

<LA><LA><LA><LA> ←*Press LEFT ARROW four times.*

COPY ←*Remains on the screen.*

<DEL> ←*Press DEL to skip one.*

<F3> ←*Press F3 to display all.*

COPY234 ←*The 1 was skipped.*

<ENTER>

<F3> ←*Display all.*

COPY234 ←*This is the new template.*

<LA><LA><LA> ←*Press LEFT ARROW three times.*

COPY ←*Remains on the screen.*

<INS><1> ←*Press INS key. Press 1 (no space before 1).*

<F3> ←*Copy the remaining template.*

```
COPY1234     ←This is displayed. 1 was inserted; 234 was "pushed" to
               the right to make room for the 1.

<ENTER>     ←Creates new template.

<F3>     ←Copy the new template.

COPY1234     ←This is displayed.

<LA><LA><LA><LA><LA><LA>     ←Press LEFT ARROW six times.

CO     ←Remains on screen.

<RA><RA><RA><RA><RA><RA>     ←Press RIGHT ARROW six times.

COPY1234     ←This is displayed. RIGHT ARROW copies template one
               character at a time.
<ENTER>     ←Press ENTER.
```

COPY-ONE KEY (RIGHT ARROW OR RA)

The previous example introduced you to the RIGHT ARROW key. When you press RIGHT ARROW one time, one character is copied from the template.

COPY-UP-TO KEY (F2)

F2, the Copy-up-to key, makes it easy to copy characters in the template up to but not including the typed character. F2 should always be followed by a character in the template. Nothing happens when you press F2. Pressing the next key immediately copies the template up to that character. Nothing will appear on the screen if the character of the key you press is not in the template. However, if you then press ENTER, the template will be erased.

SKIP-UP-TO KEY (F4)

F4, the Skip-up-to key, is the complement of the Copy-up-to key. Pressing F4 followed by a character will move the invisible pointer to that character in the template. Nothing will be displayed on the screen. The next key that you press determines what will be displayed. The following example demonstrates the F2 and F4 keys.

COPY1234 ←*This is the current template. It should be displayed on the line above the immediate line.*

<F2><1> ←*Press F2 and then 1 to copy up to the 1.*

COPY ←*This is displayed.*

<F3> ←*Copy the rest of the template.*

COPY1234 ←*This is displayed.*

<ENTER> ←*Press ENTER.*

<F4><1> ←*Skip up to the 1.*

←*Nothing is displayed. The pointer is on the 1.*

<F3> ←*Display the rest of the template.*

1234 ←*This is displayed. If you press ENTER, 1234 will become the new template. Do not press ENTER.*

<LA><LA><LA><LA> ←*Press LEFT ARROW four times.*

←*Nothing is displayed. The pointer is on the 1.*

<LA><LA><LA><LA> ←*Press LEFT ARROW four more times. This pushes the pointer back to the beginning of the template.*

<F3> ←*Copy the current template from the pointer.*

COPY1234 ←*The entire template is displayed.*

<ENTER> ←*Press ENTER.*

To complete this tutorial, you will practice the original problem posed at the beginning of this appendix. You will simulate, within EDLIN, copying of several files using the DOS editing keys. The following keystrokes will take you through the various steps.

`COPY P&LREGN1.DAT B:` ←*Key this entry.*

`<ENTER>` ←*Press ENTER. This simulates the first DOS command to copy from drive A to drive B.*

`<F2><1>` ←*Copy-up-to 1.*

`COPY P&LREGN` ←*DOS displays this much.*

`<2><F3>` ←*Key 2. Press F3 to display the remainder of the template.*

`COPY P&LREGN2.DAT B:` ←*This is the complete command display.*

`<ENTER>` ←*Press ENTER to simulate execution. This becomes the new template.*

(We will now change to a DOC file .)

`<F2><2>` ←*Copy-up-to 2.*

`COPY P&LREGN` ←*DOS displays this much.*

`<1.DOC>` ←*Key this to replace the 2.DAT in the template.*

`<F3>` ← *This displays the rest of the remainder of the template.*

`COPY P&LREGN1.DOC B:` ←*This is the complete command display.*

`<ENTER>` ←*Press ENTER to simulate execution. This becomes the new template.*

(We will now add a 2x.TXT file.)

<F2><1> ←*Copy-up-to 1.*

COPY P&LREGN ←*DOS displays this much.*

<2><INS> ←*Replace the 2 and begin Insert mode. Characters to the right will be pushed to the right.*

<x> ←*Key the x after the 2.*

<RA> ←*Copy the period. Insert mode is canceled.*

<INS><TXT> ←*Start Insert mode and key TXT. Remaining part of template is pushed to the right.*

<DEL><DEL><DEL> ←*Press DEL three times to delete DOC.*

<F3> ←*Copies the rest of the template.*

COPY P&LREGN2x.TXT B: ←*Full template, on the command line, is shown. Pressing ENTER simulates command execution.*

NEW-TEMPLATE KEY (F5)

The F5 key allows you to establish a template without actually carrying out the command you enter. This can be done from the DOS command line. It allows you to set up a template to be used or changed without causing DOS to carry out the entry. Using this key causes the current line to replace the line entered previously.

◆ *Summary*

Figure B-1 is a summary of the DOS editing keys. These keys may be used on the DOS command line. They may also be used within the EDLIN line editor, which is explained in Appendix C.

Figure B-1. Summary of DOS editing keys.

DOS Editing Key	Key	Purpose
CANCEL	ESC	Throws away the line.
BACKSPACE	BACKSPACE	Erases the character to the left.
	LEFT ARROW	Same as BACKSPACE.
COPY-ONE	RIGHT ARROW	Copies one character from the template.
COPY-ALL	F3	Copies the entire template.
COPY-UP-TO	F2	Copies the template up to the entered character.
SKIP-ONE	DEL	Skips over one template character.
SKIP-UP-TO	F4	Skips to the entered character.
INSERT	INS	Enters new characters, pushes existing template characters to right.
NEW-TEMPLATE	F5	Creates new template without executing command.

Appendix C

The EDLIN Line Editor

◆ *Overview*

EDLIN.COM is a line editor on your DOS master disk. It allows you to create and edit text files. You can use it to create or modify CONFIG.SYS, AUTOEXEC.BAT, and other files. This appendix will tell you how to operate EDLIN.

EDLIN is not a screen editor. A screen editor allows you to move the cursor to any part of the screen and modify or add to the text at the cursor position. EDLIN is a line editor. A line editor will only allow you to work with a line as a unit. You can display the line while you edit it, but you cannot move the cursor to any location on the screen. Text editing on each line is not very convenient. Instead of retyping the entire line, you can use the DOS editing keys to make changes.

As a line editor, EDLIN will not display your entire file at one time. It does not permit scrolling among lines. The editor will automatically list 11 lines before your current line and 11 lines after it. To see long files, you must change the current line frequently before listing.

EDLIN can edit long files. However, it will load only enough lines to fill 75 percent of available memory. The remaining 25 percent will be reserved for additions. In this book, you will use EDLIN with short files, so memory constraints will not be a problem.

The following sections introduce the most frequently used EDLIN commands. These will be the ones you will need to handle DOS file creation and modification. You should turn on your computer and follow the examples in order to gain additional familiarity with the EDLIN commands and file-handling techniques.

STARTING AND STOPPING EDLIN

To create a file or edit an existing one, enter the EDLIN command followed by the file name. Include the extension in the name. For example, the command syntax is EDLIN <filename>. If the file exists, EDLIN will load it and display the message "End of input file." The file has been loaded into memory, but EDLIN does not automatically display the file. You must enter the List command to see any of the file contents.

If the file you name does not exist, EDLIN displays "New file" to tell you that a new file has been created. If you know that the file you wish to edit exists, then the "New file" message will let you know that you have entered an incorrect file name. If this occurs, you must leave EDLIN and re-enter the command with the correct file name.

For example, to stop editing and leave EDLIN, enter Q. Respond with Y and EDLIN will stop without saving your file. Enter E and EDLIN will first save your file on the disk and then exit. Use Q to stop without saving. Use E to save your work before exiting.

KEY-ENTERING COMMANDS

After EDLIN has loaded an existing file or is prepared to create a new file, it will display an asterisk as its prompt. When you see the asterisk, you know that EDLIN is awaiting a command. One of the first commands to enter is the List command, which will display the first lines of the file.

EDLIN commands are entered as single letters. Sometimes a number precedes the letter to tell EDLIN the line number with which to work. Key-enter L in uppercase or lowercase to list lines from your file. List (L) will display up to 23 lines of your file. If the file is longer than 23 lines, you will see the first 23 lines if you have just loaded the file. If you are working on line 15, for example, the List command (L) will show the 11 lines in front of line 15 and the 11 lines following it. You will see lines 4 through 26. List always shows you a "window" of lines around the current line.

The current line is preceded by an asterisk. The asterisk shows you which line EDLIN considers current. This asterisk moves as you work through the file.

EDITING A FILE

When you start a new file, you must tell EDLIN to begin inserting lines. Pressing I begins the Insert mode with line 1. Each time you press ENTER to complete a line, EDLIN stays in the Insert mode and moves to the next line. Press CTRL-C to leave the Insert mode. The asterisk prompt will reappear at the left edge of the screen.

Turn on your computer. At the prompt, enter EDLIN PRACTICE.BAT. EDLIN must be in the current directory, or you must first enter its path. Follow the example below.

```
C>EDLIN PRACTICE.BAT

New file
*I                                ←Key-enter I for Insert command.
        1:*This is line 1.        ←Key-enter.
        2:*This is line 2.        ←Key-enter.
        3:*This is line 3.        ←Key-enter.
        4:*^C                     ←Press CTRL-C to stop Insert.

*L                                ←Key-enter L for List command.
        1: This is line 1.
        2: This is line 2.
        3: This is line 3.
*4I                               ←Key-enter 4I to Insert at line 4.
        4:*Add line 4 here.       ←Key-enter.
        5:*^C                     ←Press CTRL-C.

*L
        1: This is line 1.
        2: This is line 2.
        3: This is line 3.
        4: Add line 4 here.
*                                 ←Awaiting next command.
```

To begin inserting at the end of the file, either enter the last line number and I or enter #I. The pound symbol tells EDLIN to start after the last line number. EDLIN will show you the next line number and wait for input. Press ENTER and you will still be in the Insert mode. Press CTRL-C (BREAK or ^C) to leave the Insert mode.

To practice, insert a new line after line 4, as shown below. Key-enter #I, and key-enter "Add another line in 5." (without quotation marks).

```
*L
        1: This is line 1.
        2: This is line 2.
        3: This is line 3.
        4: Add line 4 here.
*#I

        5:*Add another line in 5.
        6:*^C
*
```

To insert one or more lines in the middle of existing lines, pick the line before which you want the new text to appear. Then enter this line number followed by I. Existing line numbers will increase to allow for the new inserted line(s).

To practice, list your file, then insert the following line in front of line 4: "This is line 3b." Your screen will look like this.

```
*L
        1: This is line 1.
        2: This is line 2.
        3: This is line 3.
        4: Add line 4 here.
        5: Add another line in 5.

*4I
        4:*This is line 3b.    ← Adds line after line 3.
        5:*^C

*L

        1: This is line 1.
        2: This is line 2.
        3: This is line 3.
        4: This is line 3b.
        5: Add line 4 here.          ←Renumbered by EDLIN
        6: Add another line in 5.    ←Renumbered by EDLIN
```

To edit a line, key-enter the line number. EDLIN will display the line number and its contents. Below this, it will redisplay the line number and wait for you to change the line. The following display shows line 5 being edited. Use all of the DOS Function Key editing features as described in Appendix B. For example, press INS, key "(Old line 4)," press INS again, and then press F3 (Copy-All key). The following lines will result.

```
*L
        1: This is line 1.
        2: This is line 2.
        3: This is line 3.
        4: This is line 3b.
        5: Add line 4 here.
        6: Add another line in 5.

*5

        5: Add line 4 here.                ←Existing line 5.
        5: (Old line 4)Add line 4 here.    ←Edited line 5.

*
```

Refer again to Appendix B to review the DOS editing keys. Use these to modify lines in EDLIN. With these, you will be able to modify any parts of your batch or CONFIG files.

LEAVING EDLIN

As described in the section on starting and stopping EDLIN, press Q to quit without saving your work. EDLIN will request verification. Press E to end by first saving the file and then exiting the line editor.

EDLIN COMMANDS

Figure C-1 lists the EDLIN commands. If you are using a DOS version earlier than 2.0, the EDLIN.COM program will not have all of these commands. Some of the commands are designed to make EDLIN more versatile. For example, you are able to search for specified text and replace

Figure C-1.
EDLIN commands.

Key	Explanation
A	Append—Add more lines from disk to those in memory.
^C	Break—Stop inserting.
C	Copy—Copy a range of lines.
D	Delete—Delete lines.
#	Edit—Edit line # or current line if ENTER is pressed.
E	End—Write file and end.
I	Insert—Before the current line.
L	List—List lines before and after the current line.
M	Move—Move one or more lines.
P	Page—Display an entire screen of lines.
Q	Quit—Quit without writing file.
R	Replace—Search and replace text.
S	Search—Search for text.
T	Transfer—Bring another file into the current file.
W	Write—Write lines in memory to disk.

it automatically if you wish. You may also copy or move lines. Still other commands make it convenient to add lines from another file to the file you have in memory. You may feel free to practice these commands; however, you will not need this greater capability to complete the simple files in this text. Consult your DOS reference manual for instructions on how to use these commands.

Appendix D

Computer System Fundamentals

◆ *Overview*

This appendix is designed to provide a basic introduction to computer system fundamentals. Beginning computer users will find basic discussions of computer system hardware and the essential concepts needed to start and stop the system. Experienced users who would like a short review should also read this appendix.

HARDWARE COMPONENTS

You have already learned about some of the components of the computer system. If you are a beginning user, you will find additional facts about the computer system and its components in the following paragraphs. This abbreviated information is designed to raise your awareness. It will not explore details or make you an expert.

The Computer

The basic computer consists of the cabinet and the various electronic circuits. Differences in types of computers today involve speed and memory size. The engineers have designed faster, smaller, and generally more complicated circuits in order to improve computers. At the same time, engineers have also been able to reduce the number of circuit chips, and so computers have become smaller and less costly.

In the early 1980s, IBM introduced the PC or Personal Computer. This was followed by the Personal Computer XT, which added a hard disk. Next came the IBM Personal Computer AT, which was faster, and the IBM PC AT with the 80386 microprocessor, which was faster still and offered greater memory capacity. IBM then introduced the Personal System/2. The Personal System/2 offers new technology that includes more memory and can run more than one program at a time. Current technology is using the 80386 and the newer and faster 80486 microprocessor.

In simple terms, computers are usually characterized by the types of central processing units they contain. The CPU is the chip that accomplishes the fundamental calculations and data manipulations that allow the computer to work.

CPUs are commonly named by their part numbers. The earliest IBM PC contained the 8086 CPU. Later came the 8088, a faster model. The Personal Computer XT contained a hard disk, but it used the same CPU as the PC. The Personal Computer AT has the newer 80286 chip, whereas today's fastest systems have the 80386 and 80486. In general, each CPU advance has meant faster computer operation and greater memory capacity. Both of these capabilities have made possible bigger, faster, and more versatile computer programs.

Disk Drives

Disk drives store and read data to and from magnetic media. The term "magnetic media" refers to smooth surfaces that can hold magnetic signals the way recording tape does. Some floppy disk drives work with 5¼″ floppy disks, which are round, thin platters. These floppy disks are made from magnetically coated plastic. They are flexible, portable, and convenient to carry.

Smaller diskettes that are 3½″ in diameter hold about twice as much data as do the 5¼″ floppy disks. These disks have a more rigid outer case to protect the magnetic media, which contributes to their greater durability and storage capacity.

Hard disk drives serve the same purpose as floppy disk drives, but hard disks hold more data, operate faster, and are usually not portable. They are named for the hard surface on which data is recorded. They spin faster because of their greater rigidity, and they can read and record data more quickly than diskettes can. Hard disk drives are scaled units and contain mechanisms called read/write heads that find or record data in the correct spot more rapidly than the heads in floppy drives.

FLOPPY DISK DRIVES A floppy disk drive is one that will accept a floppy disk. These drives are located on the front of the computer. They may be side-by-side or stacked. If two floppy drives are side-by-side, the drive on the left is known as drive A and the drive on the right is known as drive B.

The IBM Personal Computer XT contains one floppy drive and one hard drive. Some may contain two floppy drives stacked on top of each other next to the hard drive. The hard drive is covered with a plain plate containing a small light that comes on when the drive is running.

The IBM AT-style computer contains one or sometimes two floppy drives and a hard disk drive. The A drive is usually a special floppy drive called a high-density floppy drive. See the section below on high-density floppy drives and disks.

Some new, powerful 80386 and 80486 computers come in "tower units." These are cabinets which can sit on the floor and are tall and thin rather than flat. The keyboard and monitor sit separately on the desk and are connected to the tower by cables.

HIGH-DENSITY FLOPPY DRIVES The AT-style computer has a high-density floppy disk drive as drive A. Such a drive permits about three-and-a-half times more data to be stored on a floppy disk than does a regular drive (1200K versus 360K). Special high-density floppy disks must be used or the additional data cannot be recorded reliably.

The high-density floppy drive will act like a standard drive and read 360K floppy disks. A high-density drive can start up the computer from a standard start-up disk. Additionally, high-density disks will work automatically in the drive. Care must be taken in creating high-density disks and standard disks in the high-density drive. Additional information on this step is provided later.

THE HARD DRIVE A hard drive, as previously described, is a hardware device with room to store many more programs and data than can be stored on a floppy disk. It is located inside the computer cabinet. The hard drive is also known as the C drive. Unlike floppy disks, the hard drive is not removable by the user.

A hard disk can hold 20M, 60M, 100M, or more. The letter M stands for megabyte, or a million bytes. A hard disk can be partitioned or divided into two or more drives. This means that a part of the platter can be reserved as drive C, while another portion of the surface can be drive D.

DOS 3.3 and earlier versions are limited to no more than 32M within a single hard disk partition. Because hard drives are being made today with 40M, 80M, and higher, the partitioning technique is necessary to turn a large physical disk into two or more "virtual" or electronically separate drives. However, DOS Version 4.0 introduced a SHARE program to make it easier to use large disks. DOS Version 5.0 has eliminated this program and can use hard disks without partitioning. Partitioning will be covered in more detail in the section on preparing a hard disk.

Monitor

The monitor displays the information entered into the computer or generated by it. Connecting the computer to the monitor is the graphics display card. Monitors and display cards must be matched in order to properly display the computer's output.

Early computers came with monochrome, or single-color, monitors. The Color Graphics Adapter (CGA) standard came later. This display mode provided up to a four-color display. The next advances were the Enhanced Graphics Adapter (EGA) and the Video Graphics Array (VGA). Some color graphics monitors can provide 256 color choices.

The other important display advance has been resolution, or the amount of detail that can be exhibited. With each increase in technology, more scan lines were available. More scan lines permit higher resolution and greater screen clarity. The practical effect of this increase in resolution has been to allow greater amounts of detail to be displayed. This, in turn, has opened new computer applications, such as electronic publishing, drafting, and detailed art and drawing work. In addition, improved display resolution makes computer work more enjoyable and less tiring to the eyes.

Printer

Today, several types of printers are used with personal computers. The dot-matrix printer creates words and pictures by moving a head across a sheet of paper while tiny pins are rapidly extended and retracted in synchronization to create marks on the paper. New technology and engineering have allowed the dot-matrix printer to create more legible output and do it faster.

The daisy-wheel, or fixed character, printer makes a character by striking a formed-character device against the paper. The entire character is imprinted, much as letters are struck on a typewriter. This technology continues to produce very legible printed material, but its low speed and lack of flexibility for graphics printing are making it a declining choice as a printing device.

Laser printers and ink-jet printers are quickly growing in popularity. Laser printers form characters in a complex process similar to that of the copying machines used in offices today. The laser printer can clearly and quickly form characters of many types and shapes. Ink-jet printers form characters from tiny droplets of ink.

Printers use either parallel or serial data connections. Parallel printers receive data from the computer in groups of signals that travel side-by-side along parallel wires contained in a single, flat cable. Serial printers receive data one signal at a time through a single wire. Parallel printers are generally more popular, and in some cases faster, than serial printers. However, the printing mechanism is the slowest part of the machine, and differences in data transmission rate are usually not noticeable.

Keyboard

The keyboard allows you to issue commands to the computer. From a basic layout resembling a typewriter, keyboards have grown in size and complexity. Extra keys permit different computer commands to be entered with a single stroke. Other common keyboard features include function keys, which initiate special commands; keyboard lights, which indicate keyboard status; and numeric keypads, which facilitate entry of numeric data.

Before starting the computer, you must be familiar with the keyboard and some common keys. Some keys are used to enter computer control commands or application data. Figure D-1 shows some of the most important keys you will use when working with DOS. The explanations describe the operation of these keys. Your keyboard may use different names or spellings for some of these keys.

Figure D-1. Common keys and their functions.

Common Keys	Functions
ENTER	This key is located on the right side of the keyboard. It may contain a bent arrow pointing left, instead of the word "Enter," on the key face. It is used to end a command and to instruct the computer to execute the command.
CTRL	The CONTROL key may be labeled Ctrl. It is on the left side of the keyboard. It is always pressed along with another key to alter the meaning of that key. For example, CTRL-C means to press the CTRL and C keys simultaneously.
ESC	The ESCAPE key may be labeled Esc. Its location will vary depending on the computer you are using. It generates a special code that many programs use to "back out of" or "escape from" some operations. It can, however, be programmed for other purposes.
ALT	The ALTERNATE key (Alt) is similar to the CTRL key; it must be pressed together with another key to generate a signal to be used in a program.

Figure D-1. Continued.

BREAK	"Break" is often printed on the front of the SCROLL LOCK key. A "Break" signal is generated when CTRL-BREAK is pressed. Such a signal will override other computer activity and has the effect of stopping or breaking the activity in progress.
BACKSPACE	The BACKSPACE key has a left arrow on it. When pressed, it will move the cursor one space to the left, erasing any character that is there.
SCROLL LOCK	This key is used in various application programs to cause the display to become attached to the cursor; movement of the cursor results in movement of the entire screen.
CURSOR CONTROL KEYS	The keys with up, down, right, and left arrows control the movement of the cursor. Some applications will move the display up or down a full screen when the PGUP (PAGE UP) or PGDN (PAGE DOWN) key is pressed. Home moves the cursor to the beginning of a document or file; End moves it to the end of the file.
NUM LOCK	When on, NUM LOCK cancels the cursor control keys and enters the number of each key pressed on the numeric keypad. With NUM LOCK off, pressing the SHIFT key at the same time as one of the numeric keypad keys produces the same effect as turning NUM LOCK on.
CAPS LOCK	When pressed, CAPS LOCK causes all letters to be entered in uppercase. It does not affect other keys.

STARTING AND STOPPING THE COMPUTER

Two of the most frequent operations you will perform are starting and stopping the computer. These operations require specific procedures. Improper starting procedure may result in a computer stoppage, requiring you to perform the correct procedure. In some cases, stopping the computer the wrong way can cause loss of data.

Starting the Computer

When you apply power to your computer, it goes through a memory check procedure and then turns on drive A. It looks there for the start-up program that is on every start-up floppy disk. If drive A is empty, the computer will try drive C, if there is one. If all drives are empty and there is no hard disk, the computer proceeds by automatically starting BASIC, a programming language built into the machine.

If drive A contains a disk that does not contain the DOS start-up program, the computer will stop and display a message that the disk is not a start-up disk. You should insert a start-up disk to start the computer. The computer then waits until the correction is made and a key is pressed, signaling that it is all right to proceed.

If you wish to start up the computer from drive A, insert a disk containing the DOS start-up program into drive A. Turn on the power switch on the side of the cabinet. Nothing will appear to be happening for about 15 to 30 seconds, but the computer will be automatically performing an internal memory check. If the computer finds a problem, it may display a message about the location of one or more bad memory chips. Write this information down, and try to continue. It may be possible to use the computer even when it has a bad chip. However, this is risky because you could lose data. Instead, take your computer to a repair person.

When the memory check has been successfully completed, the computer will beep and the light on drive A will come on. During this time, DOS will be loaded from the disk into the computer's memory. If the disk does not contain DOS, the computer will stop and a message will say that a start-up disk is needed.

If your computer has a hard disk, loading DOS is accomplished by turning on the power with drive A empty. DOS will be loaded from drive C once the computer determines that no floppy disks exist in the other drives.

The computer will display the current date and time and ask you to update them. Some computers have internal clocks that allow them to automatically read the date and time. If your computer does not have an internal clock, you must enter this information each time you start it.

Once the time and date have been set, the computer will automatically date and time stamp each file you save to disk, a useful feature for sorting through many data files. However, you may bypass setting the date and time by pressing ENTER. Thereafter, the computer will use a meaningless date and time, which will not be helpful if you want to see when you saved your files.

After these procedures are complete, the computer is ready to do your work. The system prompt, which is usually the drive letter followed by the greater-than (>) symbol, will be displayed followed by the blinking cursor. DOS, the disk operating system, is awaiting your command.

Stopping the Computer

There are several ways to stop the computer and its operations. One way is simply to turn off the power. You should end any application program in which you have been working. Turning off the power from within an application program may damage files or leave temporary files on your disk, and this may inhibit your next use of the files.

You should always make backups of your work files before turning off the computer. Make backups frequently, such as once every other day or once per week. Backups are valuable when something happens to erase or damage your files. You will lose all of the time you spent in creating the files if you do not have backups.

You can reset and restart the computer without turning off the power by performing a "warm boot." A warm boot is accomplished by pressing CTRL-ALT-DEL simultaneously. This will abort any application with which you may be working. Any data you have created but not saved to disk will be lost. You will have to do this if the computer "locks up" and will not respond to any keyboard commands, or if you just want to restart the computer. This is known as a warm boot because you clear the computer's memory and make it reload DOS, but you do not turn off the power switch. When you press CTRL, ALT, and DEL simultaneously, the computer resets. The screen will blank, the computer will beep, the drive will come on, and DOS will be loaded.

Another way to stop an operation is to enter CTRL-C or BREAK. This allows you to cancel a command you have keyed if you have not pressed ENTER. It also allows you to stop an operation in midstream. Pressing CTRL and SCROLL LOCK together generates a break signal. Both CTRL-C and BREAK have the same effect: commands are interrupted and programs in progress are stopped. Sometimes, application programs ignore these keys and respond instead to their own internal break keys.

PREPARING A HARD DISK

In Chapter 2, you learned about the FORMAT command and how to prepare new diskettes for use in the computer. A hard disk is prepared once when it is new; after that, you probably will not need to reformat it. Also, when a hard disk computer system is new, the vendor may perform the preparation step. Nevertheless, the following information is offered to those who obtain a new hard disk and must prepare it for use.

FDISK

FDISK is a program that you can use to "partition" the hard disk. A partition is a subdivided section of the entire hard disk. The total of all of the partitions equals the complete disk. Partitioning the hard disk involves selecting two or more separate sections into which the operating surface of the hard disk will be divided.

DOS is only one of a number of operating system programs. The FDISK program allows you to set up several partitions, each of which can run a different operating system. This is like having several computers in one. You can work with programs in DOS and then switch to another operating system.

Start your computer from a floppy DOS disk. Run FDISK from the DOS master disk. A menu will appear that allows you to create, change, or delete partitions. Choose creation of a DOS partition, and indicate if you want to use the entire disk for DOS or only a portion of it. If you choose to use only a portion, you may come back later and change this. Unless you work with other operating systems, you would partition the entire disk to DOS.

FDISK performs some setup operations on the disk before you are prompted to restart the system. After the restart, you are ready to format the disk. Formatting an entire hard disk is no different from formatting a floppy disk. You key-enter the FORMAT command, indicate that you want to proceed, and wait while the entire disk is formatted. If the hard disk has already been formatted and contains data and programs, you will erase everything by formatting it again. Once a hard disk has been formatted, you probably won't need to reformat it.

Organizing the Hard Disk

The best time to plan your hard disk organization is before you load files. By planning ahead, you can avoid a lot of file copying and deleting. Some commercial programs offer a MOVE command, which combines copy and delete in one action; however, even this can be avoided. See Chapters 3 and 4 for more ideas about hard disk organization. You can change the system you set up if you are not happy with it; however, this will be time-consuming.

Loading Files

Once the hard disk has been formatted, you load programs and data files onto it. Begin by deciding on the directory structure you want. Create the appropriate subdirectories in the root directory. Create subdirectories within those subdirectories that require added storage compartments.

Copy data files from your data disks to the appropriate directories. Most programs must be installed on the hard disk with their own installation batch files. In some cases, you may simply use the COPY command to put the program files in place.

RENAMING AN AUTOEXEC.BAT FILE

This section is for those who have discovered that the disks they are using to start their computers contain AUTOEXEC.BAT files. You may wish to change the AUTOEXEC.BAT file so that it will immediately run a certain program or do a particular task. This section will show you how to rename the AUTOEXEC.BAT file so that it does not work when the computer is started. You will be able to rename it again later without losing its contents.

Follow the steps below very carefully. If necessary, refer to Chapter 2, which discusses the RENAME command.

1. Start the computer with the DOS start-up disk. Either wait for the AUTOEXEC.BAT file to complete its work, or follow any instructions that are printed on the screen. The file will be done when the DOS prompt (A> or C> with a blinking cursor beside it) shows on the screen.
2. Enter carefully the command that follows this step. Check to see that it is correct before you press ENTER. If you have made a mistake, press the BACKSPACE or LEFT ARROW key until the mistake has been erased, and then complete the line correctly. When it is correct, press ENTER. If your AUTOEXEC.BAT file is on drive C, key-enter C: instead of A: in the command.

   ```
   RENAME A:AUTOEXEC.BAT AUTOEXEC.OLD
   ```

   The spaces are important. When the AUTOEXEC.BAT file has been renamed, DOS will not be able to find it, and it will not be run as a part of the start-up sequence.
3. Continue with the exercises in the text. You can reinstate your existing file by renaming it again with its original name, or you can create a new AUTOEXEC.BAT file.

PREPARING AN AUTOEXEC.BAT FILE

This section provides instructions for those who wish to make their own AUTOEXEC.BAT files. See also the first hands-on exercise in Chapter 5.

1. Your computer should be on, and the DOS prompt should be showing. Drive A is the current drive.
2. Place your start-up disk in drive A.
3. Key-enter COPY CON AUTOEXEC.BAT. The cursor will move down a line and await your entry. What you now type will appear in your AUTOEXEC.BAT file.
4. Key the DOS commands that you would like to be executed whenever you start up your computer. Press ENTER at the end of every line.
5. Press F6 after the last line to insert an end-of-file (^Z) marker.
6. Press ENTER to complete the command. The AUTOEXEC.BAT file will be created on the disk in drive A.
7. Start the computer with this disk.

Appendix E

Suggested Responses to Exercises

CHAPTER 1—GETTING STARTED: ANSWERS TO EXERCISES

1. DATE
   2/13/91 or 2-13-91
2. Key-enter TIME; respond to the prompt with 8:30
   Key-enter TIME.
3. Look at the time and date stamps on each file. You can match these with the days the experiments were run. You can also make sure that the time stamp corresponds to a time after the last daily experiment is complete.
4. Look at the date and time the files were last saved. The most recent file is probably the one to use.
5. You inserted your disk in drive A but did not change the logged drive. The DIR command attempted to read the directory in drive B, which was empty. Press A (to abort), insert your disk in drive B, and continue; or key A and press ENTER—you have just made drive A the current drive.
6. A parameter tells the computer where the command should be executed, or on which devices (drives, for example). A switch tells the computer how to execute or which features to include.
7. Press the BACKSPACE key to erase the incorrect characters, and then proceed. An alternative procedure is to press CTRL-C, ESC, or CTRL-BREAK to abort the command, and then retype it correctly.
8. The file name is the same for all files; the extensions are different. You want SALES.DAT because the other two files are batch and program files, respectively.

9. DIR displays the disk directory. If there are 32 files in the directory, enter DIR /P (to pause after 23 files) or enter DIR /W to display a wide directory.

10. Free space is listed after all files have been displayed following the DIR command.

11. Examples of legal DOS file names to fit this situation are EXPER1.DAT, RESULTS.DAT or TEST.DAT, and SUMMARY.TXT or CONCLUSN.DOC.

12. EXPERIMENT.DOC is too long. TEST REPT.DAT contains an illegal space character. CONCL%1.TEXT contains an illegal % character and has a four-character, instead of a three-character, extension.

The following answers were derived using PC-DOS Version 3.1. Your answers may vary.

13. ANSI.SYS: 1651 bytes
    RECOVER.COM: 4050 bytes
    MODE.COM: 5295 bytes
    VDISK.SYS: 3307 bytes

14. Student to supply directory

15. Number having 3 characters: 1
    Number having 4 characters: 8
    Number having 5 characters: 8
    Number having 6 characters: 12
    Number having 7 characters: 3
    Number having 8 characters: 4
    Total number of files: 36

To derive the answers to exercise 15, key the command DIR ??? and press ENTER. Record the number of files listed. Press F3 to repeat the last DOS command, add another ?, and press ENTER. Record the number of files listed. Repeat this process, adding another ? each time. Subtract the count of each cycle from the count of the preceding one. The difference is the number of files with the corresponding number of characters. The total should equal the number listed after the DIR command entered alone.

CHAPTER 2—INTRODUCTION TO DOS: ANSWERS TO EXERCISES

1. First, you may have misspelled the command. If it was entered correctly, then perhaps the file does not exist. If you are using a DOS disk,

the version of DOS you are using may not contain the XCOPY command. Next key-enter VER to see the version you are using. XCOPY is available with DOS Version 3.2 and above.

2. Two regular-density 5¼″ disks have a combined capacity of 720K; two high-density 5¼″ disks, 2400K; two regular-density 3½″ disks, 1440K; and two high-density 3½″ disks, 2880K. The total is 7440K, or 7.44M—1.44M more than is needed.

3. Use the FORMAT command. If you add /S to it, you will transfer the DOS system to each disk, making it a start-up disk. This will take up valuable storage space and is not needed to store copies of files.

4. Use SYS to transfer system files to one of the already formatted disks. Use one of the disks that has no files on it. The SYS command will work only if sufficient disk space exists on the disk. Then copy COMMAND.COM to the new disk.

5. Use the LABEL command (if you have PC-DOS Version 3.0 or MS-DOS Version 3.1 or above). If you had known about this requirement earlier, you could have used the /V command. With DOS Version 4.0, the FORMAT command would have prompted you for the label automatically.

6. CHKDSK tells you if there are hidden files on a disk. The hidden files are probably the DOS system files.

7. A directory holds a limited number of file names, as well as their dates of creation and sizes. It is a part of the disk format. A subdirectory contains directory entries. It can hold an unlimited number of files depending on the disk space available. It can also hold additional subdirectories.

   An advantage of using XCOPY (if your version of DOS contains it) is that it can copy all files in several subdirectories and duplicate the subdirectories as well as the files. It will stop when the target disk gets full, so it will have to be used several times with the /M switch, which tells it to ignore the files it has already copied.

8. Use DISKCOPY to duplicate the 5¼″ disk. DISKCOPY will produce an exact duplicate of a disk, and some DOS versions will format the new disk first if needed. Because you have only one 5¼″ drive, you must issue the command DISKCOPY A: A:, and then swap disks in the first drive.

   Use the COPY command to get the files onto the 3½″ disk. DISKCOPY cannot be used with drives of different sizes. FORMAT the 3½″ disk first, or use XCOPY, which formats before copying.

9. If the current drive is A, the command is COPY SMALL.COM B: /V.
   If the current drive is B, the command is COPY A:SMALL.COM B: /V.

10. TYPE will list the contents of a file on the screen or on the printer. In this case, display the file on the screen to search for a single line. These address files are longer than one screen, and the first lines will scroll off the screen before they can be read. Press CTRL-S to stop and read the display. Press CTRL-S again to resume displaying the file.

11. ERASE removes the file names from the directory. DEL is another form of the same command. To remove these files, issue ERASE or DEL with each filename. Another approach is to use DEL *.DAT. However, this can remove other files which have DAT extensions. Another approach is to use ERASE ???.DAT. This will remove only those files with three characters in their names, and is still dangerous because other three-character files could be removed.

12. Use the RENAME command, in either of the following forms:

    A>RENAME B:TAX88.WKS TAX89.WK1
    A>REN B:TAX88.WKS TAX89.WK1

13. With today's programs, you cannot copy installation disks and expect the copies to work. You must use the manufacturer's Install program, which will decompress the files, create the necessary subdirectories, and check your equipment. Second, if the files have already been installed on one computer, it would be illegal to install them on another computer unless the license allows the program to be used on multiple computers.

CHAPTER 3—DEEPER INTO DOS: ANSWERS TO EXERCISES

1. You cannot find the files you want quickly, and you can see that disk space is being wasted by duplicate files. Also, you will soon fill up the root directory and will not be allowed to add more files.

2. You can install the word processing program on one floppy disk. There will be room for only 150K of data files. Set up drive B to hold data disks, while drive A holds the program disk. Change the data disks as they get full or as the subject changes.

3. One way to organize the files would be to install the outline, word processing, and drawing programs in their own subdirectories. Data files could be kept in these same subdirectories. Alternatively, the

program subdirectories could have their own subdirectories for the data. Knowing that data files need to be moved for use on another computer, you should consider keeping the data files directly on floppy disks. Of course, the files could be copied from the hard disk to floppies for transport, but keeping them directly on floppies saves this step.

4. A subdirectory is a special file that holds the names and locations of other files on the disk. A subdirectory has its own name, with an extension if desired. You can see it in the directory listing of which it is a part. There is no limit to the number of files a subdirectory can hold other than disk capacity.

5. The path to the Bigalow spreadsheet file is \SHEET \1991 \SMALL \.

6. DOS automatically creates a double period file in each subdirectory you make with the MD (MKDIR) command. This designates the parent directory of the subdirectory in which the double period file resides. The double period (..) is an abbreviated way to refer to the parent directory of the current directory. The command would be DIR .. \.. \MATH \WED. Another correct command is DIR \MATH \WED.

7. PATH=C: \;C: \MATH \MON \;C: \MATH \TUE \;C: \MATH \WED \ ;C: \MATH \THR \;C: \MATH \FRI \

   NOTE: The command is on two lines here to fit the page.

8. Use the Make Directory (MKDIR or MD) command to create a subdirectory. The command would be MKDIR C: \SCIENCE \MISC or MD SCIENCE \MISC (either MKDIR or MD can be used).

9. Use the Change Directory (CHDIR or CD) command to make MATH \WED the current subdirectory. Enter CD .. \.. \MATH \WED or CD \MATH \WED.

10. You remove a subdirectory with the Remove Directory (RMDIR or RD) command. Enter RD \MATH \MISC or RD .. \MISC.

11. You will receive an "Invalid path, not directory, or directory not empty" message if you attempt to remove a directory that contains a file or another subdirectory. You can also receive this message if you enter an incorrect spelling of the subdirectory name.

CHAPTER 4—HARD DISK OPERATIONS: ANSWERS TO EXERCISES

1. To perform the operations described in exercise 1, key-enter the following commands.

```
DATE
TIME
CLS
DATEBOOK
CLS
TYPE AUTOEXEC.BAT
```

2. Subdirectories organized by application have one or more data subdirectories in the application subdirectory. These may be organized by subject. Subdirectories organized by user have separate data subdirectories for each user. These can be in the first level of the directory tree or be parts of each application.

   The first-level subdirectory would contain program files. Additional first-level subdirectories could be named SAUL, JANICE, THOMAS, and WILL.

3. Answers must conform to proper file name rules, and they must contain the BAT extension. Examples include:

   GAME.BAT (GAME)
   STAT.BAT (STAT)
   CLEAR.BAT (CLEAR)
   SPELL.BAT (SPELL)
   DRAW.BAT (DRAW)

   Note that batch file names cannot include regular reserved DOS command characters.

4. This is a standard start-up but should be automatic. A standard start-up prompts you to key-enter the date and the time before you are placed in the root directory. An automatic start-up is controlled by an AUTOEXEC.BAT file, which will enter and execute any number of commands automatically. According to what you have been told, the AUTOEXEC.BAT file should run the spreadsheet program automatically.

5. A shell program is one that either operates and then is removed from memory or operates in the background. Operating in the background means that it reappears after an application program stops and exits to DOS. Applications are selected from a built-in menu after you have told the shell program the proper commands to use to execute each application. Other menu choices allow you to select a variety of DOS commands instead of having you enter commands on a command line. Arguments for purchasing this type of program include time savings because it is easier to remember commands; faster training of new users; and fewer errors due to incorrect command entry.

6. You will ask if the previous day's files were backed up. If they were, work lost because of the electrical storm will not have to be redone.

7. XCOPY is better for this purpose because it can be entered to copy only those files that have been created or changed since the last backup. Thus copies of only new or changed files are made to take home.

8. The BACKUP command creates its own files containing the ones you have backed up. They are named BACKUP.001 and CONTROL.001. You must enter the RESTORE command in order to use your original files.

9. Add the /M switch to the BACKUP command in order to back up only files that have been created or modified since the last backup. If you are using the same disks, you also need to use the /A switch to add the modified files; otherwise the original files will be erased.

10. The TREE command will list all of the subdirectories in another subdirectory or on the entire disk. If you add the ?F switch, it can also list all of the files contained in these subdirectories. It helps you manage your files because it makes it easy to list all of the files in one or more subdirectories, thus making file location easier.

11. To create this list of files, you would key-enter the command DIR ¦ SORT /+25 so as to sort the files by date. You would then use an editor to remove all files except those between the requested dates.

CHAPTER 5—ALL ABOUT BATCH FILES: ANSWERS TO EXERCISES

1. a. Only files ending with EXE, COM, or BAT can be run from the command line. Data files such as the ones in this exercise must be viewed from within a word processor or by means of the DOS TYPE command.
   b. The command TYPE JAN02.DAT will display the file. Press CTRL-S to stop and read the display. If the file is not a text or ASCII file, you may not be able to read it by using this method.
   c. If written with a loop, a batch file would allow you to view several data files with a single batch entry command. This batch file would contain the command TYPE %1.
   d. Use the COPY CON command to type in the file, or use a text processor.

2. Use the TYPE command to view the contents of the batch file. Use EDLIN or the new DOS Version 5.0 EDIT command to edit the batch file.

3. A line editor such as EDLIN can work only with one line at a time. A text editor such as EDIT can enter and change text anywhere on the screen.
4. AUTOEXEC.BAT is run automatically every time the computer starts from either a cold or a warm boot.
5. A parameter is a piece of data that is entered on the DOS command line after the batch file name. The program that the command runs must be set up to accept parameters if they are present. The information the parameter represents is passed to the program.
6. A smart batch file is one that can change its operation depending on conditions present at the time it runs. Special comparison commands or parameter passing features allow the smart batch file to react differently depending on conditions and the outcomes of comparisons.
7. A batch subcommand is a key word that DOS recognizes within a batch file. Batch subcommands allow batch files to be more versatile and manage more complex situations. Some batch subcommands also work when entered on the DOS command line outside of the batch file. The subcommands provide the capability to perform additional, programmable actions depending on conditions or data passed to the batch file.
8. You would create a batch file that contains an IF EXIST command. If the specific file is in the directory, the IF command will be true. In this case, the most critical batch subcommand is GOTO, which can be used to provide a way for the batch file to handle the action you want to take if the file does or does not exist.
9. The GOTO subcommand provides a way to control execution within a batch file. Normally, execution goes from statement to statement, from the beginning to the end of the batch file. GOTO allows execution to be directed to any part of the batch file. GOTO will not work unless it is followed by the corresponding GOTO label. The label is any word or group of characters located at the beginning of a line and preceded by a colon.
10. A string is a group of text characters. It is usually used within an IF statement to compare an actual result, such as a file name or an entry, with a predetermined result.
11. A null string does not contain any characters. It occurs when you are expecting an entry and there is none. The IF statement cannot work with null strings and will issue a syntax error message when one is

encountered. A trick is to include a string containing nothing in the IF command.

12. The FOR..IN..DO subcommand permits repetitive operations to be carried out with one command. The command syntax is FOR variable IN (set) DO command. This command is repeated with the variable being substituted for every valid entry in the set definition.

13. A batch file menu system is one in which a batch file types a list of menu choices on the screen. A menu option is selected by key-entering the name of another batch file to perform the desired operation. A menu system with four choices would require five batch files.

CHAPTER 6—ADVANCED DOS FEATURES: ANSWERS TO EXERCISES

1. Common DOS devices and the corresponding DOS device names include: console (CON); keyboard (CON); serial port or communications port (COM1, COM2); printer port (LPT1, LPT2); printer (PRN); auxiliary port (AUX); and nonexistent port (NUL).

2. The keyboard and the display are both referred to as the console. The keyboard is the console for input. The display is the console for output.

3. No. A monitor with a resolution of 320 × 200 can legibly display only a limited amount of detail. Resolution is defined as the numbers of dots per scan line and scan lines per screen.

4. No. A modem is a serial device and can be connected only to the computer's serial port. Yes, a printer can be connected to either a parallel or a serial port, although connecting it to a parallel port is more common.

5. Redirection takes data flowing from one device and sends it to a destination other than the default destination. Redirect your root directory listing to a printer using DIR > PRN. Two other approaches are to press CTRL-P before issuing the DIR command, and to redirect the DIR to a file (DIR > DIRLIST.TXT) and then use a word processor to print out this file.

6. The system will lock because there is no printer actually connected to the printer (PRN) port.

7. Nonfilter approaches are to press CTRL-S or PAUSE, and to use the DIR /P command. MORE is a filter that will automatically cause the output to pause until a key is pressed. DIR | MORE is the command.

8. The command DIR | SORT > SORTDIR.LST sorts a directory listing and puts the result in SORTDIR.LST. This command sorts the directory according to file name.

9. The command that would find all such occurrences is FOR %A IN (C: \UTIL *.BAT) DO FIND /C "REM" %A. /C counts the occurrences, IN lists the line number, and /V displays lines not containing "REM." This command would be entered at the DOS command line. To enter this within a batch file, use %%A instead of %A.

10. The ASSIGN command tricks DOS into thinking that one physical drive is another. ASSIGN A=B will make the INSTALL program think that drive B is drive A. The 3½" disks can then be used.

11. You create a RAM disk (a portion of memory set aside to act like a physical disk drive) by means of the DEVICE=VDISK.SYS line in the CONFIG.SYS file. One advantage of using a RAM disk in this situation is that the database program will operate faster as it saves and writes to memory instead of to the slow disk drive.

12. A terminate-and-stay-resident (TSR) program is one that waits in the background while another program is used. MIRROR helps you by recording information about any deleted files in a special hidden file.

13. MIRROR and UNDELETE. If you had had MIRROR running in the background, it would have captured the information in SALES.BAK. By entering UNDELETE, you will be able to recover the SALES.BAK file.

14. You should develop the habit of making backup copies of your work on a periodic basis.

15. The basic approach to elimination of conflicts among TSRs is to remove all TSRs from memory and then reload them one at a time until the conflict appears. The last one added will be the culprit. Experimenting with the order in which they are loaded may resolve the conflict.

Index

A

B

C

D

I

J

K

L

M

N

O

P

Q

R

S

T

U